CRUSADE

ALSO BY JOSEPH P. DESARIO

SANCTUARY (1989)
LIMBO (1987)

CRUSADE

UNDERCOVER AGAINST THE MAFIA AND KGB

TOM TRIPODI
WITH JOSEPH P. DeSARIO

BRASSEY'S (US)
A Maxwell Macmillan Company

WASHINGTON • NEW YORK • LONDON

Brassey's (US)

Editorial Offices	*Order Department*
Brassey's (US)	Brassey's Book Orders
8000 Westpark Drive	c/o Macmillan Publishing Co.
First Floor	100 Front Street, Box 500
McLean, Virginia 22102	Riverside, New Jersey 08075

Brassey's (US) is a Maxwell Macmillan Company. Brassey's books are available at special discounts for bulk purchases for sales promotions, premiums, fund-raising, or educational use through the Special Sales Director, Macmillan Publishing Company, 866 Third Avenue, New York, New York 10022.

Tripodi, Tom, 1932–
   Crusade : undercover against the Mafia & KGB / Tom Tripodi with Joseph P. DeSario.
     p.   cm.
   Includes index.
   ISBN 0-02-881019-8 (hardcover)
   1. Tripodi, Tom, 1932– . 2. Narcotic enforcement agents—United States—Biography. 3. Intelligence officers—United States—Biography. 4. Undercover operations—United States—Case studies. 5. Narcotics, Control of—United States—Case studies. 6. Organized crime—United States—Case studies. I. DeSario, Joseph P., 1950– . II. Title.
HV7911.T78A3 1993
363.2'52—dc20
[B]   92-29730
                                         CIP

Designed by Maura Fadden Rosenthal

10 9 8 7 6 5 4 3 2 1
Printed in the United States of America

To Carrie,
a Saint

CONTENTS

PREFACE

It was a Sunday morning. I had just settled in at the kitchen table with a copy of the *Chicago Tribune*. On page three, a picture caught my eye. At first I thought the AP Laserphoto had been taken in Beirut or some other war zone. The carcass of a demolished automobile chassis stood with others in the rubble of what once was a highway. A huge section of road had been destroyed, along with whatever vehicles happened to be in the vicinity.

I read the caption: "Anti-Mafia crusader killed in Italy." I read further and learned that on May 23, 1992, just outside of Palermo, Sicily, Judge Giovanni Falcone had been killed by a bomb along with his wife and three others. I looked for more details, but unfortunately that was the extent of the paper's coverage.

Immediately, I called Tom Tripodi. For more than two years we had been working on Tom's memoirs. The first draft of *Crusade* had been polished off only weeks before. In early April, we had finished a passage that recalled a conversation between Tom and Falcone that had occurred in 1980, shortly after a series of Mafia executions of Italian law enforcement and judicial figures. Tom had warned Falcone, saying, "You're next."

I described the photo to Tom, then started to read the caption. Before I even mentioned Falcone's name, Tom interrupted me: "They got Falcone, didn't they?"

Over the next few days, more details about the assassination surfaced. It was determined that more than a ton of high explosives had been used in the attack. Falcone's armor-plated car was no protection against a blast that was more powerful than a direct hit by a SCUD missile.

It had taken the Mafia more than a decade to eliminate Falcone, a magistrate who had been in the forefront of the Italian government's effort against it. The murderers seemed bent on compensating for the slowness of their vengeance with the excessive ferocity of their attack. Old myths about the Mafia never killing wives or bystanders expired with Francesca Falcone and the three others who happened to be caught in the blast.

In July 1992 the Mafia struck again in Palermo. A car bomb killed another anti-Mafia judge, Paolo Borsellino, and his five police bodyguards. Borsellino, the likely successor to Falcone, was visiting his mother and sister. The powerful explosion injured twenty innocent people.

For Tom Tripodi, these episodes have poignancy beyond the death of old friends and colleagues. Falcone and Borsellino are the latest in a long line of dozens of heroic Italians who have been murdered by the Mafia since 1978, when Tom spearheaded a Palermo-based campaign code-named Operation Caesar. All too many of those whom Tom worked with on that precedent-setting operation and the campaigns that followed have fallen to the Mafia executioners. Tom, himself, escaped from Sicily under heavy police escort after death threats were made against him. He learned later that the Mafia had put out a murder contract on him, a contract that he believes would become effective if he ever again sets foot on the island of Sicily. Any speculation that the passage of time has caused the contract to lapse now seems mute. Once again, the Mafia has proved itself to be patient, as well as ruthless.

Our paths first crossed in February of 1990. Tom Tripodi's literary agent had been floating a book proposal. As the story came back to me, an editor who saw the proposal recommended that Tom's agent contact me regarding a possible collaboration. After only a few conversations with Tom, I could already see that the story of his life as a federal agent offered more than enough action and intrigue to support a book-length project.

In the realm of drug law enforcement, Tom's career spanned the days of the Treasury Department's old Federal Bureau of Narcotics to the present-day Drug Enforcement Administration, from "hitting flats" in Harlem to heading a White House task force. His work for the CIA took him to JMWAVE, the secret base in south Florida where Cuban exiles were being prepared to take their island back. He was at the center of the controversy over the authenticity of KGB defector Maj. Yuri Ivanovich Nosenko. He helped track South American revolutionary Che Guevara. He questioned *Cosa Nostra* informant Joe Valachi and challenged the importance of the "Valachi Papers." He debriefed high-level mafioso Tommaso Buscetta. He was the first U.S. agent to work on extended assignment against the Mafia in Palermo, Sicily. His efforts there and his extensive knowledge of the Mafia were the subjects of a memorable "Sixty Minutes" interview after the U.S. government suggested him as most knowledgeable about the Mafia worldwide.

Crusade is Tom's story, the tale of his passage through the big events that we've heard about and the small ones that perhaps even better define the life of a federal agent. Essentially, these are his memoirs. My contribution has been limited to putting his words down on paper and to organizing the various episodes into kernels that I hope will prove tasty to the interested reader.

Tom's version of an event does not always square exactly with accounts already in print. Often he has something to add to the accepted version. I find these amplifications fascinating, as it is often that which has been left out of a story that proves most illuminating. I believe that it is by listening to those who have worked behind the scenes of history that we really learn to understand it fully.

Having worked with Tom over the better part of two years, I have come to appreciate his sense of history, his devotion to accuracy, and his incredible memory. He can relate a murder perpetrated by a CIA agent in Southeast Asia to the killing of an OSS major in Nazi-occupied Italy during World War II. He can tell you how *La Cosa Nostra* really got its name. He can recall what a dope dealer was wearing during a surveillance in 1961. I am amazed by his powers of recollection and his ability to integrate events into the bigger picture.

Readers will note that very little of Tom's personal life is recounted within these pages. It was decided early on to concentrate the book on Tom's professional life. As the Falcone and Borsellino murders so painfully illustrate, the Mafia now has no reservations about extending the scope of its violence to include family members and innocent bystanders. Tom's love for and devotion to his children forced him to avoid much of the material about them that he would have liked to include. I know they understand this was meant to limit their exposure to the violent world that their father has traversed during his career as a federal agent.

For those interested in the writing process that brought this book to fruition, it is necessary to understand that the inventor of the facsimile machine has cause to claim partial responsibility for this work. With Tom living on the East Coast and myself in the Midwest, it was only by burning the long-distance wires that the communication required to accomplish this book was completed. Numerous interviews were conducted over the phone and transcribed (mostly by my wife, Peg) into better than six hundred pages of transcripts. I organized the material and condensed it into a one-hundred–page synopsis. Via fax, chapter by chapter Tom supplied me with typewritten notes that augmented the transcripts. I then prepared the first draft of the manuscript and faxed it to him. Revisions were faxed back and forth until we were satisfied enough to move on to the next chapter. We trust that AT&T and the other long-distance services are happy with the healthy portion of our advance that has, over the last several months, been rerouted to their coffers.

Perhaps the hardest task we faced was deciding on a title. Unable to determine one that embraced a career as diverse as it was intriguing, we remanded the job to our capable publisher, Frank Margiotta, and our editor, Don McKeon. They suggested *Crusade*. I had always seen Tom's career as a journey, but one a bit more meandering than a crusade. As I gave the title further consideration, however, I saw that at several critical times during Tom's career, it was only through a staunch sense of purpose—a *crusader's* sense of purpose and cause—that Tom was able to survive the slings and arrows of his enemies, both those within the government and those without. My doubts vanished entirely when I realized that the crusaders of old, though headed for the Holy Land, often found themselves on unexpected adventures in uncharted realms.

This is Tom Tripodi's crusade.

JOSEPH P. DeSARIO

CRUSADE

1

NO GOOD DEED
GOES UNPUNISHED

As soon as they spotted me, the two killers spun around and charged off in the opposite direction, back toward their victim, who was sprawled across the sidewalk.

It was late spring, 1963, and I was on my way to work at an undercover CIA facility in Washington, D.C. I had just left my black 1960 T-bird in the *"U.S. Government Only"* parking zone near 9th and K streets, N.W. The sun had barely risen, but the capital was already sizzling. My white button-down shirt was wilting from the humidity. I had been tempted to loosen my tie, but now there wouldn't be time.

Two derelicts had just committed murder. In another few seconds, they would be long gone. Only their victim would remain. I had to do something—and quick.

I'm not editorializing when I call them "derelicts." That's what they were—bums. Their clothes were in tatters, they were filthy, they stank. Their movements were slow and clumsy, numbed by alcohol. But inebriated or not, they still had been capable of killing another human being.

It was their misfortune to encounter me on that steamy morning. Five minutes earlier or later and they would have had clear sailing. But now they had to contend with me. A CIA special agent. A former college football player. Even worse for them, I hadn't yet downed my first cup of coffee. This was not their lucky day.

I closed on them in seconds. It was no contest. I was in shape. They weren't. I was six foot three, 225 pounds. Together, the two of them couldn't have weighed much more.

I grabbed the first suspect by the leg, yanked, and put him down. No problem. A forearm slam to the neck dropped the second one just as easily. If they had split up, one of them might have gotten away. But they were too drunk, scared, or stupid. Or maybe they were just plain unlucky.

"Face down! On the pavement," I ordered. "Hands behind your heads."

They did it. The first guy's face was bleeding. The other one was only half-conscious. Neither offered any resistance.

With one eye holding my prisoners, I examined the victim, checking for vital signs. There was no pulse. Like the two who had taken his life, he appeared to be a vagrant. His face had been beaten to a featureless, bloody pulp. These two had pounded him but good. In dying he had lost muscle control over his bladder and sphincter. It was not a pleasant scene.

The first guy started to mouth off. When he tried to get up, I popped him one on the side of the head. After inspecting the corpse I was in no mood to take any shit. I made that real clear, and they made no further attempts at escape. Their day was over.

Just as I was deliberating what to do next, a taxi came cruising down New York Avenue. The driver was checking us out, gawking out the side window, trying to figure out what the hell was going on, probably debating with himself whether or not to get involved. Before he drove off, I yelled for him to bring the police. I don't know if he radioed his dispatcher or flagged down a patrol car, but two uniformed D.C. cops rolled up within minutes.

I quickly told the officers what had happened. They never asked me to produce any identification, and I never volunteered. I retrieved the leather portfolio I had dropped during the pursuit and continued on to work. It was just that cut-and-dried.

Fearing I'd be late, I hurried over to the three-story red brick building on the south side of New York Avenue, N.W., that housed the CIA undercover operation to which I was assigned. I was a duty officer (DO) for the Office of Security and I was due to log on at 0700 hours.

My first job was to deactivate the electronic surveillance and motion-detection equipment that secured the office during the night. Then there were a number of steel file cabinets in a vault area, each safeguarded by a combination lock, that had to be opened. These tasks had to be finished before the special agent in charge (SAC), his assistant SACs, and the rest of the staff arrived. It was routine stuff. My little adventure didn't prevent me from getting it all done on schedule.

Later that morning, I happened to mention the incident to one of my fellow agents. We were drinking coffee. Bullshitting. And I just mentioned it. "Something funny happened on the way to the office. . . ."

Within a couple of hours I was summoned to the SAC's office. He instructed me to proceed immediately to Langley headquarters for a meeting with the director of investigations. Nothing else was said.

Going to headquarters was no simple undertaking. For security reasons one could never be in possession of incompatible credentials. Since I was working undercover, the credentials I was carrying quite obviously did not indicate *CIA Special Agent*. But I would require just such "official" credentials for admittance to Langley. My "legend" credentials had to be placed in safekeeping, and my official credentials had to be retrieved. The exchange had to be coordinated and documented by the SAC.

The credential swapping and trip across the Potomac to Langley took longer than the meeting. The director of investigations was waiting for me. There was no small talk. He read the contents of a "blue memorandum" that had been prepared prior to my arrival. It was a goddamn reprimand.

He cited me for flagrant breach of security. He claimed that by intervening at the murder scene I had violated procedure and blown my cover.

At first I couldn't believe it. This kind of thing deserved passing notice at best. Maybe a "nice going, kid" or an "atta boy." But a reprimand?

I contended that there had been no breach of security, that I hadn't done anything wrong.

"The police don't know me from Adam," I argued. "I never gave them my name. Not even a false name. They don't know who I am or where I work. Nothing's been jeopardized."

"You violated procedure," he replied.

The whole thing was screwy. Even if I had identified myself using my legend, my cover was completely backstopped. It would have withstood normal police scrutiny. That was one of the purposes of covers. I reminded him that I had even testified in federal courts using the very same cover that I was currently working under.

My protests fell on deaf ears. The reprimand would stand. I was being punished for a *possibility*. Although it was never said in so many words, the message was clear: Look the other way. Don't get involved. Security rules supreme.

It just didn't matter if murderers went free!

I didn't realize it just then, but I was witnessing an early indication of a slow, insidious process that would emasculate our federal intelligence and law enforcement services over the next few decades. I was too angry at the director of investigations to see the situation in a broader context, to comprehend that men of action—like the World War II vets of the Office of Strategic Services (OSS) who had built these agencies—were being forced out by pencil pushers.

Today it's easier for me to play Monday morning quarterback. After twenty-seven years in the federal drug law enforcement and intelligence communities, I can look back and see the process at work, affecting and oftentimes undermining the cases I personally worked on: Botching the Nosenko defection to protect "official" conclusions regarding Lee Harvey Oswald and the Kennedy assassination. Coloring the Valachi testimony to make it less embarrassing to J. Edgar Hoover. Abandoning the secret army of Cuban expatriates we had trained in the Florida Everglades, leaving the drug trade as their only viable means of support. Fighting corruption within the ranks of the federal drug enforcement apparatus, only to see myself and the other reformers come under fire by those whose feathers we ruffled. Hyping the significance of media-popular cases like the Pizza Connection while retreating from the truly effective—and dangerous—Mafia-busting investigations I had begun in Palermo, Sicily.

The wimps were taking over. I may have harbored suspicions in 1963, but I certainly didn't see the transformation as an inevitable fate, pervasive and total. I had recently transferred to the CIA after serving three years in the Federal Bureau of Narcotics, and I was still jacked up about being in the spy business. I was excited at the prospect of engaging in undercover operations for my country. How could I foresee that two and a half decades later our covert capabilities would be so impotent that we'd have to deploy the U.S. Army, the Navy, the Air Force, and the Marines—more than 20,000 troops and millions of dollars worth of military hardware—just to take out one sorry asshole in Panama? Not to mention the untold numbers of innocent lives lost.

It was unthinkable in 1963. There would always be a few good men ready and able for the dirty jobs, guys who were ready to do what had to be done—as I had earlier that day. The director of investigations was handing me a crystal ball, but I wasn't ready to accept a future where the doers got punished and the ass-coverers got promoted.

When he finished chewing me out, he asked me if I had anything else to say.

I did: "I hope I never see you getting beat up—or your wife getting raped!"

It was a good zinger. It stopped him cold and gave me the last word. But basically it was a lie. It implied that I had learned my lesson—however grudgingly. It warned that now I wouldn't intervene, that I'd let him get beat up, let his wife get raped. And that simply wasn't true.

Even a spineless bureaucrat deserved better.

Even a dead bum on a D.C. sidewalk.

2

BRICKS

I grew up in Cliffside Park, New Jersey, just across the Hudson from New York City. One of the great traditions of our neighborhood was the making of wine. Every family had its own secret formula. The families would band together to make large purchases of zinfandel and cabernet grapes shipped from the vineyards of Italy, Greece, South America, and California. I'd help crank the handle that drove the wine press in my grandfather's basement. Then came the racking and the fermentation in fifty-gallon oak barrels. The result was a heavy, dense wine, dark as ink and powerful enough to put you on your butt after one small glass. I laugh now when I see television commercials showing yuppie couples holding their transparent wines up to the light. That's water. We made *wine!* And when at Sunday dinner you spilled some on your white shirt, it was marked for good. It was like iodine. No amount of washing or scrubbing or bleaching was going to erase that mark. That's how I remember my early years:

vintage days, a time that put its mark on me, indelible and set for life.

From the time I was about ten years old, I knew I wanted to be a federal agent. World War II had just started, and each day the newspapers headlined accounts of our soldiers' heroics overseas. I worked part-time for my maternal grandfather's newspaper delivery business, and so I had ample opportunity to read the stories about the campaigns in North Africa, Sicily, and later, Italy. I devoured every word. Those articles aroused in me a keen sense of history that, on reflection, could not have been typical for a boy of my age. It was a special *connected* feeling for the time and the place and the convoluted cavalcade of events that found me witnessing this volatile and crucial moment in the saga of mankind. Undoubtedly, the realization that some of our boys—neighbors, friends, a cousin, all of them not much older than I was—were fighting on the home soil of my Italian ancestry contributed to my appreciation of all that was going on. The war dispatches also triggered a surge of moral righteousness and patriotism, emotions much more typical for my age and for the era, emotions that breathed passion into all else I was feeling. History had come alive. It was right there, happening all around, tangible and malleable, challenging men of action and moral fiber to leave their mark. To a boy of ten, federal agents were such men.

Federal agents were always in the right, always inclined to action in the pursuit of their goals, which were, of course, the collective and proper goals of our country as a whole. As a profession, being a federal agent seemed both ideal and idealistic. It was exciting work, dangerous, adventurous, and violent. You carried a gun and punched out bad buys. What else could a ten-year-old ask for? Nobody told me then that most federal agents spent their days in the calculated regimen of avoiding action, that careers and institutions counted for far more than any abstract notion of right and wrong, that those who wore badges often prospered off the nefarious operations of those whom they were chartered to remove from general society. I probably would have taken a swing at anyone who said such things. I was ten years old. My world was the black and white of motion pictures; shades of gray didn't exist yet.

My family's neighborhood in Cliffside Park was a working-class one populated mainly by first- and second-generation Italian-Americans. As a community, we struggled through the sometimes traumatic passage away from Old World values, traditions, and loyalties—a process that was perhaps prolonged by the economic hardship of the Depression and the political turmoil of the years immediately preceding the bombing of Pearl Harbor. Our household underwent the same cultural evolution that was occurring throughout the neighborhood and in Italian-American homes across the county.

I was forbidden to play jazz records on the family phonograph; opera was the only "officially" permitted music. Women attended Mass while men kibitzed on the church steps, just like they did in the Old Country. My aunt was ostracized by the rest of the family because she remarried too soon after the death of her husband, thereby forsaking the mandatory lifelong period of mourning.

My grandfather, like many others of his generation, supported Mussolini and the Italian Fascist party. On weekend afternoons during the summer he'd dress in Blackshirt regalia and march along with the brown-shirted Nazi Bund down Nungessers Avenue. My parents and their contemporaries, on the other hand, were squarely behind Roosevelt and the New Deal.

Sunday meals were all-day events—antipasto, homemade pasta with sauce from tomatoes grown in the backyard garden, roast beef or pork, roasted chickens, fruit, and wine that had fermented in the basement. The Sunday dinner table, with never fewer than ten people gathered around it, was the forum for heated political debates that pitted the generations against each other. Those discussions, as much as the newspapers and the radio, provided me a window on the world and also demonstrated that men of honor can disagree.

Once the war started, the arguments ceased. Everyone rallied behind the cause of the Allies. The philosophical discussion of foreign politics was quickly overcome by the reality of the war effort. Victory gardens, saving tinfoil, collecting scrap iron, gas rationing, food stamps—we did our part. The flags came out, and my grandfather's black shirt got tucked away in the dresser drawer, never again to see the light of day. Relatives, friends, and neighbors went off to war. If the Depression had prolonged our assimilation into the American mainstream, then the war, itself, certainly accelerated it. And just as the Depression had brought hard times, the war ushered in an era of prosperity. Even as a young boy, I couldn't help but see the connection between economics and patriotism. You just didn't bite the hand that feeds you.

My father, Carmello Tripodi, had been born in Buenos Aires,

Argentina, the son of Italians who had emigrated from a small Apennine town in Reggio Calabria five miles up the coast from the fabled Rock of Scilla, where sirens of myth lured ships to their doom. During the great periods of immigration around the turn of the century, many Southern Europeans sought their dreams in South America, a fact often ignored in North American chronicles of the era. My grandparents' dreams of a better life were not realized in Argentina, however. When my father was four years old, the family moved back to Italy. My father remembers little of his early few years in South America. His heritage, his memories, his culture are those of an Italian. At the age of seventeen, he decided to pursue the New World dreams abandoned by his parents. He immigrated to the United States, settling in the "Little Italy" he found in northern New Jersey. In December of 1929, he married first-generation American Chiara Pitetti, my mother.

My maternal grandparents had emigrated in the early 1900s from Guardiagrelle in the Abruzzi region about one hundred miles east of Rome. My grandfather started and ran a successful construction business until an industrial accident rendered his right arm useless. With his savings, he then purchased the equivalent of a modern-day 7-Eleven. Back then it was simply called a candy store, although one could purchase just about anything from coffee and cigarettes to the latest edition of *Il Progresso*. Eventually, my grandfather sold the candy store and founded the newspaper delivery business that would usher me into the world beyond Cliffside Park.

My younger brother, Daniel James Tripodi, was born on March 13, 1939. I woke up that morning to find the house filled with a bucket brigade of aunts and neighbors running around with pots of boiling water. I didn't know then and I don't know now the connection between birth and hot water. To me, those women looked more prepared for the arrival of a dozen Maine lobsters than the birth of my baby brother. I watched the commotion as I ate my breakfast of toast, oatmeal, and espresso. Then I left for school. When I returned, most of the water-boiling contingent was gone and I got my first look at my brother. Throughout our lives we've stayed quite close. With pride, I watched his academic and athletic achievements during his school years. He received a B.S. in bacteriology from the University of Delaware, where he also played football. He passed up professional football opportunities with the Baltimore Colts to pursue a master's degree in microbiology, which he then followed with a Ph.D. in immunology from Temple University. He went on to enjoy a distinguished career with Johnson & Johnson.

One of the ironies of the Italian immigrant experience was that many of us first encountered our own cultural heritage in the American public school system. Before coming to America, many immigrants—Southern Italians especially—had not traveled beyond the confines of their hometown. Most were poor and had received little formal education. But in America, they—or their offspring—learned about the grandeur of the Roman Empire; about the magnificent works of Dante Alighieri, Michelangelo, da Vinci, Rossini; and about the exploits of Columbus, Verrazano, John and Sebastian Cabot (Giovanni and Sebastiano Caboto), and Amerigo Vespucci. Later in life, after my work for the Drug Enforcement Administration (DEA) had taken me all over Sicily and Italy, I told my father about the wonders I had seen in his homeland. As he listened, he became agitated. Finally, in desperation, he interrupted me.

"You have been all over Italy," he said. "You worked with high officials of the Italian government, stayed in the best hotels, ate in the best restaurants. You saw all the famous works of art. In Italy I never traveled more than fifty kilometers from my home in Ceramida-Pellegrina. You are more Italian than I am."

My father was a tradesman, a skilled stonemason. During the Depression, like so many others, he was unable to find work. Finally, he had to settle for a factory job in order to make ends meet. By the end of the thirties, with the country on the road to recovery, he was able once more to take up his chosen profession. The construction industry, then like now, was dominated by the unions. The regular-time work week was limited to five seven-hour days. Saturday labor cost was double time, and predictably enough, no work was scheduled beyond the normal five-day week. However, on most Saturdays, the tradesmen would gather and contribute their labor to the construction of a house for one of their co-workers. If a plumber was building a house for his family, his friends in the trades—stonemasons and brick masons, electricians, plasterers, carpenters—would work for free. They all knew that when their turn came, the plumber would reciprocate. Under their communal system, the cost of a house was limited to materials. Everything else was "sweat equity." In 1941, my father, with the help of his buddies, built us our first house on Westend Avenue.

The most visibly prosperous members of our community were mobsters. They had the biggest houses, the fastest cars, the fanciest clothes. To the casual observer it must have appeared that crime *did* pay—and pay well. Certainly, crime afforded the fastest track to the good life that was at the heart of the American promise.

Through the efforts of the mob, northern New Jersey became the bookmaking capital of the entire country. When New York's Mayor, Fiorello La Guardia, threw the mobsters out of the city, they simply set up shop across the Hudson River. Voluntarily, otherwise honest homeowners were drawn into the operation when they leased their basements for use as wire rooms. One family I knew, over a period of six years, received $175 per week in such rent, a veritable fortune back then. And at the same time, they were selling the bookmakers sandwiches, coffee, and beer at a dollar a throw. Under such an arrangement, notions of right and wrong were easily confused, especially since the mafiosi had purged the neighborhood of drugs and petty crime. To many, they were knights protecting the old order. Criminals or patrons? The difference was hard to discern.

Two of my boyhood friends were Albert Anastasia, Jr., and Joe Doto, Jr., both sons of Mafia kingpins. The three of us were altar boys at Epiphany Catholic Church. Albert went on to become a priest; Joe followed his father into the rackets. That was the hard choice we all made—the straight life or the life of crime. I was a big, tough kid. I had been in my share of fights. I had a reputation. It would have been easy to follow my friend Joe. The action and the danger certainly would have appealed to me, but fortunately, the bookmakers had never been invited into our basement. My family hadn't let us become seduced by the image of the gangster as a benefactor. In our house, things were pretty clear-cut: Crime was crime, good was good, bad was bad. My parents weren't confused, and neither was I.

Only Italian was spoken in our home. When I started grammar school, I really didn't have a firm grasp of formal English. Trying to make the transition from one language to another caused me to develop a stutter. Fortunately, through the efforts of Miss Slater, my second-grade teacher, I overcame my speech impediment. For three years, at a time when there was no such thing as a speech therapist, she worked with me and others after school. Without extra compensation and probably without recognition, she put in long overtime hours tutoring immigrants and first-generation Americans. Miss Slater, a career teacher, ranks high on my list of those who made a difference in my life as well as in the lives of others.

In high school I did some boxing, most of it at a local gym where Gus Lesnevich, the light-heavyweight champion of the world, trained. By the time I was sixteen, I was sparring with some pretty credible heavyweights, including eighth-ranked Bernie Reynolds. Every time Reynolds and I matched up, he kicked my butt, one time even knocking me out of the ring. But he never did put me down on the mat. After one beating, Lesnevich evidently felt that Reynolds had gone too far. He climbed into the ring and thoroughly trounced Reynolds. In the squared circle I learned how to give a beating *and* how to take one. Both lessons served me well—and often—after I became a federal agent.

In the tenth grade I started playing football. I loved everything about it: the idea of team, the discipline, the work ethic, the contact. By the time I finished high school, I was big enough and good enough to win a scholarship to Loyola of Los Angeles. There, Assistant Coach John McKenna, another one of those who made a real difference in my life, convinced me that the *complete man* required development of his mind as well as his body. McKenna was a classmate and Villanova teammate of my high school coach, Sam Monaco. He persuaded me to major in philosophy. "You can't be a good lawyer, a good doctor, a good engineer, until you're first a good man," he argued. According to McKenna, philosophy, which presupposed a strong grounding in literature and history, was the study by which I would become a good man.

When Loyola dropped football in my sophomore year, I transferred to Villanova. Three professors, in particular, shepherded my academic progress—Dr. Roland Houde (philosophy), Dr. Henry Rofinot (history), and Dr. John Mitchell (literature/rhetoric). I was on the football team, playing center for the offense and linebacker for the defense, and I threw the discus for the track team. I majored in philosophy.

Athletics instilled a sense of fair play that has remained with me throughout my life. As a federal agent, I had opportunities to fire my weapon and didn't because I felt it more fair to use my bare hands.

There were situations that definitely warranted gunfire, situations where it even may have been more prudent to discharge my weapon, yet I didn't. On two different occasions during my very first year with the Federal Bureau of Narcotics, suspects tried to kill me at close range—one with a gun, one with a sword. In either case, I would have been fully justified in pulling the trigger. Faced with the same situations, many of my peers would have thought nothing of blowing the suspect away. Still, in both cases, and in others, I refrained.

In life-or-death confrontations, reactions occur in a split second, with the heart pounding and the adrenaline gushing. What happens in a fraction of a second is molded by what has gone before, the long years of training and character formation. Courts can take years to determine the rightness or wrongness of one flash decision. You live with the outcome of your actions for the rest of your life.

It's easier in life-or-death situations to *do* something, to shoot back. It's the natural response. You almost have to *choose* not to do something, and there's really no time to choose. Your most basic instincts of survival tell you to blast away. If you don't, it's logical to believe that your restraint must spring from some deep, inner source of strength that's as vital and as fundamental as your will to live. It's perhaps dangerous to overanalyze periods of my life that can be counted in seconds, but nonetheless, I attribute my restraint to a deeply embedded sense of fair play that somehow signaled to me, automatically, without doubt, that I could prevail without killing the perpetrator.

Perhaps I never really made it off the gridiron. There are rules, everybody starts even, the best man wins—all of which is not to say that I didn't, quite literally, take things into my own hands when the need arose. I never had any pangs of conscience about beating the hell out of dope dealers, especially if they had just tried to send me to my maker.

In 1954 I was drafted into the army and had to leave Villanova. I underwent basic training at Fort Jackson, South Carolina, and then went on to Cryptographic and Signal Corps schools at Camp Gordon, Georgia, and Fort Devens, Massachusetts. After training, I was stationed in Augsburg, Germany. Signal Corps duty put me on the periphery of the intelligence business, and my boyhood desire to become a federal agent was temporarily rekindled.

After the army, I returned to Villanova to complete my degree.

Shortly thereafter, I evidently came to the attention of a "spotter," a quasi-official recruiter for such government agencies as the CIA, the FBI, and the Federal Bureau of Narcotics. At most major universities, there are usually a few professors, coaches, and/or staffers who work for these agencies as talent scouts. In those days, they were looking for jocks, action-oriented guys who could get things done. The CIA approached me while I was still on campus. They expressed interest, but first I had to finish my schooling.

I graduated *cum laude* in 1958, the first jock to come out of Villanova with a bachelor's degree in philosophy since McKenna had done it in 1938. Seduced by the late-fifties vision of the yuppie good life, I then began study at Seton Hall University Law School. Attorneys occupied high positions within the community, made a lot of money, and exercised considerable power. I turned my back on my boyhood dream of becoming a federal agent and dived headlong into the pursuit of a successful career in law. While other students were relying on canned briefs, I was burning the midnight oil, reading each and every case and briefing them myself. I even studied the philosophy of law.

After only a year, I knew I had made a colossal mistake. There are no two more opposed disciplines in all of creation than philosophy and law. The former attempts to determine truth; the latter seeks to evade it, deny it, overturn it, and, at all cost, avoid it. One is about ethics, while the other is about loopholes. For me, there was—and *is*—no way to reconcile the two. It was all made clear to me when I came upon a passage in one of my reference books. "The study of law," it read, "sharpens the mind by narrowing it." That did it for me. I decided not to let my brain shrink down so that it could better prosper off the problems of others.

My disdain for the legal profession began in earnest during my one year at Seton Hall. It has only grown since, as through the years I've watched the lawyers institutionalize crime in America. The link between organized crime and corrupt law enforcement has been documented to death, but the more basic interdependence of the criminal and legal professions has been generally overlooked. Lawyers launder the dirty money, supervise evasive tax strategies, set up the front investments in legal enterprises, and represent the criminal in court, on appeal, at hearings, and before the parole board. On the other side there's a formidable army of prosecutors, investigators, politicians, and bureaucrats—all with law degrees. Viable strategies like drug interdiction by the armed forces will never be given a fair chance simply because its success would put too many attorneys out of work.

This is not to say that there aren't some good lawyers out there: honest, ethical professionals who have never strayed from the origin of their calling—namely, to be a public servant. It's just that in a country that now produces twenty attorneys for every engineer, as opposed to Japan where engineers outnumber attorneys ten to one, it's getting harder and harder to find one that values *the law* more than *lawyering*.

For the six months following my departure from Seton Hall, I led a confused, disillusioned existence. I had a degree, but there wasn't a strong job demand for a philosopher in the body of a linebacker. My boyhood dream of becoming an agent seemed ever so distant and unattainable, a teasing mirage blurred further by my time at Seton Hall. Still, I applied to the FBI and the CIA. Finally, I drifted back to the skills my father had taught me, brick masonry.

My life was about to change, but I didn't know it yet. I did my job, setting the bricks one by one. All that had gone before, like those bricks, had built up to something. The foundation was solid, but the final design was still uncertain.

3

GANG BUSTERS

A BADGE AND A GUN

The Federal Bureau of Narcotics (FBN) required that all applicants for the position of narcotics agent have a degree in either business administration or pharmacology. I had neither. An applicant for an *undercover* position, however, could qualify for a "Schedule A Excepted Appointment." After three years of experience—assuming the undercover agent lasted that long—the other requirements were waived.

George H. Gaffney was New York district supervisor for the FBN. He interviewed me during November 1959.

"If you're fluent in Italian and one or two of the more popular dialects," he said, "we'll consider you for a position as an undercover agent."

Italian was as natural as English to me. I explained that I also spoke Calabrese and some Sicilian. To a lesser extent I could get by with my Neapolitan.

Gaffney triggered the intercom and summoned Administrative Officer Ben Trullio into the office. He bounced into Gaffney's office rattling off Italian, slipping in and out of various dialects. I responded in kind.

That was it. The interview was over, and I was sent home.

The connection to Gaffney had been made through Hank Hayman, a college buddy. Hayman knew the assistant U.S. attorney for the Southern District of New York, William Walsh. Hayman had contacted Walsh and told him about me. Walsh spoke to me by telephone and, evidently pleased with what he had heard, passed my name on to Gaffney.

Although I had also interviewed with the CIA and the FBI, at the time I really preferred employment with the Federal Bureau of Narcotics. If I landed with the CIA, there was always the possibility I'd get shipped off to China or Africa or some other godforsaken place. The FBI had made it clear that I would never be stationed for more than two years in any one particular spot. But if I got into the FBN, I'd be assigned to New York, just a hop, skip, and a jump from my New Jersey home. And I could stay there as long as I wanted. Everything else considered, that sounded pretty good to me.

A few weeks later, a couple of days before Christmas, Gaffney called and offered me the position of narcotics agent. That was the best Christmas present I could have imagined, a dream come true if ever there was one.

On January 11, 1960, I left the house at seven o'clock in the morning. I took two buses and the subway for the long trip to the Federal Office Building at 90 Church Street in Manhattan. Intent on making a good first impression, I wore my best three-button, dark gray, Ivy League suit, a white-and-black-striped tab-collar shirt, a very *in* narrow tie, suspenders, and jodhpur boots. I made it to Gaffney's reception area on the ninth floor by 8:30 A.M., a half-hour early. At 9:15 A.M. I was sworn in as a grade GS-7 agent.

Harry Massi, an administration officer, ushered me up to the tenth floor, which housed the office of Naval Intelligence. There, pictures were taken for records and credentials. Evidently the FBN, which possessed an impressive inventory of surveillance cameras, didn't have the budget for passport photographic equipment. Massi then issued me a badge, a U.S. government driver's license, and a Colt Detective .38 Special.

First day. Not even noon yet. No training. But I had a badge and a gun—not that I knew what to do with either. This was going to be one hell of a job!

Firearms Officer John Tagli led me down to the firing range in the basement where he qualified me in the use of the .38. He quickly ran through an explanation of the firing progression and instructions on the alignment of the three-point sights. After some dry firing, he handed me some wad cutters, target ammunition that, unlike combat issue, produces clean holes upon impact. I fired at traditional ringed bull's-eye targets, scoring well enough to please Tagli. Today, black human silhouette targets are used, a practice that generates some provocative commentary—some good natured, some not—between white and black shooters. Tagli was unable to equip me with a holster. I'm left-handed, and the FBN didn't stock any left-handed equipment. Lucky for me my trousers were tight, and I was able to slip the Colt inside my waistband.

My appointment was provisional for a one-year period. Because of budgetary restraints, there would be no formal training until I'd proven myself in the field. New agents basically received on-the-job training under the tutelage of senior agents who would make assessments and recommendations. Getting along with them and their supervisor was crucial. After about six to nine months, assuming I performed to their satisfaction and made the cut, they'd send me to the U.S. Treasury Law Enforcement Officers Training School (TLEOTS) in Washington, D.C. Of the one hundred new agents appointed in 1960 by the New York office, only six were retained.

The New York FBN office had four Enforcement Groups, each consisting of about twelve men. In addition, there was a Registrant Group responsible for registration and inspection of medical doctors, pharmacists, and others who legally handled drugs. An eight-man Conspiracy Unit, a small Courthouse Squad, and an administrative staff were also based at 90 Church. There were satellite offices in Buffalo, Newark, and Paterson, New Jersey. All in all, about ninety agents and administrative personnel, charged with the impossible responsibility of stopping the illegal drug trade in New York State and northern New Jersey, worked for Gaffney.

I was assigned to the Fourth Enforcement Group under Supervisor Joseph Amato, a great guy and a very effective undercover agent. Diminutive, nondescript, and fluent in Italian, Amato had developed a network of organized-crime informants who were used to corroborate information and verify intelligence. It was Joe Amato who would later introduce me to organized-crime law enforcement by bringing me to clandestine meetings with his highly placed contacts. For all his reputation, Amato was nonetheless considered somewhat of a jinx by the rest of the Fourth Group agents. On a few occasions, with Amato present, routine arrests had erupted into gunfire. Subsequently, agents went out of their way to have him elsewhere when busts were going down.

Within the Fourth Group I was attached to Senior Agents Joseph Hermo and Bill Carrozo. They gave me a desk and a copy of the *Agent's Manual*.

"Stick around," Hermo ordered. "We've got work to do tonight."

Then they headed for the door.

"What should I do?" I asked.

"Read the fucking manual," Carrozo barked.

I devoured the half-inch-thick book in about fifteen minutes. (Today the *Agent's Manual* consists of three volumes, each about two inches thick.) Secretary Rosalind Corbellini made introductions as other agents came and went through the office. The agents treated me as I imagined veterans treated rookies in most professions. They were friendly but distant, maintaining a careful aloofness interlaced with the usual curiosities: "Where are you from? What did you do before?" These were overworked, very busy guys, and I was just the new kid on the block, sitting behind a desk and looking useless. I didn't pick up on it just then, but their restraint was edged with suspicion. Corruption inquiries had begun to surface from the Washington, D.C., office of FBN Deputy Commissioner Wayland Speer. Having come in cold as an excepted appointment, they naturally suspected that I had been covertly inserted into their midst.

I called my folks in New Jersey and told them I'd be late. They knew nothing about my being an agent. Tomorrow morning I'd tell them that I had accepted a job as a criminal investigator for the Treasury Department—something very white collar with nothing at all to do with drugs, with the streets, with the Mafia. I didn't want them to worry.

Hermo and Carrozo picked me up around eight o'clock. I squeezed into the back of Carrozo's 1958 two-door DeSoto. Carrozo drove as Hermo talked on the two-way radio. Hermo was a former military police officer. A fanatic for discipline, especially around junior agents, he told me to keep quiet. He didn't have to tell me twice.

At a luncheonette near 96th Street and Lexington we met up with three NYC Police Department Special Investigative Unit (SIU) detectives. Over coffee, they consulted their notebooks and exchanged names, addresses, and phone numbers obtained during previous arrests. It was obvious that they assumed that any such information gleaned from drug pushers or drug users just had to be drug related. I listened, hanging onto every word.

The shop talk then turned to "hitting flats," a euphemism for midnight raids without search warrants. At the time, the FBN and the U.S. Immigration and Naturalization Service (INS) were the only law enforcement agencies in the country that could conduct discretionary searches and seizures without a warrant. The FBI, the Secret Service, the state and local police—no one else could break down a door without a warrant unless a felony had been committed in their presence. It was an awesome power, and we were the only ones, along with the INS, who had it. And from what I was hearing, we weren't afraid to use it.

"You kick in the door. If you make the case, fine. If not, you're Detective Andrews from Homicide."

I was to learn later that local police were involved in these raids because probable-cause restrictions would disallow such cases from the federal courts. Federal narcotics agents may have possessed the power to break into and enter a suspect's dwelling, but it was the state courts that actually tried the cases. It was a mutually dependent relationship where the New York cops racked up easy busts and federal agents earned collateral credit for their periodic performance reviews.

We finished our coffee and drove to the vicinity of 7th Avenue and 117th Street. We exited the cars at thirty-second intervals. Nobody explained anything to me. When my turn came, I fell into the loosely spaced single-file line of agents and detectives walking toward god-knows-where.

I followed them into a tenement, stepping over a wino who was slumped on the front steps. It was my first time in a slum. Nothing I'd seen previously had prepared me for this kind of oppressive poverty. Trash was piled in the vestibule. Paint was peeling off the walls where the plaster hadn't been torn down altogether. The lights were dim. The stench was overpowering.

Without a word, we climbed six flights of stairs. On the landing, one of the detectives finally addressed me.

"We're going in there," he said matter-of-factly, pointing to an apartment door. Then he pointed to a door at the other end of the corridor. "The apartments might be connected. If anyone comes out that door, you stop them."

Without any further instructions or explanation, the five of them smashed through the first door and charged into the apartment. Warily, I approached the other door, the one I was supposed to watch. From inside the apartment I heard screams, furniture crashing, bodies careening into the walls. Seconds later, the door—*my door*—exploded open.

"Halt! Federal agent!" I shouted, reaching for my badge.

Duly impressed by my first command as a federal narcotics agent, twelve men stampeded through the doorway and ran right over me. I went down with my hand still fumbling in my pocket for my badge, as if that would have made any difference.

I heard two gunshots, deafening blasts in the narrow hall. A detective had fired from the first doorway, hitting two of the suspects. One of them collapsed beside me and proceeded to bleed profusely all over my new Ivy League suit.

What happened next is a little bit fuzzy. I suppose I was a bit dazed by all that had occurred. I do remember that someone called for ambulances. Both of the wounded men were wheeled away. There was the bedlam of arrests and charges and gathering evidence, but I recall few details. The night ended at a bar. The detectives and agents drank to their success. I sat there silent, shell shocked.

I got home at 3:00 A.M. My folks were waiting up for me, wanting to congratulate their son on his first day on the job. After all, I was the first son of this immigrant family to be born in America. That I had an important job with the federal government was something to be proud of. I had to think of something quick to explain the blood.

"The guys threw a party for me," I lied.

There had been a fight at the party, hence the blood. It was believable. They could envision a celebration in my honor, and they could easily imagine their son getting into a brawl. God knows I'd been in enough of them before.

When I reported for work on my second day, only Amato and Corbellini were in. Amato summoned me to his office. Evidently, Hermo and Carrozo had called in to report the events of the previous night. I figured I'd blown it—and badly. I half-expected Amato to ask for the badge back. Instead, he told me that I had handled myself well.

"You're ready for phase two of your training," he added.

What the hell ever happened to phase one? Biting my tongue, I kept the thought to myself.

"We make buys undercover," he continued. "It's standard U.S. government practice, but there are some important rules. Whenever you buy drugs, you have to be under the surveillance of other agents. It's for security and corroboration—and to keep you from getting burned. To overcome the burden of entrapment, you've got to make two buys from the same guy."

Amato's lecture went on for a few hours, touching on the importance of appearance and the need to "assimilate into the environment." I was given a handful of documents to read: reports, case summaries, and guidelines issued by the U.S. Attorney's Office. And that was it for "phase two" of my training.

"Go home. Change your clothes," he ordered. "Frequent the vicinity of 111th and Madison. Spanish Harlem. I don't think the blacks or Italians are going to accept you. Try the Puerto Ricans."

The black and Italian narcotics operations were well established and quite sophisticated. They were cautious, suspicious of new faces. Amato wasn't ready to put me up against such savvy opposition. The Puerto Rican gangs, on the other hand, were the up-and-comers in New York's criminal melting pot. They were more aggressive and undisciplined. They were hungrier and more likely to make a mistake.

Amato then handed me my official advance fund (OAF), $300 that I was to use for buying heroin. Serial numbers were recorded so that when the money was later found on the dope seller's person, it could be used as evidence against him. Today OAF money is photocopied prior to issuance. Agents were personally liable for the OAF if purchased substances turned out not to be illegal drugs. Honor among thieves doesn't exist in the drug trade. It was—and continues to be—common practice for drug sellers to substitute harmless powders for the heroin they purport to deliver. If an agent bought "turkey," as we called such substitutes, he was responsible for the purchase money. To protect themselves from being burned, some agents routinely reserved real heroin that they had confiscated in previous seizures to resubstitute for turkey. Later on, laws would change so that even persons selling turkey could be prosecuted if it was represented as being heroin or other controlled substances.

For the next three days I hung around Spanish Harlem. I made dozens of cold approaches, trying to buy a half-ounce of heroin. Everywhere I went, people ran from me. One guy told me I looked too healthy. Another said I looked like a cop. Finally, I developed the "legend" that I had a girlfriend dancing on Broadway who had the habit. In the name of love, I was trying to help her and her friends. One guy bought my story, probably because he was drunk at the time. He was a small-timer, a "go-fer." When he left to get the stuff, I called in to arrange the necessary surveillance. The buy went down without hitch: one-half ounce of 8 percent pure heroin.

As a narcotics agent, I later experienced my share of close calls, but perhaps none was closer than an incident that occurred in the late summer of 1960. With phases one and two of my training taking all of twenty-four hours, it's not hard to accept that within seven or eight months I was actually leading a team of agents, mostly other young guys like myself. They called us the Dawn Squad because we'd start hitting flats early on Friday morning. We'd be at it by 5:00 A.M., and we'd have our prisoners and evidence processed by 1:00 P.M. We scheduled it like that in order to get a head start on the weekend. There are priorities, and there are *priorities!*

During one of our dawn raids, five of us hit a second-floor apartment. It was the kind we called a railroad apartment, a long corridor with rooms branching to either side. I was the first one in. The first guy in has responsibility for the room farthest away from the entrance. The second guy gets the room second farthest away and so on. Gun in hand, I charged down the hall and smashed into the bedroom door football blocking style. It flew off the hinges on the first hit. A guy sat up on the bed. He had a Colt .45 semiautomatic in his hand. He pulled the trigger, and I heard the most beautiful-sounding click I ever heard in my life. If that gun hadn't jammed, my life would have ended right then and there. There wasn't time to contemplate my good fortune, though—not with the suspect trying frantically to work the slide on the Colt manually. I leaped up on the bed and kicked the son of a bitch in the jaw before he had another chance to pull the trigger. His skull slammed back into the headboard, and his eyes glazed over. I threw him off the bed, into the dresser. He slumped to the floor. His mouth was bleeding, and I could see that his jaw was broken. There was no more fight in him.

While another agent handcuffed him, I examined the Colt. I removed the magazine. It was fully loaded. I pulled back the slide and found a cartridge in the chamber. There was a neat little indentation in the primer where the firing pin had struck. Looking at the cartridge more carefully, I found it to be World War II surplus. Probably because of age or because it had been stored in wet or damp conditions, the primer had failed to detonate. Manufactured to kill Nazis and the forces who had bombed Pearl Harbor, the bullet had refused to kill me.

Justice is where you find it.

"BOBOES" AND SCAMS

In 1960, the Federal Bureau of Narcotics only had about 250 agents throughout the world, but it accounted for more arrests and criminals sentenced to the federal prison system than the FBI, which had more than 7,000 agents at the time. Part of the old FBN's effectiveness stemmed from the unique enforcement powers it possessed, but its success was also in no small part due to the wide latitude afforded street-level agents. Unfortunately, there were those who abused their autonomy—and others who were outright dirty. It didn't take me long to see that corruption had become institutionalized.

I accompanied a group of five senior agents to an apartment building in Washington Heights. I was instructed to remain on the street and watch the fifth-floor windows in the event that the subjects tried to throw out evidence. The other agents entered the building, and within a few minutes I could hear the unmistakable sounds of a raid in progress. Although one of the windows did shatter, nothing but shards of broken glass made it down to street level. Once the commotion had abated, another window was opened. An agent leaned out and motioned me to come up.

I was elated. Still a green rookie, I jumped at any opportunity to enter the *sanctum sanctorum* of the pros. I took the stairs two at a time and bounded into the apartment, stepping over the shattered door that lay at the entrance. Immediately I saw a dresser standing in the middle of the living room. It struck me as odd. What was a dresser doing in the living room? *In the middle of the living room?*

When one of the other agents told me to search the dresser, I definitely knew something was screwy. They had already been inside about fifteen minutes. They had searched everywhere else. Why hadn't they searched the dresser that was standing in the middle of the room? You didn't have to be a mental heavyweight to know something was not right.

I opened the top drawer. Inside was a packet about eight inches long and three inches wide. Maybe an inch thick. All wrapped in aluminum foil. Just sitting there in the otherwise empty drawer, just waiting to be found by a young, immature agent. I really don't know why—call it instinct—I pretended there was nothing there. I shut the drawer, then searched the other five or six drawers in the dresser.

"What did you find?" asked the agent who had given me the order to search the dresser.

"Nothing," I answered.

He was really pissed off. "Search it again," he commanded.

I went through the whole charade a second time while the other agents and three suspects watched in silence. Again I pronounced it clean.

"Get the fuck out!" shouted the senior agent.

I did just that.

A few minutes later, the five agents stormed out of the building, piled into their cars, and left me standing there. I had to take the subway back to the office, where I was greeted with stony silence. I didn't know what had just happened other than that I had really annoyed the guys I worked with, guys whom I relied on in dangerous situations. But still, I felt that the whole episode was *wrong*, that they had tried to use me somehow.

It wasn't until about a month later that I learned the truth. A group of us were having drinks at the Terminal Bar, which was located only a block from the office. We were celebrating the successful conclusion of a significant investigation. I happened to be seated next to one of the agents present the day I was asked to search the dresser. After a couple of hours of heavy drinking, I asked him, "What the hell was that all about?"

He explained that one of the residents of the apartment was a large-scale kilo dealer in heroin. His street name was Sheets. The agents wanted to recruit him as an informant, hopeful that he would lead them to even bigger dealers. In order to get him to flip, to turn informant, they had to provide suitable motivation. They needed to arrest Sheets, then trade the bust for information. Unable to collar him legitimately, a stash was placed in the dresser for me to find. Sheets would see that I was not part of the frame-up. He'd have no choice but to go along with the plan. Ignorance being bliss, not knowing that it was a setup, I was supposed to discover the package—which contained heroin pilfered from another seizure—and then be in a position to honestly testify under oath. But then I fucked everything up.

I was furious. Even though I was sitting down and he was standing, I hauled off and knocked him ass over teacups. He flew back into the oak railing that ran parallel to the bar. It snapped. He bounced onto a table and then dropped to the floor. Rolling over, he pulled his revolver and got off two quick shots, which hit the bar about a foot to my left. Lucky for me his aim was off just enough.

Needless to say, I didn't sleep much that night. It's bad enough being shot at by junkies and drug dealers, but to have a fellow agent try to take me out—well, it certainly prompted me to reevaluate my career plans. I seriously considered resigning. But as often happens, things have a way of resolving themselves if you just let them. Word quickly got around that you couldn't fuck with Tripodi. I'd "made my bones." I wouldn't play the game. They knew on what side of the line I stood, and if anything, it limited the number of compromising situations that I was exposed to. In a way I was lucky. I would have less temptation to contend with. That one day I would be involved in anticorruption work can probably be traced back to that goofy dresser and to a decision made more from instinct than anything else.

On another occasion, on the basis of an informant's information, I led a raid against a suspected heroin dealer who also happened to run a numbers bank. We found an ounce of heroin in the window box, exactly where our informant said it would be. Later, the informant confronted me.

"Just give me my cut," he demanded.

"What the fuck are you talking about?" I asked.

"I watched the whole thing from the alley," he explained. "When you went upstairs to look for the junk, your buddy found the bank. It's a lot of money, man. Just give me my cut!"

I believed that he had watched us. He described the raid in perfect detail—how many of us took part, who searched what part of the flat, everything. But I couldn't believe that my partner had pocketed numbers money. In those days, that kind of graft was called "making a bobo" (a bonus). I confronted him. Of course, he denied it. Given the choice of taking the word of an informant or an agent, I elected to side with the agent. Now I have my doubts.

Other times I'd report to work on a Monday morning and find a group of agents already in the office, busy at their typewriters, preparing reports, processing evidence. Obviously raids had occurred without my knowledge over the weekend.

"Why didn't you call me?" I'd ask.

The answers were always lame. "Your phone was busy" and "we didn't have time to call" were favorite excuses. The reports and busy-work were just a bullshit paper trail designed to mask raids on floating crap games. Typically, acting on a tip, agents converged on a game in an alley somewhere, drew their guns, and told everyone to get the hell out. Without the money, of course, which was then divvied up among the raiders.

The corruption in New York wasn't limited to the old FBN. Even the IRS got its share. Responsible for enforcing the gambling laws, IRS agents had easy pickings when raiding book joints, gambling establishments, and numbers banks. And then there were the boys in blue. New York's finest certainly knew a good thing when they saw it.

Once I was working with a New York cop on a surveillance. Time passed, and we got to talking. I found out this guy had been a dentist in Brooklyn. He gave up his practice to become a narcotics cop. Dentists make a lot of money. Even back then. Yet he felt he could make more as a New York cop.

He was probably right.

4

"COMMODIOUS"

Early in that first year with the FBN, still working with Hermo and Carrozo, I participated in the investigation of suspected heroin kilo dealer Marco DelGado. My partners had already made one buy from DelGado, but they hadn't been able to complete the required second purchase. One day, during a surveillance, we trailed DelGado all the way to Derby, Connecticut, a fairly upscale residential community about fifty miles north of New York City. Having followed him out of the gridlocked congestion of the Upper West Side and on up the Henry Hudson Parkway, it was embarrassing when we lost him in the quiet little country town. We sensed that he was about to lead us to someone important. We'd learn later that our instincts were right on the money.

Simultaneous to our ongoing investigation of DelGado, another team from the Fourth Enforcement Group was developing a case on a different suspect, a heroin junkie and dealer named FNU (first name unknown) Soto. Working with fellow agents George Rahas, Arthur Krueger, and James Ceburre, top undercover agent Al Garafalo made a number of buys from Soto. When they busted Soto, I was included in the raiding party. We broke into his apartment and dispersed to our assigned search areas. Rahas and myself were the first ones to come upon the suspect. As soon as we placed him under arrest, he dropped to the floor choking and panting, clutching his chest.

"Heart attack!" he gasped.

"Get an ambulance," Rahas ordered.

I flew out of the apartment as Rahas attempted to make Soto comfortable. I was racing down the stairs when I encountered Soto's twin brother, whose identity was known to me from previous surveillances.

"Your brother had a heart attack," I said, thinking that the brother could provide information that would prove helpful in rendering aid.

"That son of a bitch," he replied, to my surprise. "He ain't having no heart attack. He's a big actor. He does this all the time."

I spun around and ran back up to the apartment. Rahas was bent over Soto, worry in his eyes, doing everything he could to make the asshole comfortable. To Rahas's utter astonishment, I popped Soto one square in the jaw. I thought Rahas was going to have kittens.

"What the fuck are you doing?" he screamed. "Are you crazy? You're going to kill him!"

"If he's gonna have a heart attack, I'm gonna give it to him," I answered.

I was wrong. I shouldn't have hit Soto, but it really pissed me off that he had suckered us like that. And who knows what he might have tried with me out of the room and with Rahas's guard down?

Needless to say, Soto never had a coronary. Once busted, he flipped. He was easily "persuaded" to introduce Garafalo to yet another dealer, FNU Rodriguez. Buys were arranged, and Rodriguez was also arrested and flipped. Motivated to cooperate, Rodriguez then cut Garafalo into two merchant seamen, José Pena and Raul Santiago. At this point the case held the promise of progressing beyond the local dealers to the importers, perhaps even to the very source of supply.

The idea that criminals never rat on each other is strictly the stuff of movies and myth. A great deal of the FBN's work proceeded on the basis that little fish lead to big sharks. If we nailed a minor offender, we gave him a choice: Give us someone bigger or do time. Usually a good informant produced a number of arrests, each of which could be prosecuted or flipped, leading to yet more arrests. Sometimes we encountered resistance and had to resort to our own brand of salesmanship. "Help us out or we're gonna put you away for fifteen years. Within the first week you're gonna go queer for half the cell block. And while you're getting bent over in the joint, the friends you're protecting back here are gonna be banging your old lady. And when we do get them, however long it takes, we're gonna tell them you gave them up anyway."

All in all it was a fairly effective pitch. If it seems less than honorable, just remember that we were dealing with heroin peddlers caught red-handed in the act of buying, selling, or possessing dangerous drugs. I sure never lost a night's sleep over motivating some low-life dope seller to rat out some other low-life dope seller.

When it was thought that a suspect was likely to cooperate, care was taken to keep the actual arrest as quiet as possible. The fewer people who knew about it, the better. The very fact that a dealer or a junkie had been arrested was enough to undermine his credibility on the street—even if he wasn't working with us. Once arrested and flipped, the U.S. attorney made representations to the judge for the purpose of setting a low bail. By copping a plea, the informant had, in effect, waived his right to a trial. The only step left in the legal process was his sentencing, and that would be determined in large part by the nature and productivity of his impending cooperation. He would still do time, but it would be a small fraction of what the original charge would have garnered. In effect, he had a chance to "work off his case"—and that's exactly what we called it.

We tried to get an informant back on the street as quickly as possible, hopefully with his bona fides intact. It was then the informant's task to introduce an undercover agent to the agreed-upon target. As soon as sufficient trust had been established between the undercover agent and the target, the informant was moved out of the picture.

The agent's job was to maneuver the target to a public place—a bar, a restaurant, an airport terminal—to conduct a transaction under the surveillance of other agents. Of course the dope dealers understood our modus operandi and were justifiably suspicious of any such meeting places. They preferred quiet, private spots to conduct business. We obliged as best we could, usually with hotel rooms that had been rigged in advance with electronic monitoring devices. Sometimes we were forced to get a bit more creative. Once I used a yacht, which really impressed the suspect before we nailed his ass. Another time I used a Lear jet.

Garafalo had already met with Pena and Santiago a number of times when I was called in. His bona fides had already been established. Garafalo was the quintessential undercover agent. Thin. Pallid. Chain-smoking. Nervous. His eyes were always darting about, checking doorways, scrutinizing suspicious movement, scoping the action. He looked and acted more like a criminal than a lot of the guys he busted. He was a great negotiator, too, always haggling for a better price or demanding higher purity of the narcotics being purchased. A lot of agents just go for the first offer, and of course, that's a dead giveaway. Garafalo was a master at maneuvering suspects to locations conducive to surveillance or arrest. And he was good in court. His testimony was always rock solid and credible.

I accompanied Garafalo to a dockside bar in Hoboken, a rough joint catering to seamen from the merchant ships. He played the part of an outfit hood, a big-time connected buyer. I was his bagman and bodyguard. It was my first time undercover. I didn't do much besides stand around looking nasty and listening to everything that was said, but it felt great just the same. It was the feeling of possessing this incredible secret. I was a U.S. narcotics agent, which was still hard enough for me to believe. I knew it, and they didn't. There was a sense of power in that. Invigoration. Control.

Eventually, after a number of meetings in Hoboken, Pena and Santiago agreed to introduce Garafalo to Clarence Asperlund. A Dutch national, Asperlund was ship's cook on the *Excalibur*, the same vessel that employed Pena and Santiago. Showing good faith, Garafalo went alone to the first meeting. The encounter took place at Asperlund's home—*in Derby, Connecticut.*

Asperlund proved tougher to crack than any of the others, however. Whether suspicious or just shrewd, he refused to come to terms with Garafalo on a major buy. Reluctantly, it was decided to stop the investigation and raid Asperlund's house.

There were eight to ten of us in the raiding party. While two supervisors stayed with Asperlund and his wife, the rest of us split up and searched the large house. We looked everywhere—in drawers, closets, under rugs, in the rafters, between the beams, everywhere. I was assigned to a large unfinished room on the third floor. Attached to the room was a bathroom, also unfinished except for a commode. No shower. No tub. No wash basin. Just a commode.

A chain-smoker at the time, I was polishing off one Camel after another as I searched the premises. The more frustrated I became, the more I smoked. Each time I finished a cigarette, I flipped it into the commode and flushed. Having an urge, I took a leak and noticed that the butts were still floating in the bowl. I flushed and worked the handle, but nothing helped. Still, it didn't strike me as anything but a malfunctioning toilet. After all, the room was obviously under construction. I just figured that Asperlund hadn't gotten around to fixing it yet. Or maybe he was just a lousy plumber. Before I made things worse, I retreated into the adjoining room and continued my search, ripping the moldings off the walls.

By now Rahas had had enough. He was a bull of a man. Two hundred and fifty pounds of solid muscle packed into a body just under six feet in height. He grabbed a fire ax and drove the blade into the living-room floor. He turned to Asperlund and said, "We're going to tear down every fucking wall in this house until you tell us where it is." Nobody doubted that he meant it.

That Dutchman must have really liked that house. He caved in immediately and led the raiding party right to his stash. To my embarrassment, 2.5 kilograms of pure heroin were hidden in a trap under what turned out to be a false commode. It wasn't hooked up to any plumbing at all. The water in the bowl had been placed there. The whole contraption was on a hinge. He swung it back, and there was the dope. Right where I had pissed and doused my cigarettes. Needless to say, I incurred a major helping of well-earned sarcasm.

Asperlund was arrested and charged. Facing more than fifteen years in federal prison, Asperlund, like those before him, decided to cooperate. He told us where the remainder of the heroin was secreted on the *Excalibur*. Working on his information, the U.S. Customs Service was engaged to search the ship. An additional 3.2 kilograms of heroin was found in an egg crate in the ship's bakery, exactly where Asperlund said it would be.

Under interrogation, Asperlund confessed that over the previous eight years he had personally imported more than eight hundred kilograms of heroin from the Aranci brothers, a source in Marseille, France. During World War II, Marius, George, and Joseph Aranci had been active in the French underground. After the armistice, however, they applied the clandestine arts they had mastered during the war to the drug trade. They were considered top targets by the FBN. Their organization was thought to be worldwide.

Asperlund was bailed out and convinced to set up a delivery of three kilograms of heroin from the Arancis to Garafalo in New York. Garafalo accompanied Asperlund to France, and all went as planned. A courier was dispatched by the Arancis to bring in the heroin. Upon delivery to Ralph Cianchetti, a known New York drug trafficker, both the courier and Cianchetti were arrested. Simultaneously, French authorities nabbed the Aranci brothers in Marseille. Further work by the French succeeded in dismantling a major processing laboratory. However, if the French ever learned the true extent of the Arancis' operations, they didn't share their information with us. Nor did they extend interrogation privileges. Suspicions quickly surfaced that one or more of the Arancis had a "relationship" with someone in the French intelligence community.

Other arrests were made in the States, including Marco DelGado, the guy who had originally lost us just a few blocks from Asperlund's house. DelGado skipped bail and was eventually re-arrested in Boston. I was sent there to testify at the extradition hearing. In Boston, the court maintains the old English custom of standing at the docket. I took my place, they swore me in, I looked across toward the defendant's table, and I identified DelGado, which was all that I was required to do at the proceeding. DelGado bolted to his feet, pointed at me, and screamed, "I'm going to see you in a bathtub with salt!" I didn't know what it meant at the time, but I later learned that when hit men wanted to get rid of a body, they soaked it in a bathtub using a salt-and-chemical solution. Eventually the corpse actually dissolved and simply ran down the drain.

The Asperlund case represented a classic bottom-to-top investigation. As such it's still studied by narcotics law enforcement professionals today. It proved, beyond a doubt, that given the time, effort, motivation, and energy, you can start with a junkie and go all the way back to the source of supply. It was possible in 1960, and it's still possible in the 1990s.

Those of us who had worked the case felt pretty good when it came to a successful conclusion. We figured we owed ourselves a little celebration, and so a bunch of us headed on down to the Terminal Bar. That was the night I decided to ask about a certain dresser in Washington Heights and wound up being shot at by another agent.

5

GETTING THE
BREAKS

When we didn't have anything scheduled—no surveillances, no buys, no raids, no arrests—we cruised the streets of Harlem looking for something to do. We'd try to catch a deal going down. If we spotted somebody running or acting suspiciously, we'd act on it. Basically, we just went out looking for trouble, which wasn't all that hard to find.

The obvious problem with this approach is that it's purely reactive and therefore highly subjective. Not all is as it appears to be at first glance. Not every guy running down a Harlem street is a dope dealer. Once, three of us took down a teenager being chased by a uniformed cop. Our guns were out. Two of us hit the kid in our effort to get him under control. Then the cop told us that the kid had run out of a deli without paying for a slice of pie and a glass of milk. We couldn't believe it. We had almost killed this poor kid over a lousy piece of pie. That's how on-the-edge we were, how reckless, how hair-trigger ready to jump into action.

Oftentimes we'd pass groups of people gathered at intersections. When it was really slow, it was not unusual for us to break up these street corner congregations, line the individuals up against a wall, and pat them down. Most of the time, these random searches produced illegal weapons or drugs. Today, law enforcement officers are prohibited from stopping a suspect without "sufficient probable cause." For fear of being disciplined or sued for false arrest, most won't even ask a guy's name unless they feel they have proper cause.

Although we dressed in street clothes, we really didn't try to conceal our identities as law enforcement officers. Three white guys cruising Harlem—what else could we be? In the summertime, the biggest problem was figuring out where to hide the gun. We couldn't just parade around New York City with revolvers strapped to our hips like a bunch of cowboys. Most of the guys wore their shirts out to conceal their weapon. Others had elaborate tailoring done to their clothes. Still others just opted to carry their guns in brown paper bags. Because of my size, I was able to get away with slipping my gun under the front of my waistband. I could still tuck my shirt in as long as I folded it over in front to allow easy access.

During the summer of 1960, I was patrolling with Hermo and Carrozo one night when we decided to introduce ourselves to a group of unsavory-looking characters loitering on a street corner. Hermo and Carrozo ordered the men to line up against a nearby wall. There were about fourteen of them, and we quickly got them in place with their hands on the bricks and their feet spread wide and set well back from the base of the wall. I was given the job of patting them down. I'd done it before, but never so many at once and certainly never with an audience. Hermo hovered over me and itemized, for my benefit and for the benefit of all within earshot, the myriad lapses of proper procedure in my novice technique. His criticism was detailed and enthusiastic. After about the fifth search, however, he backed off. Maybe he gave up on me, figuring I was a lost cause. Or maybe I passed his test. It was hard to tell with him sometimes.

I found contraband on each and every one of the suspects. Shiny chrome Saturday night specials. Switchblades. Straight razors. Marijuana. Heroin. When I put my hand on the back of the last man in line, he bolted, sprinting down the street. I took off after him. I was still in pretty good shape back then, and with no trouble at all I caught up to him within a half-block. He was only about 150 pounds. It was no contest. I pushed from behind. He went down easily, but then popped back to his feet and shoved something into his mouth. It looked like a small glassine bag. I tried to hit him in the stomach, thinking I'd force him to cough it up. But just as I swung, he doubled over. My left fist—I'm left-handed—caught him in the right eye. My thumb broke when it hit his cheekbone, what doctors call a Bennett's fracture and what fighters call "boxer's thumb." He got the worst of it, though. My knuckles, carrying the full force of my punch, went unimpeded into his eye, which popped out of its socket.

We rushed him to the nearest hospital, hoping that the damage could be repaired if we got him there quickly. I stayed with him while the doctors tried without success to save his eye. The doctors made it clear they had no use for me. I guess they figured it was a case of police brutality. Or maybe they just didn't like narcs. They had no way to know what had happened on the street, that the injury was completely unintentional. It was only after they finished treating my prisoner that they reset my thumb and placed it in a cast.

A lot of the senior agents used "equipment" during arrests—saps, jacks, gun butts, billies. My sense of fair play, the legacy of my football days, told me that if you can't hit a guy with your bare hands then forget it. Punch him or shoot him. One or the other. Now, with my good hand in a cast, I started to understand why the veterans augmented their fists.

Two weeks later, I accompanied Hermo and new agent Leonard McNeil to Fox Street in the East Bronx, then one of the toughest neighborhoods in all of New York. Our assignment was to arrest a guy named FNU Rosa. Another agent, Ray Maduro, had already made a couple of buys from Rosa. For some time Maduro had been trying to negotiate a major buy. His plan was that a meeting would occur during which Maduro would show Rosa the money and Rosa would show Maduro a sample of the heroin. Once Rosa had given sufficient representation that he was in possession of the total quantity of heroin under negotiation, Maduro was to signal for other agents to close in. The agents were to arrest Maduro along with Rosa, thereby maintaining Maduro's legend as a dealer.

The plan went sour. Rosa either couldn't put the deal together or refused to. Maduro phoned us and instructed us to hit Rosa's apartment. We were simply to arrest him and seize whatever we found on the premises.

The apartment was on the third floor. Hermo and I ran up the stairs. McNeil stayed in the car, manning the radio. I hit the door with my shoulder. It gave way so easily that my momentum carried me right down to the floor. I landed on my hands and knees. My left hand was still in the cast. My gun was in my right hand. Rosa was waiting behind the door. I looked up, and there he was, swinging the biggest sword I'd ever seen in my life. A big, two-handed samurai job. From my perspective on the floor, with the blade slicing toward my head, it looked like it was about twelve feet long. It whizzed over my head and stuck in the door jamb.

I jumped up, shoving my gun into his considerable gut. The barrel disappeared into his blubber. I could have shot him right then and there. It would have been perfectly justified. He had a deadly weapon. It was still in his hands. He had demonstrated intent to kill. He had resisted arrest by a federal officer. I had him cold, but again my sense of fair play kicked in. Instinctively, instead of pulling the trigger, I swung my dominant hand, my broken left, at him. The cast drove into his jaw. It hit him solid—and my thumb broke. Again.

I lost it. A dope peddler had just tried to decapitate me. My hand felt like it had just been caught under a pile driver. I was not in a good mood. I drop-kicked that son of a bitch from one end of the apartment to the other. I took him apart. I hit him hard and often. When I saw him weeks later at his sentencing, he told me he wished I had killed him.

"You'll have to take care of that yourself," I replied.

Obviously, I still hadn't learned my lesson about using "equipment." My thumb had to be reset, and a new cast had to be applied. Weeks later, after the cast was removed, I spent many days squeezing a rubber ball, trying to regain the strength in my left hand.

The injury forced me to cut back on my duty time. Compounding the situation, Hermo and McNeil—who had replaced Carrozo—were both on leave. I was flying solo with a bad wing, and I needed some overtime to compensate for all the time I'd lost. I contacted another group, and they indicated they could use some help. They were planning a bust near Madison Avenue and the 120s. They just wanted some additional backup. They doubted I'd be involved in the arrest. It sounded like just what I was looking for.

They assigned me a partner for the night. A new guy. It was his second night on the job. He was a New York law school graduate.

Columbia, I think. Soaking wet he didn't weigh 150 pounds. On tiptoe he might have been five foot five. I drove a 1960 Bonneville convertible to the prearranged point and parked. All we had to do was watch the street and listen to the two-way radio. For about fifteen minutes we engaged in the usual small talk. Then a call came over the radio.

"Tripodi! Pick him up. He's coming your way."

"What's he look like?" I radioed back.

"Biggest black guy you ever saw!" came the reply.

They weren't lying. Coming around the corner *was* the biggest black guy I ever saw. More than 300 pounds. At least six foot seven. This guy was a walking oak tree.

I jumped out of the car, held up my badge, and shouted, "Federal agent! You're under arrest."

He laughed. Then he swung at me.

I swung back—you guessed it—with my left hand. He dipped his head, and my hand collided with his skull. This time I broke my pinkie, as well as a number of other bones between the finger and the wrist. In about four different places. And for all my trouble, the object of my aggression wasn't even breathing hard.

I glanced over at my partner. There he stood with his brand new .38 Colt Detective Special in his shaking hand, looking like he wanted to be anywhere else in the world but where he was. With all of one day's experience to draw on, he pulled the trigger. The suspect took the bullet in the gut. He didn't fall. He just sat down. Slowly, under his own steam, the behemoth settled to the ground and leaned back against the wall of a building.

My hand hurt like hell. My gut-shot prisoner was quite possibly bleeding to death. My partner was babbling to himself, walking in circles, and otherwise being totally useless. The other teams couldn't respond to my radio calls because the buildings were interfering with my transmissions. Fortunately, an ambulance drove up. I don't know if an onlooker called for it or whether it just happened to be driving down the street. The attendant got out and informed me that the prisoner had to be restrained.

"For what?" I asked. "The guy's dying."

"Union rules," he answered, as if that was the last word in last words.

Disgusted, I retrieved the handcuffs from where I kept them on the emergency-brake handle. It was going to be difficult manipulating the cuffs with one hand, but I could see that my partner was incapable of rendering assistance. As it turned out, it didn't matter. The prisoner's wrists were so enormous the cuffs wouldn't close anyway.

Again I debated with the ambulance attendant, and again he answered with that most unassailable of arguments, "Union rules."

I requisitioned the prisoner's belt, tied it around his wrists, and pronounced him "restrained." The attendant reluctantly agreed, then added, "But he's too big for the stretcher."

The prisoner had heard enough. Bullet or no bullet, stretcher or no stretcher, he was going to the hospital. He got to his feet and walked, with our help, to the ambulance. As soon as the big man was settled in the back of the ambulance, I stepped up on the bumper, intending to ride along. The attendant put his hand on my chest and said, "We can't take more than one at a time."

"Why the fuck not?" I asked.

"Union regs," he answered predictably.

By this time the pain in my hand was unbearable. I was going to the hospital, and I was going that very moment. I pulled my gun, stuck it in his face, and said, "Drive!"

He did.

Evidently there was no union regulation prohibiting the commandeering of an ambulance by a federal narcotics agent. Or if there was, he didn't bother to mention it.

I found out later that the prisoner's wound was not as serious as it looked. All that fat had prevented the bullet from reaching any vital organs. I don't think he spent more than two or three days in the hospital.

After the third break, I reluctantly took to using a palm sap, a piece of leather wrapped around the hand with a small pocket of sand or buckshot in the palm. One day we were searching the apartment of a heavyweight fighter. He followed me all around, shadowboxing, sparring, generally showing off. At first he kept his distance, but then he threw a left hook into my shoulder. I spun and slapped him on the right ear. I had suede gloves on, and under the left glove was the palm sap. He crumbled to the floor, clutching his head and mumbling.

"Jesus! You should be in the ring," he moaned.

Sure. Just as long as I have the right "equipment."

6

"WHO'S FIRST?"

In August of 1960, during my eighth month on the job, I was finally sent to the Treasury Law Enforcement Officers Training School (TLEOTS) in Washington, D.C., for the official training program. TLEOTS was located on 12th Street, N.W., between New York Avenue and H Street in a nondescript building that had been subdivided into classrooms. By no stretch of the imagination could you call it an academy or a campus. It was more like a vocational school or a small inner-city commuter college with very little in the way of special facilities. Since there were no dormitories on site, we were given per diems to pay for room and board. Such arrangements were left entirely up to us. If you wanted to sleep on a park bench, eat sardines, and pocket the per diem, it was perfectly satisfactory, just as long as you showed up for class at the appointed time. Most of the trainees, however, opted for transient hotels or apartments that rented by the week.

I roomed with Roger Warner, a narcotics agent from Chicago who later transferred to the Secret Service, and Paul Landis, who was already with the Secret Service. Both were great guys, but except for sporadic telephone calls through the years, we all went our separate ways after TLEOTS. The apartment we shared was on Meridian Hill, near the foreign embassies. At the time, the neighborhood was renowned for its European gardens and was considered quite desirable.

TLEOTS training was a cooperative venture. The Treasury Department believed in agency collaboration and synergism. Thus, it was not unusual for FBN agents to share training with counterparts from the IRS, the Customs Service, the Secret Service, the Coast Guard, the Alcohol and Tobacco Tax Unit (ATTU), and other entities then under the Treasury Department. Such fraternity is nonexistent today, with each enforcement operation jealous and suspicious of the others. The current realities of budget and career survival dictate isolationist strategies that pit agency against agency. In fact, it's not uncommon to find two departments within the same agency working at cross-purposes in an adversarial climate.

Under the Treasury Department, federal drug law enforcement was based primarily on the very tough customs regulations and tax statutes. Today, with the Drug Enforcement Administration (DEA) within the dominion of the Justice Department, the main antidrug legal weapons are the much-less-stringent interstate commerce laws. Thus, the evolution of federal drug law enforcement over the last thirty years has seen the agencies entrusted with enforcing the laws split into factions and the laws themselves diluted.

On the surface it might appear that all was well in 1960, with several diverse agencies interacting and singing off the same sheet of Treasury Department music. While the situation did have its merits, those same agencies also shared in the Treasury Department's longstanding reputation for rampant corruption. Going back to the fabled T-men, whose ranks included such straight-arrow figures as Eliot Ness, it was the Alcohol and Tobacco Tax Unit agents—the so-called revenuers—who had the most opportunity for graft. For every Eliot Ness, there were dozens of others who found ways to participate in the illegal gains of their supposed adversaries.

During Prohibition it was common practice for New York bootleggers to sail their illegal booze out on barges to meet incoming ocean liners from Europe. The liquor was smuggled aboard ship and later off-loaded under the label of *Imported Scotch. Imported from Brooklyn* would have been far more accurate. The practice did not escape detection by the Coast Guard and the ATTU, but yet it flourished. When the Coast Guard did intercept the smuggled shipments, the confiscated goods were often sold back to the bootleggers or to their competitors. After enough such disruptions of their lucrative trade, it was possible to earn payoffs from the mobsters just by threatening an interdiction. Similar parasitic schemes operated on the drug and gambling rackets.

Corruption within Treasury was almost a tradition. It existed as a given, as an established means of doing business. Effectiveness was the rationalization. Crooks were being put in jail. Drugs were being taken off the streets. If some ill-gotten gains were finding their ways into the pockets of agents, it was, after all, dirty money anyway. Mob money. Drug money. When the arrest and conviction rates of Treasury Department law enforcement entities became, by comparison, an embarrassment to the FBI, J. Edgar Hoover often went on the attack, holding up his own people as paragons of virtue and condemning the T-men as corrupt and unprofessional. The T-men, on the other hand, tended to characterize the FBI as a do-nothing collection of bureaucrats more interested in their own press releases than in law enforcement.

It was during the latter stages of the Treasury Department's involvement with drug law enforcement that I attended TLEOTS. Eventually, the Coast Guard, along with its considerable interdiction abilities, would be moved over to the Department of Transportation. The FBN would evolve into the Bureau of Narcotics and Dangerous Drugs (BNDD) and be placed under the Justice Department. An era was coming to a close. The Treasury Department monopoly on drug law enforcement would soon end. So would the interagency camaraderie. The corruption, however, would continue.

Our daily TLEOTS training regimen usually started at 6:00 A.M. at the shooting range in the basement of the U.S. Treasury next to the White House. From there we'd head to classrooms where we'd be instructed on fingerprinting, interrogation, arrest procedures, search techniques, surveillance, undercover craft, report writing, and other aspects of law enforcement. Sometimes we'd be assigned to street exercises, dispersing into the capital to apply what we'd learned in class.

After eight months of on-the-job training in the streets of New York, there wasn't a whole lot for me to learn at TLEOTS. Our educational system usually progresses from the theoretical to the practical, from concept to application. In the FBN, it was the reverse. I'd already done it. Now I was learning it by the book.

My eight weeks at TLEOTS weren't an entire waste, however. Every night after class a group of trainees would meet at the Officer's Club at 21st Street and R Street, N.W. One of our classmates, a Captain White of the Coast Guard Intelligence Service, was staying there. He got us in even though admittance was supposed to be restricted to officers in branches of the armed forces. We'd rendezvous with a group of girls we'd befriended. Typically, we'd have cocktails at the O Club before heading out to a restaurant for dinner. All in all, it wasn't tough duty.

I began seeing one of the girls regularly, a former cheerleader for the University of Maryland. I'll call her Patricia. One night I was having a few beers with Patricia at the O Club when Ben Scotti, the defensive halfback for the Washington Redskins, strutted up to our table and pointed his finger in my face. Right behind him was former Notre Dame All-American Ralph Guillermi, the Skins' quarterback.

"You keep away from her," Scotti threatened. "She belongs to my buddy Ralph."

"I don't see any sign on her," I shot back. "I don't think she belongs to anybody. The chick can do what she wants."

With that, he tried to cheap shot me, but I saw it coming. He telegraphed a right, which I caught. I left hooked and came back with a solid right. Before it could go any further, my friends from TLEOTS intervened and broke it up. I was satisfied to let it be, but Scotti decided to go for an Academy Award, struggling to break free and hissing all kinds of "let me at him" threats. Finally he gave it up and headed for the door.

"We'll be waiting for you outside," Scotti warned.

"Fine!" I answered.

Scotti had the rep of being a tough, street-smart punk from South Jersey. The rumor around town was that while he and his brother were playing college ball for the University of Maryland, they severely beat up another player in the locker room after a loss. Scotti's hard-guy image certainly benefited from the story.

After about two more hours, we decided to head out for dinner. My friends from TLEOTS were still around. They offered to tag along. I declined. I didn't need an escort. I was sure that two big-shot ball players like Scotti and Guillermi had better things to do than wait around outside for two hours on a chilly October night.

I was wrong.

As soon as Patricia and I stepped out of the O Club door, we saw Scotti, Guillermi, and tackle Franny O'Brien waiting by my car. Scotti's jacket was off. He was warming up for the main event, shadowboxing and yelling threats.

They started for us.

One on one I might have tried it. But not three at once. I pulled my Colt .38 Detective Special, pointed the two-inch barrel in the air, cocked the hammer, and said, "Who's first?"

O'Brien and Guillermi backed off, but Scotti still wanted a piece of me. He kept running his mouth until finally his two teammates succeeded in pulling him back to their car.

I was one lucky junior agent. Had they kept coming at me, I would have had a very tough decision to make: take one hell of a beating or shoot three local football heroes.

I don't want to even think about explaining that one to the D.C. police, let along my superiors at the FBN.

7

UN PEZZO DI NOVANTA

They called him *"il muto."*

The mute. The quiet one. Someone who could be trusted. Someone who wouldn't talk.

He went by the name of Tarantino. Funereally attired in a black suit, black overcoat, white-on-white shirt, and white tie, he was the prototypical Mafia hit man. A "torpedo," as the dark profession was more commonly called back then. Nerves wore thin throughout the Toronto underworld when this mysterious stranger hit town during the winter of 1961. A gang war was raging between Italian and Jewish factions over the control of gambling and service businesses such as restaurant supply and liquor distribution. Any unexplained new arrival in Toronto's Italian community was sufficient cause for concern, but such a brooding, potentially lethal presence demanded even closer scrutiny and care. No one was quite sure just who Tarantino was after. Or maybe he was just looking for work, in which case it made far more sense to become his employer than his target.

After taking up residence at the King George Hotel, Tarantino began frequenting mob hangouts. One of his haunts was a combination espresso club and pool hall where he sat quietly for hours in the corner cleaning his fingernails with a pocketknife. When approached for conversation, his replies were seldom more expansive than a grunt or a nod of his head.

I was Tom Tarantino. The *"il muto"* bit—my rep for being close-mouthed—actually evolved from necessity. Confronted with obscure Sicilian dialects I didn't understand, my only recourse was to bluff my way through the conversations by saying as little as I could get away with. That such noncommunication served to reinforce my torpedo legend was an unexpected, and greatly appreciated, side benefit.

My undercover activities in Toronto started with a fugitive investigation. A fugitive warrant is issued when an arrested or indicted suspect has been released on bail and then fails to appear in court. Every law enforcement office has more fugitive investigations on file than it can handle, and often they're treated as last priorities. Generally they're pursued only during times of extremely light case loads. Ironically, such investigations often yield results beyond the apprehension of the target fugitive. Information uncovered during fugitive investigations can augment other cases or even cause new investigations to be opened. The so-called French Connection case actually sprang from such an investigation.

The fugitive I was after was one Settimo Accardi. Born in Tunisia and raised in Sicily, Accardi had been arrested along with a number of others in connection with the substantial heroin traffic he was conducting between Sicily, Canada, New York, and New Jersey. Released on bail, he quickly skipped town, leaving behind his wife and two sons who resided in New Jersey.

The initial focus of my investigation centered on Accardi's family. It was obvious they were receiving money from unknown sources on a regular basis. His family was being well provided for, and we had good reason to believe that the steady flow of money was originating with Accardi. The cash was being filtered through an intricate network of banks in Sicily and Venezuela. Besides trying to track Accardi through the complex paper trail of international bank records, we also started mail and toll-call surveillance on his family and known friends.

Mail covers were initiated by a written request on official FBN letterhead to the U.S. Postal Service. We were then provided with a description, including postmarks, dates, and return addresses, of each and every letter and parcel delivered to the address under investigation. In full compliance with constitutional protections, the letters and parcels were never opened. Such covers often went on for months or even years at a time. Today, mail coverage requires a subpoena.

Toll coverage was simply a listing provided by the telephone company of all long-distance calls emanating from a specific phone line. We were required to provide a subpoena for toll coverage, but the subpoena was typically supplied after the fact. For instance, one subpoena would be submitted on a monthly basis for all the toll covers activated the previous month. The current practice is to submit one subpoena in advance for each phone line to be covered.

Mail and toll covers continue to be important investigative tools. They establish patterns of calls and correspondence that often prove helpful in tying one suspect to another or in branching an investigation off into new territory. If a cover is productive, the documentation can be used as evidence to support a request for a court order to install electronic surveillance on a particular phone line. Pen registers, devices that don't require the constant attention of agents, are often used to capture the phone numbers of incoming and outgoing calls. Pen-register data, toll covers, and informant affidavits are all used to back up requests for intercepts, which allow telephone conversations to be recorded. Typically, an apartment is rented undercover and set up as a listening post (LP). Equipment is installed at the site to monitor calls related to several different ongoing investigations. An agent can stop by periodically, pick up the tapes, and distribute them to the interested investigators.

The covers on Accardi's home indicated significant activity between New Jersey and Toronto. Intelligence coming in from other sources suggested that Accardi often traveled to Toronto to meet with his family and business associates. Surveillances were established on the New Jersey family home and on one of Accardi's sons who was a student at an upstate New York university located less than one hundred miles from Toronto. When the surveillances proved unproductive, it was decided to try an undercover approach.

At the time, my undercover experience was extremely limited, but I had participated in several surveillances of undercover operations.

I had watched, and hopefully learned, something about the under-cover craft. Many of the surveillance sites had been bars, restaurants, and espresso shops in the Italian sections of New York and Newark, fertile training ground for the environment I would experience in Toronto's Little Italy. Still, I just couldn't blow in and start asking for Accardi. I had to establish a plausible legend that would allow me to penetrate the local underworld and then, through those contacts, eventually find my target. I sought out the three agents within the New York office of the FBN whom I considered to be the top under-cover pros—Al Garafalo, Joe Amato, and Patty Biase. Garafalo, de-spite his nervous idiosyncrasies, was the coolest undercover agent I ever encountered. Amato's effectiveness derived in large measure from his inscrutability; you just never knew what he was thinking. Biase used style and flair; he did it with sharp clothes and a cavalier attitude. Together, we analyzed the situation in Toronto and came up with the hit man legend. It was perfect. The Toronto gang war was taking its toll, and the demand for experienced torpedoes was high.

It wasn't long after I arrived in Toronto that one of the local wise guys was tasked to check me out. He introduced himself simply as "Toto," a common nickname for Salvatore. Squat in build and a bit flabby, he said he worked as a seaman off and on. He always dressed neatly, but he never wore a tie, an indication to me that he was probably of very low rank within the local criminal organization. A perpetual five o'clock shadow—he always seemed to need a shave—and a toothless smile were his most memorable features. He wasted no time in asking all the predictable questions:

"Where you from?"

"Where do your people come from in Italy?"

"Why are you here?"

"Do you have relatives here?"

"Do you need something?"

The interrogation was in Sicilian. My background was Calabrian and Abruzzese. I may have been able to bluff my way into the FBN by demonstrating some command of other Italian dialects, but there was no way I could con Toto. It took all my concentration just to translate what he was saying. I got it more by inference and guess-work than by direct translation. By absolute necessity, I kept my answers brief and evasive:

My people were from "down below"—that is, they were from

Sicily. I was in town looking for work, "anything that paid well and let me have long vacations."

I could see that he understood. Beyond my baited comment, my appearance, and my demeanor, it's possible that Toto had been previously assigned the job of recruiting hit men, a task he had perhaps accomplished in the past by drawing on a small, trusted pool of Italian drivers, runners, and couriers. He may have *wanted* to believe I was a torpedo.

Without breaking character, I looked for opportunities to throw my arm fraternally across his shoulders or to walk arm in arm with him. Such physical contact was in keeping with accepted Italian custom and reinforced the idea of a budding friendship. It also allowed me to covertly search for concealed guns and knives. He never impressed me as being muscle, but I never doubted he was the kind who could sneak up from behind and cooly insert a shiv between my ribs. It didn't hurt to be careful.

It wasn't long after my first meeting with Toto that I began hearing myself referred to as *"il muto."* I understood what that meant, but I was confused by the meaning of another moniker that some of the old-timers had hung on me: *"Un pezzo di novanta"*—a piece of ninety. I hadn't heard that one before. I had no idea what the hell they were talking about. It troubled me, but since it was said with obvious respect—perhaps even dread—I assumed it could only help to establish my hard-guy legend.

Two nights after the initial conversation with Toto, I was approached by Tanino (short for Gaetano) and Mimmo (short for Domenico). They befriended me, and we hung out together for several nights, hitting their favorite Italian restaurants and bars. As with Toto, the conversations, most of which centered on food and drink, were in Sicilian. Although obviously lacking in formal education, they were extremely streetwise. Their profanity and penchant for curses would cause a sailor to blush, assuming he could understand them. Most of all, they just struck me as being homesick for the Old Country; they missed the *paese* (hometown) back in Sicily. On two occasions, on my way back to the hotel, I noticed that I was being followed. They had swallowed the bait, but still they were being very prudent.

One night they took me to a pizzeria and introduced me to the owners, Baldassare Accardo and Benedetto Zizzo. It was clear that these two guys weren't mere restaurateurs. I was being taken up the chain of command and showcased. If I was to be accepted, it was important that I be exposed to loftier plateaus of the mob hierarchy. Accardo and Zizzo were men of weight, men who could make life-or-death decisions. Unlike the others, who had identified themselves simply with first names, Accardo and Zizzo were presented to me formally and introduced by their full names. I was referred to as "*un amico* from New York." Accardo and Zizzo nodded, shook my hand, and then disappeared into the back room.

On the way back from the pizzeria, Mimmo said, "If you can hang around for a few months, we'll have some work for you. It'll pay very well. Afterwards you can go on a long vacation."

After Mimmo and Tanino dropped me off, I called Joe Amato from a pay phone. I couldn't chance using the hotel telephone. It was likely that the Mounties or the provincial police had tapped the line. I suspected that they were no less interested in me than the underworld factions. If I was in town to hire out as an assassin, then it was logical to assume that the responsible law enforcement agencies would try to thwart my efforts. In any undercover activity of this type, there always exists the possibility of attracting the attention of law enforcement agencies, which, usually for reasons of security, have not been apprised of the operation.

I was really jacked up. I'd conned the mob. They had accepted me. They were ready to give me a contract. I gave Amato all the details. To my dismay, he ordered me back to New York.

I arranged lunch with Toto the next day.

"I have to leave for a couple of days," I told him.

"Why?" he asked suspiciously. "We've got plans for you this weekend."

"Got to pay my dues," I answered, trying to be as vague as possible.

"I understand," he replied. "Every man has to service his woman."

I'm glad he understood, because I sure didn't. How he got from "pay my dues" to "service his woman" was beyond me. In any event, thanks to another communications gaffe and Mafia machismo, it appeared I could get out of town without undermining the progress I had made.

When I returned to New York, Amato explained that agents from another group were in the midst of a large undercover operation involving Italians in New York, Sicily, and Toronto. Two of their primary suspects were Accardo and Zizzo, the supposed pizzeria owners. They didn't want me messing up their play. I had to abort my operation in Toronto to protect a far more important ongoing investigation.

Eventually Settimo Accardi was apprehended in Sicily through the tedious backtracking of the funds he had transferred to his family. After prolonged diplomatic wrangling, he was extradited to the United States, tried, convicted, and sentenced. He died in jail.

The night of my return to New York, I related the "cultural achievements" of my trip to my father—namely, the improvement of my mastery of Sicilian. I told him about the foods I had eaten, many of which were similar to those we were accustomed to: a pasta dish with broccoli, cauliflower, and eggplant; *trippa*, tripe in a red sauce; *pasta con broccoletti*, pasta mixed with a special bitter variety of broccoli. Finally, I asked him about *"un pezzo di novanta."*

"That's what they called me. What's it mean?" I asked.

"Ooo! That's bad," he answered quickly.

"What the hell does it mean?" I demanded.

"I don't know," he replied. "I've got to look it up in the dream book."

So-called dream books dealt with the interpretation of dreams and the assignment of numerical equivalents to human activities and attributes. They were widely used throughout the immigrant community of Southern Italians. Most dream interpretations were simply rooted in the principle of opposition. If one dreamed of a birth, it meant someone close, a friend or a family member, was about to die. A dream about a wedding usually portended marital strife. The numerological components of the dream book journals had infiltrated the immigrant lexicon to the extent that criminal elements sometimes used the numbers as a kind of code. A woman was seventy-seven, the long stems of the sevens denoting two legs. Food was ten. Sex was seven. And fear was ninety.

Those Sicilians in Toronto had been saying that I was a man to be feared.

They had that right. I may not have been the hired assassin they thought I was, but I had penetrated their organization. It was an accomplishment I marked as my coming of age as an undercover agent. Unfortunately, I never had the chance to return to Toronto and finish what I had started.

8

CHARLIE CIGARS

Late on a Friday afternoon during September of 1961, Gaffney ambled up to my desk and asked me if I'd like to go to headquarters in Washington, D.C., for a "TDY" (temporary duty assignment). I inquired about the nature of the assignment, but Gaffney was unable to elaborate.

"All I know is that you'll be working for Siragusa," he added, as if nothing else was cogent to the decision at hand.

Charlie Siragusa was the assistant deputy commissioner of the Federal Bureau of Narcotics. Also known as (aka) "Charlie Cigars" because of his fondness for stogies, a mild heart attack would eventually divorce him from his beloved El Productos. The fourth man from the top on the FBN's organizational chart, Siragusa was clearly the least political of those enmeshed in a power struggle for control of the bureau. A former naval intelligence officer detailed to the

OSS during World War II, Siragusa had helped set up the Central Intelligence Group (CIG), the forerunner of the CIA.

Siragusa believed in the Mafia. Throughout the years prior to Joe Valachi's testimony, while the FBI's J. Edgar Hoover, ostensibly the nation's top law enforcement officer, was still vehemently denying the very existence of organized crime in general and the Mafia in particular, Siragusa had repeatedly seen the Mafia in places where others did not. So adamant were his allegations that many at the time accused him of "inventing" the Mafia. Italian-American groups routinely castigated him, feeling that his charges were undermining the reputation of the entire nationality.

Charlie Cigars had been a key figure in the disruption of the famous Apalachin Mafia conclave of 1957 and in the legal battles that ensued thereafter. Just weeks after the murder of mafioso Albert Anastasia as he reclined comfortably in a barber chair with his face covered by hot towels, *capo* Vito Genovese called for a meeting of the *Commissione*, the ruling council of Mafia family chiefs from all over the country. The meeting was to take place in the upstate New York hamlet of Apalachin, at the country home of Buffalo crime family lieutenant Joseph Barbara. One of the agenda items was what to do about the increasingly troublesome Federal Bureau of Narcotics. Siragusa's tactics had so rattled the Mafia that some of the family bosses had begun to advocate the elimination of known FBN agents.

Shortly after the limousines began pulling up Barbara's driveway, they were noticed by a New York state trooper. It's possible that the trooper had been notified by the FBN's New York office, whose agents or informers would have spotted the migration of so many Mafia notables out of the city. A choking noose of roadblocks was quickly thrown around the house. The meeting ended then before it ever had the chance to begin as the Mafia bosses scattered throughout the countryside. Sixty of the delegates were picked up by the troopers. The routed Mafia chieftains were indicted—albeit, several months later—for conspiracy to obstruct justice. All were convicted, only to be released when the verdicts were overturned on appeal.

Siragusa had contributed significantly to the development of the conspiracy prosecution as the federal government's most effective legal weapon against organized crime. Essentially, conspiracy is the communication of a criminal intent in conjunction with the commission of an overt act that sets the criminal intent in motion. For instance, if Jones and Smith decide to sell heroin, they have communicated criminal intent. When Jones lends Smith his car for the purpose of delivering the heroin and Smith gets busted with heroin in the trunk, an overt act has been committed. The heroin in Smith's possession is considered "substantive" evidence. Although Smith has been caught red-handed, Jones can be picked up and charged with conspiracy—assuming there is evidence, say by way of surveillance or informant testimony, of the preceding conversation between him and Smith.

With Siragusa pioneering much of the legal maneuvering, the FBN was in the forefront of the conspiracy prosecution attack on organized crime. Siragusa enjoyed some success in expanding the tactic to embrace the controversial concept of continuing conspiracy. If Johnson and Smith had engaged in heroin trafficking two years prior to Smith's episode with Jones—and Johnson knows of Smith's current activities—then Johnson could also be busted on the basis of a continuing conspiracy.

The threat of continuing conspiracy prosecutions so unnerved Vito Genovese that he was quoted in 1957 as saying, "You can go to jail just for talking to somebody." Unfortunately for Genovese, he didn't heed his own warning. In July of 1958, Genovese was indicted for conspiracy to violate the U.S. narcotics laws. He went to trial in 1959, was convicted, and was sentenced to fifteen years in prison. Because of his advanced age, it was, in effect, a death sentence.

The continuing conspiracy case against Genovese largely rested on the testimony of Nelson Cantellops, a drug dealer who had been busted and flipped by the FBN. Cantellops, "working off his case" by going undercover for the FBN, attempted to cut a dope deal with Joseph DiPalermo (aka Joe Beck), a Genovese lieutenant. Beck insisted on checking Cantellops's bona fides, and the two men engaged in a cat-and-mouse game of "whom do you know?"—all under FBN surveillance. Finally, Beck asked Cantellops if he knew "Don Vittone." Cantellops assented, only to have Beck further insist that the relationship be corroborated by Don Vito Genovese himself.

During World War II, Genovese had worked for German intelligence and had even traveled to Germany on a few occasions. There, he had developed a fondness for German cuisine. (To me, that was his biggest crime.) Genovese's affinity for pig knuckles and red cabbage would contribute to his undoing, for it was at a German restaurant that his fateful meeting with Beck and Cantellops took place. As Genovese was preoccupied with his meal, Beck tapped him on the shoulder and said, "Do you know this guy?" As much to dismiss the intrusion as anything else, Genovese waved and replied, "Yeah, he's all right."

And with those few words Don Vito Genovese earned his death sentence, for seated at the bar were FBN agents Jim Hunt and Frankie Waters. Both would later testify that they had witnessed and overheard the conversation. By vouching for Cantellops, an admitted dope peddler, Genovese sealed his fate. It made him guilty of a continuing conspiracy.

So thin was the evidence against Genovese that even J. Edgar Hoover, that self-appointed guardian of American morals, came to his defense. Hoover was outraged by what he considered to be the FBN's transgression of the Constitution. I saw a letter he wrote to FBN Commissioner Harry J. Anslinger asserting that the Genovese case was a frame-up. Hoover referred to it specifically as "a travesty of justice."

Most of the groundwork for the organized crime conspiracy prosecutions was done by field agents in the Third Enforcement Group of the FBN's New York office. However, even while engaged in these critical cases, many of those very same agents were under investigation for corruption. The man leading the corruption probe was FBN number-three man and Siragusa's archenemy Wayland Speer.

Backed by a strong congressional lobby, Speer, who held the position of special assistant to the commissioner, was the only member of the FBN's elite caste who hadn't come up through the ranks. He had served in the military and had been stationed with the occupation forces in postwar Japan, where he became involved with narcotics law enforcement activities. After his discharge from the service, he gained a political appointment to the FBN, an entrance that did little to ingratiate him to his peers. When he later embarked on a solo crusade to clean up the bureau—which, if successful, could only embarrass those others who ran the FBN—he, in effect, ostracized himself. No one at headquarters, or anywhere else within the FBN, would give Speer the time of day.

Although I came to be aligned with those who saw Speer as the enemy, I later realized that much of his corruption work had merit. In many ways, his probes foreshadowed the investigations I would take up much later in my own career. Watching the entrenched forces line up against Speer should have prepared me for the resistance and backstabbing that awaited me as a corruption fighter. But, of course, it didn't. Some lessons you just have to learn the hard way.

Speer was a workaholic. He arrived every morning at six o'clock and often came into the office on Saturdays. He made it a point to read each and every memorandum and field report that came into headquarters. He prepared written responses to each one and oftentimes critiqued the content. *Why didn't the agent fully describe the subject in paragraph 4, page 5? What was the ambient lighting in which the subject was viewed? What was the distance?* And so on and so forth. Speer was a one-man intelligence analysis unit. He was smart, and he was morally clean, but he was also one colossal pain in the ass.

Some of Speer's tactics were questionable, as well. He liked to summon agents to his New York hotel room at two or three o'clock in the morning for an interview. Sometimes he'd conduct the interview in his pajamas or underwear. On one occasion he made disparaging remarks about an agent's Catholic religion and the number of children the agent had fathered. Such indiscretions played into the hands of Speer's detractors. The practices were eventually brought to the attention of the Civil Service Commission. Speer was reduced in rank and transferred out of headquarters. With his transfer, the corruption probes were shelved within the FBN.

Among the beneficiaries of Speer's fall were top man Harry J. Anslinger, the commissioner of the FBN; and his second in command, Deputy Commissioner Henry L. Giordano. Anslinger was already a legend in law enforcement circles—mostly for his unceasing disdain for J. Edgar Hoover and the FBI. He had been appointed in 1929 when the FBN was established. Almost from the outset he had locked horns with Hoover over the issue of organized crime and the Mafia. At the time of my transfer to headquarters, Anslinger was paving the way for his impending retirement and the passing of the baton to Giordano, his handpicked successor. Speer's embarrassing, persistent allegations of corruption were a threat to Anslinger's reputation and to his plans for the future of the FBN.

Naive in the ways of Washington intrigue, I walked into this Machiavellian labyrinth—a veritable political square plodding straight in and leading with my chin. I accepted the transfer to headquarters and, ever anxious to demonstrate my enthusiasm, reported to work at 8:00 A.M., an hour early. FBN headquarters occupied the third and fourth floors of the Coast Guard Building at the corner of 13th Street and E Street, N.W. I was ambushed by Speer as soon as the elevator door opened onto the third-floor corridor. Fresh from New York, where his probe was focused, I was of keen interest to him as a potential new source of information. He grilled me for more than an hour, asking repeatedly if I'd witnessed any wrongdoing. He questioned me specifically about individual agents, some of whom I considered to be the very best in the FBN. To say I was confused is a gross understatement. There I was, within the hallowed halls of FBN headquarters, in a big shot's office, on the first morning of the first day of a major new assignment, and I was being asked to incriminate guys I worked with and considered to be dedicated, effective law enforcement professionals. It wasn't what I expected. Not even close.

Shortly after nine o'clock, frustrated that I had nothing juicy to give him, Speer released me. I asked somebody for directions to Siragusa's office and then reported to his secretary. Rather frostily she said, "Mr. Siragusa has been looking for you." Then she announced my arrival into the intercom. I heard Siragusa's voice rasp back through the speaker: *"Send him in!"* He did not sound like he was in a good mood.

Siragusa had a large office with a view. Two chairs were faced opposite an immense executive desk. I sat down in one of them.

"Who told you to sit down?" he barked.

I immediately jumped to my feet and snapped to attention. It was a reflex response, a flashback to my army days.

"First day and you're late," he continued.

"I wasn't late. I've been here since eight o'clock," I explained meekly.

"What have you been doing? Hiding in the john?" he asked sarcastically.

Actually, given the amount of coffee I had ingested earlier, that wasn't such a bad idea. But the coffee, like Siragusa's anger, was just something to be endured.

"I've been in a conference with Mr. Speer," I replied, feeling confident that Siragusa would understand. After all, we were all on the same team. Speer was technically his superior. Everything would be fine.

Siragusa's eyes narrowed. His face reddened. "With Speer?" he snapped. His expression and inflection clearly indicated that all was *not* well. Things were *not* fine. *What had I gotten myself into?*

"Sit down," he ordered.

I did.

"Look," he said, "your name ends in *I*. My name ends in *A*. We come from the same country. We're almost *paesani*. You're Calabrese. I'm Sicilian. Whenever that Dutch-Texan-Protestant son of a bitch tells you something, I want to know about it."

Just so clearly and unequivocally was my allegiance established. Things may not have been as black and white as I would have preferred, but on this point there was no room for doubt. Siragusa was telling me where I stood, and he wasn't leaving me so much as one inch of leeway.

My primary job at headquarters was working on the *Mafia Book,* a compendium of the bureau's intelligence on all the Mafia personnel who were catalogued on another FBN document appropriately labeled the *Mafia List.* I worked under the capable tutelage of Agent Armando Muglia, a research expert who instructed me on data collection and correlation procedures. Each page of the *Mafia Book* was devoted to an individual organized-crime suspect. The book recorded such items as date of birth, address, description, criminal history, current activities, specialties, and known associates. I'm sure much of the information, originating oftentimes from dubious sources, was questionable or exaggerated. There were actually two Mafia books, a green one and a black one. The green one was periodically distributed to other law enforcement agencies. The black book was classified, and its distribution was tightly restricted. We also prepared summary reports on major Mafia figures and did groundbreaking research into the mob's investments in legal enterprises, the latter representing some of the earliest investigative work done in the area of money laundering. Additionally, Siragusa often requested our assistance in overviewing ongoing major investigations and prosecutions.

Not only was I privy to all the FBN's data on the Mafia, but I was also exposed to the details of the top cases under Siragusa's supervision. I had almost unlimited access to some of the most sensitive information known to the FBN. It wasn't long that word got out that Tripodi was "connected." I began receiving all kinds of phone calls from "friends" I never knew I had. Agents in distant offices would call me to check out rumors of transfers, assignments, and disciplinary actions. I had no knowledge of such matters, but still the calls persisted.

It never ceased to amaze me just how quickly and how accurately the rumor mill worked. Once I received a call from an agent in New York inquiring about an agent assigned to our New Orleans office. According to the caller, the agent from New Orleans, while in Washington, D.C., on special assignment, had been arrested by the Metropolitan Police and charged with homosexual activities. I thought it laughable. I had been out with the agent in question and a few other guys a couple of nights previous to the call. No way was this guy gay.

No sooner had I hung up than Siragusa summoned me to his office. "This morning I'm going to give you a lesson in interrogation," he said. "I'll do the interrogation, and you take notes."

"What's it all about?" I asked.

"The cops arrested one of our agents last night," he answered. "The guy's queer. Before I fire him, I want to learn all about the other queers in the bureau."

That agent in New York sure had some pipeline. Never again would I doubt the power of the office grapevine.

The actual interrogation of the allegedly homosexual agent proved anticlimactic. The agent arrived and immediately presented Siragusa his badge, his gun, and his credentials. Then he headed for the door. Siragusa exploded out of his chair and shouted, "Stop!" He then fired off a number of questions. The agent from New Orleans let Siragusa finish before answering with a simple "Fuck you!" With that he was out the door and out of the FBN. Siragusa wheeled around and told me to "write it up." That was the shortest memorandum of interrogation I ever prepared.

In February of 1962, the name of a former South American ambassador to the United States emerged as a suspected courier of heroin from Europe to this country. Our interest in the former ambassador had developed as a result of a previous investigation of a number of Latin diplomats who were smuggling heroin in their diplomatic pouches. Although no longer acting as an ambassador, the suspect had been granted continued diplomatic immunity, a protection that effectively shielded him from arrest and prosecution.

Siragusa suggested that I contact the suspect, who was then maintaining a residence in Washington. Following Siragusa's instructions, I met the diplomat at the University Club, where he was a member. After about an hour of verbal sparring, I got to the point.

"The FBN is considering initiating steps to have you ejected from the country. We're about to advise the INS that you're a suspected heroin trafficker. That might be enough to get your resident-alien status revoked."

The threat worked, as Siragusa had anticipated. The diplomat agreed to cooperate with us. Although we recruited him as an informant, we still considered him to be a suspect, and we maintained his name on all the watch lists, the lists of suspects whose activities we needed to monitor. I continued managing him as an asset until well after I had transferred to the CIA, where I was eventually obliged to relinquish control over him back to the FBN.

The diplomat's information never led to a seizure or an arrest. However, one of his disclosures did aid in an intelligence operation. During one of my debriefings, I explored his relationship with the vice president of the South American country he had represented. The vice president was an avowed Marxist and the head of the Communist party in his country. In time, my informant delivered to me letters written by the vice president's wife to the ambassador from another South American country. The vice president's wife was a professional model and quite attractive. The letters clearly indicated that she was having an affair with the other diplomat. My informant furthermore indicated that the woman was having an affair with him, as well. As proof, he offered a number of Polaroids he had taken showing the vice president's wife cavorting in the nude in a Washington hotel room.

The pictures were delivered to Siragusa, who passed them on to the CIA. The CIA was interested because the vice president had decided to run for president of his country. On the heels of Castro's ascendancy in Cuba, the last thing that the CIA wanted was another Marxist regime in the Western Hemisphere. As the case developed, I established a relationship with Paul Gaynor, the director of the CIA's Security Research Services (SRS), a relationship that would continue to grow after I transferred to the CIA. The Polaroids were eventually employed in a black propaganda operation in the South American country during the presidential campaign. The former vice president lost.

Another case I worked on during my tenure with Siragusa involved the notorious gangster Salvatore (aka Charlie ["Lucky"] Luciano) Lucania. We learned that writer/producer Martin Gosch had been in contact with Luciano, who was then living as a deportee in Italy. Gosch had contracted to produce a film on Luciano's life. Consistent with Hollywood's tradition of never being confused by the facts, the contract stipulated that the script could not depict Luciano as a murderer or a dope peddler.

Gosch's connection to Luciano had been through U.S. Army Maj. H. J. M. Melaro. Gosch had first come to know Melaro when Gosch's son had been stationed in Spain with Melaro. The producer had approached Melaro and offered his services in the preparation of training films. Melaro later transferred to Italy, and from there he came to work at the Pentagon. It was while Melaro was stationed at the Pentagon that Gosch came to him with the idea of contacting Luciano. Melaro knew Luciano from his time in Italy. The major was also an attorney. He not only had access to Luciano, but he also had the legal expertise to negotiate a contract.

Knowing in advance about the meeting with Luciano, we arranged to have it monitored by the Italian authorities. FBN agent Henry Manfredi acted as the bureau's liaison to the Italians. During the meeting, Luciano, who evidently was running out of money, agreed to sell the movie rights to his life story for $100,000.

On January 24, 1962, the Italians picked up Luciano for questioning. They detained him overnight even though Luciano was quite ill. On the day of his release, he went to the airport, under the surveillance of Manfredi and his Italian counterparts, where he met Gosch upon his arrival. Luciano died in the producer's arms.

Gosch was then pulled in by the Italian authorities for questioning. They extended interrogation privileges to Manfredi. After a day and night of intense questioning, Gosch was understandably angry. When he was released, he boarded a plane for the States and headed directly to the White House. Immediately, we felt the blast at headquarters.

Some time later, I established contact with Major Melaro at the Pentagon. I told him that I was interested in seeing a copy of the script. Melaro indicated he had a copy in his office. Although he was willing to give it to me, he needed Gosch's permission before passing it on. I apprised Siragusa of the situation. He told me not to accept a copy. He felt that Gosch was trying to wangle an FBN approval of the material. When Melaro got back to me, saying that he had secured Gosch's permission to show us the script, I had to beg off. He was pissed off at my change of heart, and he let me know it. Gosch was pissed off, too. Everybody was pissed off. While everyone was fussing and fuming, I made arrangements for an operation that surreptitiously obtained a copy of the script. I sent it on to Siragusa. It turned out to be no big deal. It provided nothing new in the way of Mafia intelligence.

My work in Washington was sensitive and important, but I began to miss the streets. Whenever the opportunity presented itself I'd assist the Washington field office, usually when the agents needed an undercover agent to play an "Italian heavy." As the junior agent at headquarters, I also drew my share of "go-fer" details and undesirable tasks. Once I was assigned to interrogate a citizen who was charging that his girlfriend had conspired with the government to have him followed.

"Government agents are following me in fire engines," he insisted.

The guy was obviously a nut case. He was wearing a big, heavy mackinaw, and I remember thinking that he could have smuggled a weapon into the building under his coat. Still, I neglected to search him. I simply took his statement and walked him to the elevator. Later I heard that he went straight to his girlfriend's house and shot her to death along with her twelve-year-old son. Then he ate a bullet himself. Even though the police speculated that he had the gun stashed at his girlfriend's house, it haunted me that I hadn't trusted my instincts and frisked the guy.

On the streets, you took action.

At headquarters, you walked a guy to the elevator.

9

LA COSA NOSTRA:
WHAT'S IN A NAME?

In October 1960, agents of the Third Enforcement Group working out of the FBN's New York office arrested Salvatore Rinaldo and Matteo Palmeri in possession of ten kilograms of heroin. The narcotics had been discovered in the false bottom of a steamer trunk ferried across the Atlantic from Palermo, Sicily, aboard the *Saturnia*. Subsequent investigation determined that the heroin had originated in a clandestine laboratory in France operated by Corsicans. It had then been consigned to Sicilians who transported it to Palermo and arranged for delivery to the United States. After the seizure, an expanded conspiracy investigation was undertaken with the cooperation of French, Canadian, and Italian authorities. On May 22, 1961, as a direct result of the FBN-led multinational investigation, a federal grand jury indicted twenty-four individuals for multiple violations of federal narcotics laws. Among those charged were Frank ("the Bug") Caruso, Salvatore Manieri, Vincent Mauro—and Joe Valachi, the man who, according to then-Attorney General Robert F. Kennedy, had provided the "biggest single intelligence breakthrough yet in combating organized crime and racketeering in the United States."

After their arrest and release on bond, Caruso, Manieri, and Mauro jumped bail. An extensive manhunt was launched, but the three fugitives proved elusive. Their flight from justice was financed by deported mobster Lucky Luciano, who, a short time later, would try to peddle his memoirs to Hollywood. From his residence in Naples, the exiled Luciano masterminded their getaway using a courier named Cristoforo Rubino to shuttle money and information between the three fugitives and himself. Working for Siragusa at FBN headquarters, I was assigned to monitor certain aspects of the hunt.

After field agents determined the aliases being used by the three men, their trail was picked up in Miami. At this point I became operationally involved in the investigation. One step behind them, I tracked them from Miami to Kingston, Jamaica. With the help of the Jamaican constabulary (at the time, Jamaica was still part of the British Commonwealth), we organized a manhunt that ranged throughout the island. We located the hotel where they had been staying, but once again, they eluded us. From airline manifests, we determined that they had fled to Caracas, Venezuela. I followed them to South America, only to learn that they had flown, by way of London, to Spain. Eventually, we located two of the suspects in Barcelona and the other one on the island of Majorca. Before arresting them, we established surveillance and bugged their hotel phone lines. The recorded conversations corroborated our earlier intelligence that they were under Luciano's protection.

While Caruso, Manieri, and Mauro were still globetrotting on Luciano's bankroll, Joe Valachi was doing his time at the federal penitentiary at Atlanta. Valachi, himself, had skipped bail on a previous narcotics case. Fellow mobster Anthony Strollo (aka Tony Bender) had supposedly "put in the fix," but Valachi didn't trust the arrangement. And evidently, the mob didn't trust Valachi. The crime bosses were upset when Valachi decided to take flight. Valachi's decampment appeared suspicious. Feeling more pressure from his partners in crime than from the law enforcement efforts, Valachi finally turned himself in. Instead of the five years that Bender had promised, Valachi received a harsh sentence of fifteen years. He had already started serving his time when he was tried for the *Saturnia* case. With

Caruso, Manieri, and Mauro still at large, Valachi received most of the prosecution's focus. In February of 1962, he was convicted and sentenced to twenty years. The new sentence was to be served concurrently.

Crime boss Vito Genovese was also doing time at Atlanta. Genovese arranged for Valachi to be assigned to his four-man cell. Ostensibly an act of loyalty and friendship, Genovese really wanted Valachi close at hand so that he could keep his eye on him. In addition to the disturbing stories Genovese was hearing from other convicts, some of whom had ulterior motives for setting Genovese against Valachi, Don Vittone had also taken keen interest in two men who frequently paid visits to Valachi.

Frank Selvaggi and Russell Dower were federal narcotics agents from the FBN's New York office. At regular intervals, they'd travel to Atlanta and summon Valachi to an interrogation room. During these sessions, Valachi scrupulously observed *omertà*, the Sicilian code of silence. His only communications were complaints that Selvaggi and Dower were trying to get him killed by creating the impression that he was cooperating with the government. He was angry that he had been "branded a rat and marked bad."

The two agents were in fact trying to portray Valachi as a stool pigeon. They were hoping to create a leper who would be ostracized by his fellow convicts. Once isolated and without the protection of his cronies, they hoped Valachi would flip, thus matching reality to the illusion they had created.

Valachi's fears that he'd be murdered, however, accelerated events beyond anything that Selvaggi and Dower could have imagined. Valachi would later claim that on three occasions Genovese tried to have him killed—once by poison, once by arranging a shower-room ambush, once by having another convict try to taunt him into a fight where he could be knifed in the ensuing confusion. None of the supposed assassination attempts could be verified, but they were nonetheless real enough to Valachi. He requested solitary confinement for his own protection. He attempted to write to George Gaffney at the FBN's New York office, offering to "talk," but really intending to buy some time until things could be worked out. He desperately tried to correspond with New York mobster Thomas ("Three-Finger Brown") Lucchese, pleading for his intervention and protection. When he heard that Joey Beck had picked up the contract Genovese had placed on his life, Valachi's fears overwhelmed him. Mistaking another prisoner for Beck, Valachi grabbed a two-foot length of pipe he saw lying on the prison floor and clubbed the imagined assassin to death. The man he killed was a small-time criminal with no connection to the Mafia. John Joseph Saupp died because he bore a fatal resemblance to a Mafia hit man.

Now faced with the electric chair, Valachi decided to talk in earnest. He was allowed to plead guilty to second-degree murder and was sentenced to life in prison. Selvaggi arranged Valachi's transfer to Westchester County Jail, where he was incarcerated in the hospital wing under the name of Joseph DeMarco.

Siragusa was copied on all the debriefing reports stemming from Selvaggi's ongoing interrogation of Valachi. Because of my involvement with the *Mafia Book*, I was often requested to compare Valachi's allegations against known intelligence. In instances where Valachi provided fresh information, I was called upon to research the data and, if appropriate, add it to our files. As usual, I assisted Siragusa in preparing the summary reports that went out under his signature.

Once, while in New York pursuing a related investigation, I actually had the opportunity to interview Valachi in person. His handlers were not happy that a headquarters type was entering the picture. Normally, if headquarters wanted a question answered, it was presented by way of a memorandum to the interrogators. They then had the ability to work it into the flow of their discussions with Valachi. They resented that Siragusa had pushed his weight around to arrange a personal interview for me.

My impression of Valachi was that he was no more than a small-timer, a peripheral player who had somehow wound up in the spotlight. He could not have understood his import because it had already gone beyond the reality of what he had been and what he knew. His phenomenon was to be manufactured according to the design of others, and he could not have imagined at that time just what role he was to play. He had landed at ground zero on a political battlefield where careers were being gambled on the basis of what he would eventually say about the existence and extent of organized crime in the United States of America. He was crude, uneducated, inarticulate, and bitter. And he was on the hot seat.

My purpose in seeing Valachi had to do with the murder of Tony

Bender and the subsequent rise to prominence of gangster Thomas Eboli. All that was known about the Bender hit was that three men had called for him at his home. He had left with them, never to be seen again. The killers had exhibited the ultimate in gangland manners by not whacking him at his home in the presence of his wife. Rather, lifting lines from an old B movie, they suggested Bender accompany them "for a ride." Good soldier that he was, Bender went along without protest. I had authored a memo quoting intelligence that suggested Eboli was behind the hit. Our sources had indicated that Eboli had taken command of the old Luciano crowd, the criminal organization sometimes referred to as the Thompson Street Gang and that included Vito Genovese among its former leaders. I was looking for corroboration from Valachi.

"Eboli's a bum," Valachi huffed. "He's a nobody running lottery slips."

I wrote up my report citing Valachi's statements, but I was disturbed that our "star witness" hadn't substantiated what we all felt was reliable intelligence.

Throughout the following several weeks Valachi's debriefing progressed, and I continued to incorporate his revelations into the *Mafia Book* data. As Valachi began to talk more about the structure and overall nature of organized crime, Siragusa's summary reports became more and more interesting to Henry Giordano who, by then, had ascended to the position of commissioner of the Federal Bureau of Narcotics. Giordano showed the reports to William Hundley of the Justice Department. Hundley passed the reports to Attorney General Robert F. Kennedy.

Kennedy had always believed in the Mafia. That belief was a major point of contention—albeit not the only one—between him and FBI boss J. Edgar Hoover. It was the FBI's position, articulated repeatedly by Hoover through the years, that the Mafia did not exist. All crime was local in nature, according to Hoover; there was no such thing as organized crime. Ever since Kennedy had worked as chief counsel for the Senate subcommittee hearings into the criminal activities of the New York Longshoremen's Union, he had been looking for a way to mobilize the vast resources of the FBI into the fight against organized crime. A number of FBN agents had assisted Kennedy during his tenure as chief counsel, and a close relationship had formed between him and key FBN figures such as Gaffney, Tom

Dugan, and Frank Dolce. When he read the Valachi reports, Kennedy realized he now had the leverage he needed.

A deal was struck. Jurisdiction over gambling, then under the purview of the IRS, would go, as Hoover had wanted for years, to the FBI. For his part, Hoover would admit the existence of organized crime and commit FBI resources. Joe Valachi would be offered to the American public as exhibit A. The whole thing would be on television. And the FBI would get all the credit.

That was the quid pro quo for Hoover. He'd get into the game, but only if Valachi was turned over to his people. At the FBN, we felt betrayed by Kennedy, our old ally, but there was nothing we could do. Under orders, Selvaggi reluctantly transferred Valachi into the custody of FBI Special Agent James Flynn.

There was one sticking point, however. Hoover insisted that organized crime be called something other than "the Mafia." It would be just too embarrassing for him to suddenly accept the name he had for so long denied. To James Flynn fell the dubious honor of renaming the Mafia.

Flynn noticed that Valachi often used certain recurring phrases in describing the mob's methodology. It was common for Valachi to begin statements with "our thing was. . . ." Over and over Flynn heard that line. "Our thing was we'd do this . . . our thing was we'd do that." Finally, the multilingual Flynn just literally translated "our thing" into Italian. The Mafia suddenly became *La Cosa Nostra*. Hoover had what he wanted: The FBI had uncovered the existence of an evil, secret, sinister cabal even more diabolical than the mythical Mafia. It was all total bullshit, but the press and the public bought it—and it's stuck for thirty years.

By the time the FBI people got done with Valachi he was saying whatever they wanted him to say. They paraded him on TV and just about broke their arms patting themselves on their backs. I knew it was all show business when Valachi testified about Eboli. All of a sudden, the guy, whom Valachi had previously called "a nobody," was running the New York rackets. I heard my own words, lines from my report—*the very one Valachi had disputed*—parroted back. In reality, it was Valachi who was "the nobody." He had disputed me because he didn't know any better. But now that he had been knighted as the FBI's all-knowing, all-telling expert on *La Cosa Nostra*, he had to sound like he was in the know on such basics as who was running things in New York. The FBI was spoon-feeding him the information, most of which the FBI got from us, to ensure that he was the credible authority it had advertised.

I don't deny that Valachi contributed to our overall view of the Mafia, but his perceptions were those of a lowly foot soldier. He was not the kingpin he was portrayed to be. Most of his truly helpful revelations were never televised because they dealt with nuts-and-bolts issues that were of interest to the FBN, but which did not advance the PR operation being orchestrated by the FBI.

I've always measured the impact of an informer's information by the number of criminals his testimony puts behind bars. As far as I know, not one single mafioso went to jail because of anything Valachi said. Valachi's real impact was the by-product of his manipulation by Robert Kennedy, namely the recruitment of the FBI into the fight on organized crime. Unfortunately, the FBI's involvement would be no more than symbolic for several years to come.

By 1967, the FBI had tired of Valachi. He had served it well, but when the media lost interest in Valachi, so did the FBI. With Hoover's blessing, the bureau dumped Valachi back on the FBN for safekeeping. There was not yet any such thing as the Federal Witness Protection Program, and there were still rumors floating around about a murder contract that had been put out on his life. Secure accommodations had to be found for him. Technically, Valachi was still serving a life term for the murder of Saupp. Suitable arrangements were eventually made at a minimum security prison in Latuna, Texas, that catered mostly to white-collar criminals. Valachi was set up in a separate cabin equipped with a TV and a kitchen. All in all, he was made to be about as comfortable as possible while still behind bars.

Henry Manfredi, special assistant to the commissioner, made it a point to visit Valachi whenever he could. Before his trips to Latuna, he'd go grocery shopping at Litterio's in Washington, D.C. He knew all the Italian specialties that Valachi liked and couldn't get in Texas. Several times, I accompanied Manfredi on his shopping sprees.

Valachi died in 1971, succumbing to cancer. According to Manfredi, during his last years he became increasingly bitter over his abandonment by the FBI. Perhaps Valachi's most profound, and certainly most ironic, legacy is the name he unwittingly bequeathed to organized crime: *La Cosa Nostra.*

10

IN THE SPY BUSINESS

During the period when Vito Genovese and Joe Valachi were both doing time at the federal penitentiary in Atlanta, it was not uncommon to find a large group of Mafia notables playing boccie on the prison grounds. The spirited matches, which Genovese was tactfully allowed to win despite his lack of ability, were often watched by other inmates, who kept a respectful distance, knowing better than to intrude on the mobsters' recreation. One inmate, in particular, was a regular spectator—a quiet, stoop-shouldered, graying man known by many in New York as semiretired photoengraver Emil Goldfus. To those who had put him behind bars, however, he was more properly known as Col. Rudolph Ivanovich Abel, "master spy" for the Soviet KGB.

Although he was arrested in June 1957, Abel's story continued to develop long after his apprehension. The unassuming little man, who, according to the press, had controlled an entire network of covert agents during the very height of the cold war, seemed to typify the insidious nature of the perceived Communist threat. Abel, the chameleon, the nonentity who had been so adept at blending into the fabric of American life, was being called the chief illegal resident Soviet agent. I followed the story with interest, augmented as it was at times by the interagency rumor mill. As the details of the case unfolded, it drew me increasingly toward a decision that was to affect the course of my career.

For some time I had been harboring doubts about my work for the FBN. Taking down narcotics offenders no longer offered enough satisfaction. The hoods themselves weren't all that sophisticated or intelligent. The challenge just wasn't there anymore for me. The Abel case, on the other hand, really seemed like the kind of work I wanted to pursue. When the opportunity presented itself during September 1962, I eagerly transferred to the CIA. There was no resignation from the FBN, just a letter from the CIA requesting the transfer and one from the FBN approving it. There was no break in my service continuity; leave, insurance, retirement, and all the rest transferred with me.

In the FBN, I was targeted mainly against Italian crime groups. Now I would be targeted against countries and institutions. The stakes were higher, the opposition more sophisticated and therefore all the more dangerous. I saw the intelligence world as separate and distinct from the law enforcement scene I knew in the FBN, although years later I had to correct that notion as the worlds of narcotics and intelligence moved toward one another. Narcotics would soon become one of the major weapons in the intelligence game. Not only did the drug traffic inflict irreparable damage to the target country, but the moneys collected paid many operational bills. The need for quick finance by emerging terrorist groups would also do much to accelerate the convergence of drugs and intelligence.

At the time, however, joining the CIA appealed to me as the next logical step in a progression toward more sensitive and critical undercover work. Even the nature of cover in the CIA was more developed. Every cover was backstopped in multiple layers. A cover as a Defense Department analyst, for instance, was supported not only with the proper credentials, but with in-place verification. If someone checked at Defense, he'd find a complete history.

It was easy for me to see the CIA's work as a global crusade of cold war combatants. Communism was the infidel. CIA agents were the Knights Templar, consigned to fight the war of intrigue that played out in the shadows of the nuclear arsenals.

I was assigned to a field unit of the CIA's Office of Security operating in the Washington, D.C., area. It was a beehive of activity. Many of our agents were doing work related to the Cuban Missile Crisis. Others were involved in paramilitary operations abroad. Still others were assigned to various defector programs. Some of the guys I worked with had been involved with the Abel case, seeing it all the way through to the spy swap of the previous February that had sent Abel back to Mother Russia in exchange for downed U-2 pilot Francis Gary Powers.

Abel's undoing, as it turned out, was really at the hands, however inadvertently, of the Campisi brothers of northern New Jersey, Mafia heavies who were into narcotics, gambling, and loansharking in a big way. The Campisis had advanced money to one of Abel's operatives, Reino Hayhanen. Using the alias Eugene Nicolai Maki, Hayhanen had been sent by the KGB to assist Abel, but unlike his boss, Hayhanen never mastered the art of assimilating into the environment. He spoke English poorly, drank too much, engaged in loud arguments with his wife, and developed a keen fondness for gambling. Habitually unlucky, he managed to run up some healthy debts, which were financed at the prevailing juice rates by the Campisis. Burdened with the usurious vigorish imposed by the mobsters, Hayhanen's troubles only grew worse.

One of Hayhanen's duties on Abel's behalf was to service "drops." Typically he would place money at a prearranged drop, a hiding place used for the exchange of money and information. For instance, one drop was in the base of a lamppost in Fort Tryon Park in New York City. After secreting money he might push a red thumbtack into the lamppost, a signal that the drop had been loaded. A drop mate would visit the park later at a specified time, see the tack, take the money, and leave some information in its place—pictures, data, microdot, coded messages, blueprints, schematics, film, whatever. The drop mate might then replace the red tack with a white one, indicating to Hayhanen that the exchange had been made. Hayhanen then had to retrieve the documents and deliver them according to instructions.

On one of the drops, Abel and Hayhanen together buried $5,000 in New York's Bear Mountain State Park. Hayhanen was ordered to return at a later date, dig up the money, and deliver it to Helen Sobell, the wife of one of the men convicted in the famous Rosenberg atomic secrets case. Hayhanen did go back to Bear Mountain, but when it came time to deliver the funds to Helen Sobell, he decided that the money would do more good in the hands of the Campisis, who had recently been pressuring him in classic loan-shark style for a payment on his mounting debt. Abel detected the treachery and advised his superiors. Soon thereafter, Hayhanen was ordered to return to the USSR for a "promotion and a vacation."

Hayhanen was to travel by ship to Le Havre, then by train to Paris and West Germany, and finally by plane to Moscow. On the long cruise across the North Atlantic, Hayhanen had plenty of time to ponder his situation. He had done nothing to merit a promotion, and his vacation was more than not likely to take place in a Siberian gulag. Once in Paris, he decided he'd rather take his chances with the bourgeois imperialists than with his socialist comrades back home. He entered the American embassy and defected to the CIA. His subsequent disclosures led to Abel.

There has been much made, then and since, in books and in the press, about the supposed discovery of Hayhanen's coded microfilm way back in 1953. According to the accounts, after being given some loose change by the Hayhanens, an alert newsboy found the film in a hollowed-out nickel. The film was reportedly turned over to the police, who then passed it to the FBI. Whether or not the story is true, it certainly had little, if anything, to do with Abel's apprehension. If FBI agents had Hayhanen under surveillance since 1953, then they certainly would have been aware of his relationship with Abel. They would have had ample time to close in before Hayhanen, fearful of the Mafia on one side of the Atlantic and terrified of the KGB on the other, gave himself up to the CIA in Paris three years later. If the FBI was indeed tipped off by a vigilant newsboy, it sure didn't act on its hot lead. In any event, I give the Campisi brothers, who wound up holding Hayhanen's worthless paper, more credit than I give the FBI.

Hayhanen died in 1961, the victim of a car accident on the Pennsylvania Turnpike. According to some accounts, he was drunk at the time. Some of the guys in our office were still griping about the mess created by the accident. It had been their job, for reasons of national security, to control any and all information stemming from the accident. Police reports, news coverage, insurance claims, eye-witness accounts—it all had to be controlled. They must have done a good job, for years later, investigative reporters were still trying to prove that an accident had even taken place.

This was one hell of a far cry from kicking down doors in Harlem. As far as I was concerned, these CIA guys were a cut above. Their equipment and operational techniques were first class compared with what I was used to. Everything they did struck me as critically important—yet nothing they did was ever exactly as it appeared. Even the official credential that I was given was not quite what it seemed: Special Agent. It was identical to the field designation used by the FBI and, therefore, suggested arrest powers, which the CIA did *not* possess. I was to learn, over time, that my badge, like so much else within the CIA, was heavily influenced by the FBI. And the more I learned, the more I realized that the CIA was going to fall short of my expectations.

The origins of the CIA can probably be traced back to the Depression years, a period during which the prevalent philosophy of the American law enforcement and intelligence communities was that gentlemen don't read other people's mail. In general, undercover operations were frowned upon as unethical. Intelligence operations were for the most part reactive. The State Department had a functioning intelligence-collection capability, but its findings were not always respected by the White House. There were no programs of penetration or other forms of aggressive espionage.

The concept of one central entity coordinating all the nation's intelligence efforts probably originated with William ("Wild Bill") Donovan. During the late thirties, with Europe and Asia already engulfed in war, he campaigned hard for the creation of such an agency. He traveled frequently to Great Britain and refined his idea with the help of the Brits, who were already accomplished in the intelligence arena. In July 1941, he prevailed upon President Roosevelt to establish the Office of Coordinator of Information, which was chartered to collect intelligence concerning enemies, actual or potential, by itself and through its brother federal agencies, both domestically and abroad.

When we suddenly found ourselves engaged in World War II, we were forced to quickly escalate our intelligence undertakings. The Office of Strategic Services (OSS) was created as part of the War

Department. The OSS absorbed all of the Office of Coordinator of Information's duties, plus the additional responsibilities for espionage, sabotage, and covert action. The government searched the nation seeking out potential OSS agents among those who had skills perceived to be of use in the widening intelligence field. The hunt even extended to Hollywood, where a Sterling Hayden could be recruited primarily on the basis of his acting ability, an ability that could now be viewed as complementary to a "role-playing" undercover assignment. Sterling Hayden went on to distinguish himself as a leader of guerrilla operations in Nazi-occupied Yugoslavia. The search for manpower also zeroed in on the Treasury Department's Federal Bureau of Narcotics office in New York, where many agents had experience in undercover operations. So it was that Charlie Siragusa, Henry Manfredi, George White, Howard Chappell, and many other FBN agents were inducted into the OSS.

One of the most successful operations undertaken by the OSS was the capitulation of the Italian government, an event that forced the Nazis to maintain a sizable defensive pressure along Italy's enormous coastline, thus tying up troops that could have been better deployed at Normandy or elsewhere. Allen Dulles, who worked out of a site in neutral Switzerland, is generally credited with masterminding the Italian operation. He would later become the first director of the Central Intelligence Agency, and with the help of Henry Manfredi and others who had participated in the Italian adventure, he would establish the Deputy Directorate of Plans (DDP), an innocuous euphemism for what was then the covert-operations ..m of the CIA. With much of the CIA's covert talent coming from the FBN by way of the OSS, a strong affinity naturally existed between the two agencies—or, at least, between the FBN and the DDP.

After the war and prior to the creation of the CIA there was a rather chaotic period during which the nation's intelligence apparatus tried to adjust to a peacetime environment. It was once more deemed appropriate to move the centralized intelligence effort under civilian control, and, in 1946, President Harry Truman created the Central Intelligence Group (CIG). Almost immediately, a political power struggle erupted.

The military fought to maintain its paramilitary and covert roles abroad. And J. Edgar Hoover, who was bitter and felt betrayed that Truman hadn't placed the CIG under his control, struggled to continue the FBI's domination of Central and South American intelligence-gathering operations, as well as other intelligence-related activities. A little-known, yet absolutely critical, event then took place—one absolutely essential to any true understanding of the history and evolution of the CIA.

Hoover, upon hearing that he was not to head the CIG, quickly RIF'ed (reduction in force) perhaps as many as five hundred of his best FBI agents. All of the fired agents had exhibited keen loyalty to Hoover and the bureau. Indeed, it was precisely because of their loyalty that they were sacked. Knowing that the CIG was desperate to hire experienced personnel, Hoover was certain that his loyal soldiers would immediately find employment at increased grade levels within the CIG. Many of the RIF'ed FBI agents wound up either in the CIG's Office of Security (OS) or Counterintelligence Staff (CIS). When, in 1947, the CIG was restructured and renamed as the Central Intelligence Agency, the ex-FBI men were already securely in place. Since the OS was responsible for the investigation of all incoming personnel, the Hoover loyalists were able to influence the composition of the CIA work force for years to come and in ways that transcended the operational charter of the Office of Security. All this came to me from some of the very men who had come over into the OS from the FBI. They felt, as do I, that J. Edgar Hoover had, through them, penetrated the Central Intelligence Agency and was able to influence its actions.

The prevailing attitude of the OS was that it carried the awesome responsibility of ensuring that the CIA conformed in all ways to Hoover's philosophy of morality and judicial propriety—or, as they were more likely to put it, their job was "to ride herd on the cowboys." More often than not, the perceived "cowboys" were the former OSS, former FBN guys working covert operations in the DDP. The men of action who had distinguished themselves during World War II found themselves being restricted by the Hooveresque, bureaucratic mind-set of former FBI agents. As age and attrition took their toll on the OSS vets, younger agents took their place, agents who had been cleared for admittance to the CIA by the OS and who therefore reflected OS-approved attitudes.

When I came over to the CIA, the agency had already evolved through fifteen years of Hoover's influence, but the effects of that influence were not readily apparent to me. Perhaps I was just too jacked up about getting into the spy business to see that the CIA was being steadily and methodically refashioned along lines more accept- able to J. Edgar Hoover, whose policies I had already come to loathe during my time with the FBN. Also, as I joined my OS field unit after twelve weeks of training, just as the Cuban Missile Crisis was winding down, I happened to hit the CIA during an exciting period when perhaps it was easier for me to overlook the increasing number of constraints and controls that the Kennedy administration was placing on covert operations.

But to me, all was right with the world.

I was in the spy business.

11

THE KENNEDY FUNERAL

November 22, 1963.

It's been said that everybody remembers exactly where he was and what he was doing at the time he first heard that John F. Kennedy had been assassinated. I was up in the Blue Ridge Mountains outside of Harrisonburg, Virginia, getting ready to go hunting.

I had driven up the previous day with three other agents from the Office of Security. Our plan called for some serious R&R. One of my colleagues owned a cabin in the foothills. We'd be up at 3:00 A.M. for a quick breakfast followed by some deer or bear hunting. Back in camp by late morning, we'd cook up our version of gourmet cuisine, play cards, and drink beer. By 3:00 P.M., we'd be back out for some evening hunting. We were all looking forward to the break.

Before we pulled off the main road to head for the cabin, we stopped at the local state police barracks. We identified ourselves using our primary-cover credentials and gave them directions to our cabin. We explained that we had left their telephone number as a contact point in the event our office needed to reach us. Then we proceeded to the cabin, unpacked, and started to enjoy our vacation.

The following afternoon, just as we were preparing for our evening hunt, we heard the news of Kennedy's assassination over the radio. Immediately, we began to speculate that the assassination was but the first shot of a much bigger operation. Were the Russians moving on us? Was it the beginning of an all-encompassing national revolution? What was Castro's involvement? We had been taught to think in patterns, to project possibilities, to prepare for worst-case scenarios. Layered over our shoptalk was the same enervating pall of grief that I imagine was afflicting millions of others across the country.

All four of us genuinely liked Kennedy. We saw him as young, energetic, dynamic—a perception I felt was shared by many of the younger agents throughout the CIA. As for the conspiracy pundits who insist on fingering the CIA for planning or abetting the assassination, all I can say is that such a theory is completely inconsistent with my observations at the time and my experience since then. The four of us felt the stinging hurt of a deep loss that day, and none of us, for even one second, amidst all else that we may have conjectured that afternoon voiced a word of speculation that our own agency might have been involved. It was unthinkable then, and, as far as I'm concerned, it's unthinkable today.

Struggling to come to grips with the situation, we decided that we'd better head back to the office. Just as we started to pack up, a state police helicopter appeared over the treetops. It touched down in a clearing. An officer jumped out and ran over to us.

"Your office called," he said, telling us what we had already anticipated. "You're to report back for duty ASAP!"

We got back to the capital as quickly as we could. When we reported for duty, we found the entire government in a state of utter confusion. Official vehicles were racing in all directions with their lights flashing and their sirens wailing. Army troops in full battle gear were all over. Agents in my office were being assigned to various details, several in the State Department to assist in providing security for the many foreign heads of state and dignitaries who were expected for the funeral. I was assigned to a group responsible for contacting informants and others to gather intelligence concerning planned assassination attempts or other acts of violence targeted against any of our government officials or any of the foreign notables.

Information came in—from exactly where I never knew—indicating that four Algerian terrorists were en route from Montreal, Canada. Their mission was to assassinate President Charles de Gaulle of France. My team interviewed a number of the same informants I had been running when I was with the FBN, characters who frequented bars and transient hangouts. We pushed them for any useful information: *Had they seen anything suspicious? Had they heard anything? Had they noticed any new faces in town?* Other agents contacted various police departments in the vicinity, instructing them to tell their informants to be on the lookout. This utilization of other law enforcement entities was the more traditional approach as it better conformed to the CIA's charter, which didn't provide for the domestic covert gathering of intelligence, a responsibility more properly belonging to the FBI. There was always sensitivity in this regard, a real reluctance to trespass into other jurisdictions—especially the FBI's.

None of our efforts turned up anything useful. We didn't know if the assassins were traveling in pairs or singly; if they were driving down, flying, or taking the train. We had no idea as to what weaponry they planned to employ—bombs, sniper rifles, automatic weapons?—or where or when they intended to strike. All we knew was that they were going to try to hit de Gaulle some time while he was in Washington. Feeling that we were getting nowhere fast, we abandoned our canvass and began concentrating on the physical aspects of de Gaulle's security.

On the 24th, the day of de Gaulle's scheduled arrival in Washington, I began making the rounds in the neighborhood of the French ambassador's residence, which was where the French president would be staying. With another agent, I visited the houses and mansions in the vicinity, getting inside as many as we could and giving them a quick once-over. Many of the households employed butlers, maids, and/or other staff help. To a person, all were extremely cooperative. We were able to ascertain the names of residents, guests, and staff. When we spotted broken attic windows, we prevailed upon the owners to board them up.

By late afternoon, we still hadn't discovered anything or anyone related to the purported threat. All we could do now was keep our eyes open and try to protect de Gaulle as best we could. At about 4:00 P.M., crowds started pressing in around the French ambassador's residence. I had been instructed to mingle with the spectators and to be on the alert for anything that could even remotely be construed as an act of violence. If I witnessed such an act, I was to respond accordingly.

Working with three other agents, we established a countersurveillance of the area. I had been provided State Department Security identification. All of us were equipped with concealed radios, and we were all receiving a play-by-play of de Gaulle's progress toward our location. We were informed when his plane landed at Dulles and when his motorcade passed various checkpoints. At about 5:40 P.M. we heard that his car was crossing the Key Bridge.

Just about then, I observed a uniformed police officer chasing two white males who were running up the drive of the residence. One of the two men was carrying a couple of large bags. The other, who was impeccably dressed, carried a leather attaché. The drive had been roped off, but these two had hopped over the barrier. I joined the chase and caught up to them just as the police officer and the two men engaged in a heated argument. As I approached, the one with the attaché addressed me, perhaps sensing that I was someone in authority.

"I am the first secretary to the French Embassy," he snapped, acting totally outraged that we had detained him. "This man," he continued, gesturing to his companion, "is the official photographer. He is here to cover President de Gaulle's arrival."

"No one is allowed on the grounds without the right pass," the police officer quite correctly explained.

The man claiming to be the first secretary shot us his snootiest-possible expression, tugged the sleeve of his companion, and started for the entrance of the residence, where the ambassador and his staff were patiently awaiting de Gaulle's arrival and watching our confrontation on the drive. I stepped in front of him, blocking his way.

"Look," I said, pointing to the ambassador, "your boss is right over there. If he wants you, he could easily tell us to let you in. But since he hasn't, I suggest you find a telephone and call him and ask for instructions."

"You son of a bitch!" he huffed, apparently not at all appreciating my suggestion.

Then, this asshole—who didn't have the right pass, who had not exhibited any identifying credentials, and who had not been recognized or acknowledged in any way by the ambassador who was standing only a few yards away—pushed me.

As far as I was concerned, that push qualified as an act of violence. Per my instructions, it begged a reply in kind. I hit him twice. That's all it took to put him on the ground. I helped him to his feet and led him, his companion, and the police officer off the premises. No one in the ambassador's entourage interceded or protested. A few minutes later, the motorcade arrived, and de Gaulle safely entered the residence.

The following day I walked with the funeral procession, a moving, emotional experience that I will never forget. No attempt was ever made on de Gaulle's life, and security for all the other visiting dignitaries was provided without serious incident.

As required, I filed a report documenting what had occurred at the French ambassador's residence. I noted in the report that I never identified myself and that after the situation had been controlled, I simply disappeared into the crowd.

A few days later I was summoned to headquarters where another one of those "blue" disciplinary memorandums was waiting for me. And I received another ass-chewing from the very same ex-FBI bureaucrat who had gotten a piece of me the year before when I bagged those two murderers. The charge was the same and just as ridiculous. He said that I had violated procedure and blown my cover.

I don't think I did.

And I don't think that the French government ever complained that an American special agent took action in an attempt to protect its president's life.

12

YURI IVANOVICH NOSENKO, KGB

Nestled in the foothills of the Blue Ridge Mountains of northwest Virginia was a former private girls' academy that the CIA had adopted as a think tank retreat. Here, agency personnel would meet away from the responsibilities of their offices and concentrate their attention on a specific agenda. The environment was country—wholesome and conducive to strategy sessions, planning activities, and certain types of training. Quarters were comfortable, if a bit Spartan. The meals were adequate. There was even a recreation room in one of the buildings equipped with a pool table, a well-stocked bar, and card tables. My first visit to this tranquil spot occurred in the early part of 1964, when I attended a high-level briefing and planning conference. The subject of our meeting was the defection of KGB Maj. Yuri Ivanovich Nosenko.

The conference was highlighted by a presentation by George Kisevalter, a longtime, highly respected CIA case officer who was well known throughout the intelligence community for his dog-and-pony shows on the Oleg Penkovsky case. Penkovsky was a colonel in the GRU, the intelligence directorate of the Soviet General Staff. He had divulged to the West critical information regarding the state of Russian missile technology. Kisevalter had acted as his case officer. In 1962, Penkovsky's revelations had proved crucial to Kennedy's hardline handling of the Cuban Missile Crisis. During the following year, Penkovsky was unmasked by the KGB, tried, and shot for treason.

Kisevalter had made his reputation in the expert handling of Soviet defectors. The heavyset New Yorker was an effective speaker who was seldom seen with his suit jacket on or with his shirttails tucked in. His ruffled appearance belied his organized, comprehensive knowledge of his subject matter. He was spellbinding in his presentation of the Penkovsky case. He compared Penkovsky to other defectors, focusing on personalities, motivations, egos. He warned us about the threat posed by the KGB and its ongoing efforts to penetrate and damage the CIA. It is my recollection that Kisevalter then told us that Penkovsky, before his arrest, had warned that the KGB was preparing for the false defection of one of its up-and-coming young officers, a rising star by the name of Yuri Ivanovich Nosenko.

Kisevalter's profile of secret agent Nosenko detailed a life that recently had been anything but secret. Nosenko had been popping up all over the place—Europe, Tokyo, Cuba. His high visibility was thought to be intentional. It was Kisevalter's conclusion that Nosenko had been showcased by the KGB in preparation for the false defection. In 1962, Nosenko had contacted Pete Bagley of the CIA in Geneva, making known his desire to defect. Working together, Bagley and Kisevalter had tried to orchestrate an "in-place" defection— that is, Nosenko would defect secretly, remaining in the USSR and working on our behalf. However, Nosenko had insisted on a physical defection. In October 1963, while the clandestine negotiations were still in progress, Nosenko, in another high-visibility episode, had participated in the unwarranted arrest of Yale Professor Frederick C. Barghoorn in Moscow.

Barghoorn had been arrested without reason or provocation by the KGB. His handling had been harsh, even by KGB standards. The entire incident, in retrospect, seemed designed solely to once more afford a stage for Nosenko. Ostensibly, the KGB had taken Barghoorn on trumped-up charges in order to force an exchange for one of their agents who had been arrested at the UN, but when President Kennedy personally intervened, Barghoorn was released without condition.

After the Kennedy assassination, Nosenko again made contact with Pete Bagley in Geneva. He pushed hard for the defection, telling Bagley that he had been Lee Harvey Oswald's case officer during Oswald's stay in the USSR. Nosenko knew that the CIA could not ignore such a revelation, coming as it did within a month following the assassination. The CIA responded as Nosenko had anticipated, abandoning its defector-in-place position and arranging Nosenko's physical defection to the West.

At that first meeting at the retreat and in others I attended over the course of the next several weeks, there was never any doubt expressed by Kisevalter or any of the others who briefed us that Nosenko was anything but a phony. Our meetings were entirely based on that premise, as were the plans we made for Nosenko's handling.

A great deal has been written about the Nosenko defection. An HBO original movie has even been made. Some of the assassination conspiracy buffs have woven the Nosenko episode into their theories. But I don't believe that anyone has, prior to now, revealed the original CIA plan for Nosenko's handling, a plan that not only illustrates to what extent the agency was convinced that Nosenko was a double agent, but in its undoing shows how far special interests will go in order to protect the Washington status quo. That Nosenko, considered from the onset to be a KGB double agent, would in the end be accepted as a consultant to the CIA is testimony to the irrepressible power of politics.

The plan we devised with the help of psychiatrists was divided into two parts. During Phase One, Nosenko would be taken to a safe house. All the creature comforts would be provided. He would be made to think that his bona fides had been completely accepted. At that point, Phase Two would be suddenly implemented. The military would storm the safe house in a hail of gunfire, grab Nosenko, and whisk him off to some remote holding cell. Nosenko would be made to believe that an interagency power struggle had occurred and that the military had wrestled him away from the civilian CIA. His ensuing treatment would be harsh, mirroring his treatment of Professor Barghoorn. The shock of the feigned military kidnaping and the new, hostile environment were considered sufficient stimuli by the psychiatrists to break Nosenko down. We'd get to the truth; we'd learn Nosenko's real agenda; we'd find out all about Lee Harvey Oswald's connection to the KGB.

Two groups were selected from the Office of Security for Nosenko's handling. The first group consisted of agents who were assigned to Nosenko during Phase One. I was assigned to the second group. We would provide countersurveillance during Phase One and then play the military heavies during Phase Two.

Nosenko arrived at Washington National Airport during the first week of February 1964 on a cold, clear night. Working countersurveillance, I picked up the entourage at the airport and followed them to the safe site. There was no evidence of surveillance by the KGB or anyone else. A day or so later, I was again on countersurveillance when Nosenko was taken to the Department of Justice for the customary meeting with a representative from the Soviet Embassy. We were extremely alert to the possibility of KGB surveillance from within the Justice Department, but again we detected nothing. Although in both cases we were looking for surveillance, we really had no concerns for Nosenko's safety. We were absolutely convinced he was a double agent. There was no reason to expect the KGB to attempt an assassination of one of its own, but we were concerned that the KGB would attempt to determine where we were housing Nosenko and then try to implement a covert method of communication with him.

For four weeks, Nosenko was housed at a posh estate in Virginia complete with an indoor swimming pool. Three or four security officers were always with him. A cleared and witting (i.e., security-cleared and briefed) husband-and-wife team took care of all the housekeeping and cooking chores. He enjoyed gourmet-quality meals, Russian vodka smuggled in from Canada, and Upmann cigars from Cuba. Whatever Nosenko wanted, Nosenko got.

Nosenko spent most of his days being interviewed by agents from the CIA's Soviet Bloc Desk as well as by representatives from other interested agencies such as the FBI and the Department of Defense. As far as I know, no one outside of the CIA had been advised of Phase Two of our plan or that we suspected that Nosenko was a plant.

On weekends Nosenko was often taken on R&R excursions. There were trips to Washington, D.C., Baltimore, New York, Miami, Puerto Rico, Los Angeles, and Hawaii. His hotel room was always equipped with covert electronic monitoring equipment prior to his arrival. Generally, the observation post was in the adjacent room. On some of these outings, he was "introduced" to a female companion, a cleared prostitute who had agreed to entertain Nosenko. On one occasion, at the Shoreham Hotel in D.C., he was drunk and became very physical with his lady of the evening. I was manning the observation post with another agent. When the woman began to scream, we decided that we had to intervene, even if it meant blowing our cover. When we approached the door, however, it became apparent that the crisis had passed. It sounded like she was dressing and preparing to leave. We went back to the observation post. In the hall, the agent who had arranged the tryst confronted the woman whose face was badly bruised. "Never again!" was all she had to say.

While Nosenko was enjoying all the various pleasures of Phase One, agents from the second unit were busy preparing Phase Two. A safe house had been found in southern Maryland. A 12-foot-by-12-foot room was readied on the third floor. Half of it was under the slope of the gabled roof, giving it the cramped feeling of an even smaller room and allowing an occupant to stand up only in the half that wasn't diminished by the roofline. There was only one window, and it had been completely sealed. No natural light could get in. Like Barghoorn's cell, the room had a metal-frame cot, a stool, and a slop bucket, and was lit by one 75-watt bulb. The plan called for uniformed guards equipped with submachine guns to be stationed all around just as Barghoorn had experienced. However, there wasn't enough time—or really any inclination—to train the security officers in the use of machine guns. And if we removed the ammunition, we felt Nosenko would be able to detect the chicanery. Thus, the machine-gun idea was dropped.

Phase Two was to kick off in late March 1964. Nosenko would be put through his normal paces at the safe house in Virginia. After a big dinner with lots of wine and vodka, and followed by brandy and cigars, he would stagger off to his bedroom and pass out as was his nightly custom. After he was sound asleep, my team would "assault" the house. Nosenko would be awakened with a gun to his temple and find himself surrounded by men in black military combat clothing. He would hear gunfire coming from the rear of the house, unmistakably the sounds of his CIA guards being systematically executed. He would then be stripped naked, led away in handcuffs and ankle chains, and thrown into the back of an old ammunition panel truck we had acquired. Since it was still quite cold, it was expected he would freeze his ass off during the long, circuitous ride that would follow. Although the Maryland site was only about forty minutes away, our route called for hours of traversing the beltway and other major highways to give Nosenko the impression he was being taken hundreds of miles from the Washington area. We didn't care if he screamed his head off because the van was soundproof.

At the new safe site, the routine called for a noisy changing of the guard every morning at 8:00 A.M. Without variation, the new shift would bring Nosenko his breakfast, a slice of black bread and a cup of black coffee. Lunch at noon would be identical except for the addition of a piece of cheese. At 4:00 P.M., he'd hear another shift change and at six o'clock he'd get his dinner, which consisted of the lunch bill of fare augmented by a chunk of well-done meat. After about a month under such a predictable regimen, the schedule was to undergo some adjustments that were designed to disorient Nosenko. Breakfast and dinner would be pushed back each day in fifteen-minute increments. The lunch schedule would creep in the opposite direction. In less than a week, breakfast would arrive at 9:30 A.M., lunch at 10:30 A.M., and dinner at 7:30 P.M. With Nosenko's internal time clock completely confused, it was thought he would be much more susceptible to interrogation. The use of drugs to further advance Nosenko's disorientation was also considered, as was utilizing the services of a hypnotist, but these ideas were quickly discarded.

Phase Two, as we had planned it, never got implemented. Certain aspects of our plan did proceed, but in watered-down versions that were far from the original concept. The same trump card that Nosenko had played with Bagley—namely, his connection to Oswald—was now being used not only to emasculate our plans for Nosenko's handling, but to undermine previous conclusions regarding Nosenko's authenticity.

While the Warren Commission was busy investigating the Kennedy assassination, J. Edgar Hoover and the FBI were taking a lot of heat for what appeared to be negligence in the FBI's lackadaisical behavior toward Oswald prior to the shooting. As early as December 10, 1963, less than three weeks after the assassination, Hoover had already read the results of a damning internal investigation. At one point he wrote, "These delinquencies in the investigation of Oswald have resulted in forever destroying the Bureau as the top-level investigative organization."

Oswald, after all, had defected to the USSR, had been under the direct control of the KGB, was married to a Soviet national, and was a known pro-Castro demonstrator—any one of which was enough to warrant interest by the FBI. Since the president's motorcade route was determined after Oswald had already begun employment at the Dallas School Book Depository, it could never be proved that he took the job for the express purpose of killing the president. But the fact did remain that Oswald, Marxist defector and Castro activist, was employed there on that fateful day in 1963. For days he had been sighting in the scope of his rifle, obviously preparing to shoot something or someone. It was clearly the responsibility of the FBI to know such critical information and to make it available to the Secret Service, the Treasury Department unit directly chartered with the president's protection. Whether the FBI people had failed to properly keep tabs on Oswald or they had just neglected to tell the Secret Service about him, the lapse was just as glaring.

To make matters worse, Hoover couldn't plead ignorance, because Oswald had recently been interviewed by the FBI and quite possibly even recruited by FBI agents to penetrate the pro-Castro movement. Not long before the assassination, while in the custody of the New Orleans police after an altercation with anti-Castro factions, Oswald began ranting about Russia, the KGB, the CIA, and the State Department. At that point the locals decided to call in the FBI, whose agents proceeded to interview Oswald at length.

Routinely, the FBI would have completed a background check at that time. In the unlikely event that the bureau was not previously aware of Oswald's history, its files certainly should have been updated at that point.

Compounding the FBI's problem was a notebook that had turned up after the assassination in a garage rented by Oswald. One page of the notebook listed the name of the special agent in charge (SAC) of the FBI's New Orleans office, along with his office telephone number and his unpublished home telephone number. Also listed in the notebook were the names of the FBI's Dallas SAC and two other FBI agents, one of whom I suspect was Oswald's handler. Corresponding office and unpublished home telephone numbers were likewise recorded. When the notebook was presented as evidence to the Warren

Commission by the FBI, the pages listing the FBI agents' names and telephone numbers were missing. However, although the FBI had been authorized by President Lyndon Johnson to collect and maintain all evidence pertaining to the assassination, both the Secret Service and the Dallas Police Department had been allowed to examine the notebook while it was still intact. Both made copies of the pages in question.

It really appeared as if the FBI had botched things but good. Not only had it failed to surveil a known Communist sympathizer and activist, but there was strong evidence to suggest that Oswald was actually working for the bureau at the time of the assassination. Hoover was being painted into a corner, and his only defense was to claim that Oswald was not what he appeared to be. Sure he had defected to Russia. Sure he had been under the scrutiny of the KGB. Sure he had demonstrated on behalf of Castro. But these were not the actions of a dedicated, dangerous Marxist. These were just the confused actions of a seriously disturbed individual. Oswald was a nut, and therefore the FBI had no real reason to consider him as a threat. After all, the FBI couldn't be expected to watch every kook that was running around loose.

Oswald, the Marxist activist, loomed as Hoover's ruination; Oswald, the lone crackpot, was to be his salvation.

Hoover's position was shaky—until Maj. Yuri Ivanovich Nosenko showed up on the scene. All of a sudden, here was corroboration in the form of the very man who had handled Oswald for the KGB. And, like Hoover, Nosenko was saying that Oswald was a nut case. If the KGB thought that Oswald was a kook, then why shouldn't the FBI? So went the logic. If the KGB did not consider Oswald competent for operations on its behalf, then why should the FBI consider him as a threat working in league with the dreaded Communist conspiracy? That it was a totally self-serving disinformation plan for the KGB to have Oswald pegged as a crackpot was overlooked by Hoover and his supporters within the CIA.

Nosenko had indeed told his interviewers that Oswald had been determined by the KGB to be deranged and of no intelligence value. According to Nosenko, Oswald had been quickly turned over to Intourist for whatever propaganda opportunities it might be able to exploit. A few months later, Nosenko said he received a call from Intourist advising him that Oswald had failed to appear for a scheduled appointment. Nosenko then went with a few other KGB agents to Oswald's apartment. They kicked in the door and found Oswald lying in a pool of blood. He had tried to commit suicide by slashing his wrists.

"If I would have known then that Oswald was going to kill President Kennedy, I would have let him bleed to death," Nosenko boasted.

There was only one problem remaining for Hoover. The CIA's Soviet Bloc Desk and Counterintelligence Staff were still absolutely convinced that Nosenko was a plant. As long as Nosenko's bona fides were in dispute, he could not corroborate Hoover's position. Nosenko's information could not be trusted if the CIA believed his mission to be essentially one of *dis*information.

Referring to the Nosenko interviews, Hoover decreed that the FBI must "dominate the situation." The former-FBI agents in the Office of Security took his words to heart. They heard what they wanted to hear—what they needed to hear. With Phase Two ready to begin, the former-FBI contingent and others sympathetic to the plight of the FBI now began to waffle on the plan. Suddenly there was hesitation about implementing a plan that all had previously agreed would quickly and decisively determine Nosenko's authenticity—or lack of it. The FBI lobby argued for watering down the individual elements of Phase Two. What remained was a mere shadow of the original plan, one that had little chance of proving anything, one way or the other.

There was no military raid on the Virginia safe house. Nosenko was simply taken to the Maryland site and given a routine polygraph examination. At a prearranged signal, I entered the room and instructed Nosenko to stand.

"We've got problems with your polygraph," I told him. "You'll have to stay here until they're resolved."

I patted him down and told him to strip. I examined his clothes for contraband—recording devices, weapons, suicide pills, etc.—and then gave him some Sears, Roebuck mechanic's overalls and a pair of shoes without laces. He should have been nervous about this unexpected turn of events—perhaps even panicky. But he was perfectly calm. It occurred to me that he was expecting something like this all along. He had been trained and prepared for it.

He was then blindfolded and brought up to the third-floor confinement room. There was no slop bucket. No drugs were administered, despite what he has said in the media since. No hypnotist was brought in. There was no "tunnel check" (rectal exam), as he has claimed. He was not roughed up or physically abused in any way. The menu, while not quite up to the gourmet standard he had enjoyed at the Virginia location, was at least adequate and nourishing. He was allowed a weekly bath; he laughed when I made a little sailboat for him and when another agent brought in his kid's rubber ducky. Time disorientation was limited to the absence of natural light. Evidently, it wasn't very effective because after months of incarceration, during a routine periodic search of his room, I found that he had been counting the days by making knots in a thread from his blanket. His calendar was off by only a day or two. He claimed that the knots were his way of passing time by "playing chess," an explanation we considered preposterous. He never admitted that the knots were a calendar; doing so would have proved that he had been trained to undergo long confinement.

During one of the interrogations, Nosenko made an interesting revelation that, if true, adds a curious footnote to the story of one of history's most diabolical villains. Nosenko claimed that he was one of the agents who had arrested Lavrenti Pavlovich Beria, the man who had been Stalin's chief executioner during the mass exterminations of the prewar purges. As head of the People's Commissariat for Internal Affairs (NKVD), the predecessor of the KGB, Beria had masterminded perhaps the most-feared secret police agency of its day. Thousands, maybe millions, died at his orders. But, according to Nosenko, when given a pistol and told to shoot himself, Beria cried uncontrollably, clutching at the boots of those who tried, in vain, to convince him to do "the honorable thing." Beria was finally shot by one of his captors. Nosenko never claimed to have been the executioner, nor did he ever deny being the one who had pulled the trigger. I think it served his ego for us to entertain the possibility that he had killed such a historic figure.

On another occasion he claimed to have been one of the KGB officers who had arrested Oleg Penkovsky. Supposedly, he gave testimony at Penkovsky's trial.

Nosenko's ability to withstand his incarceration and long, grueling interrogation sessions really impressed me. He was tough, expertly prepared, and thoroughly indoctrinated. He was in great physical shape, despite the boozing and soft life he'd experienced during Phase One. His back muscles were very well developed, much like a rower's. I do recall, however, that his hands appeared incongruously small and delicate to me. It just didn't fit with everything else I knew about him.

I never developed a genuine rapport with Nosenko. We just never hit it off. I saw him as the enemy, and I acted accordingly. For his part, I think he harbored a special dislike for me above and beyond what he might have felt for his other handlers. Clearly, I wasn't buying what he was selling, and he resented my intransigence. Whenever one of the other agents gave Nosenko a haircut, I always told him to "cut it all off," which I'm sure did little to endear me to the Russian.

I remained on the interrogation detail through November of 1964, at which time I was assigned to other responsibilities not related to Nosenko. Such reassignments were standard within the agency. Unlike the FBN where I tended to follow a case from beginning to end, work in the intelligence world was fragmented by the principle of compartmentalization. You knew your little piece of what you were working on and nothing more. If you saw the bigger picture, as I think I did with Nosenko, it was because other activities continued to bring you into contact with further developments.

One of the ways I kept tabs on the Nosenko affair was through Paul Gaynor, the head of the OS's Security Research Services (SRS) group. Like all intelligence organizations, the CIA had some unofficial and rather covert operational units. I never knew exactly what the SRS did, although it did have a regular staff who seemed to be engaged in normal research and analytical activities. Almost from the very beginning of my career at the CIA, Paul Gaynor would approach me from time to time and *suggest* certain tasks. Of course, these tasks were completely unofficial and outside of the normal chain of command. In other words, like all truly covert operations—before Ollie North rewrote the definition and began documenting his ill-conceived activities on White House memos—Gaynor's assignments didn't exist.

It was my impression that Gaynor acted as a secret operational broker on internal affairs and domestic matters for James Angleton, the powerful and influential chief of the Counterintelligence Staff. Angleton supported Pete Bagley's views on Nosenko. They were in the forefront of the group who insisted that Nosenko was "wrong," that he was a double. I assumed that the assignments I received via Gaynor had actually originated with Angleton.

When I was still on the interrogation team at the Maryland site, Gaynor approached me and *suggested* that I get close to Nosenko. He was also interested in finding out what others were doing on the Nosenko project. Getting close to Nosenko proved an impossible assignment. He hated me, and I had little use for him. I was, however, able to keep Gaynor abreast of what others in the OS were doing and talking about—as I'm sure many others reported progress to their superiors, both official and unofficial. I trust that the information was useful, because years later, in the fall of 1967, with Nosenko still under wraps and his bona fides still unresolved, Gaynor once more approached me and asked if I would be willing to participate in the reinterrogation of Nosenko. Gaynor brought me up to date on the case and pushed to get me the assignment. However, in early 1968 I was told that my name had been rejected for the project. The assignment went to Bruce Solie, another member of the SRS staff.

Solie had previously been given the job of critiquing Bagley's original nine hundred–page report on Nosenko, which had concluded he was a disinformation and deception agent sent over to penetrate the CIA. Solie quarreled with many of Bagley's key points. Basically, Solie decided that Nosenko was telling the truth when Bagley said he was lying. And in some other areas, where both reports had Nosenko lying, Solie argued that the lies were not disinformation, but rather Nosenko's attempt to build himself up to make himself appear to be a more attractive defector. The two did seem to agree on one point: Nosenko was one big liar. But on the basis of Solie's critique, and spurred on by the contingent that was still pushing for a view of Nosenko that would further the "Oswald as crackpot" theory, it was decided that Nosenko would be reinterrogated.

Eventually, Nosenko's bona fides were accepted. He was released from captivity. He acquired U.S. citizenship, divorced his Soviet wife, and married an American. But most importantly, *he became a consultant to the CIA.* If he was indeed a plant, as Angleton, Bagley, Gaynor, and even Director Richard Helms believed, then it can be said that he both succeeded and failed in his mission.

Nosenko did penetrate the CIA. That was his success. But it occurred years after he defected. The long delay could only be viewed as an abysmal failure. His priorities and objectives would no longer be relevant. In effect, he was all dressed up with nowhere to go.

My own feelings are that Nosenko was most certainly sent over as a plant, but when, after long years of confinement, he realized he could no longer complete his mission, he abandoned his KGB assignment and began looking out for himself. Bagley knew the *wrong* Nosenko, and his report reflected that view. Solie knew the Nosenko who was out for himself, and his report could only say that Nosenko was for real.

As for Oswald, none of us ever seriously believed that the KGB had used him to assassinate President Kennedy. For one thing, the weapon—a mail-order, World War II–vintage, bolt-action rifle packed in Cosmoline—was hardly the weapon of choice for the murder of the century. Nor did we think the KGB would utilize someone with such visible ties back to the USSR. The nature of Oswald's attempted escape and his own murder at the hands of Jack Ruby were also grossly inconsistent with a KGB-planned operation. Oswald's unstable nature, the reason Nosenko had actually advanced, also seemed to eliminate him as a likely KGB assassin, or for that matter, as a hired assassin for any other group as well.

We were most disposed to believing that Oswald was a low-level recruit of the KGB, sent back to the United States to serve at a later date in some as-yet-undetermined capacity—a sort of sleeper agent. We had hoped that Phase Two of our plan would answer all our questions about Oswald and his relationship with the Soviets, questions that largely remain unanswered to this day.

Unfortunately, in the Nosenko affair, politics prevailed over truth.

13

THE OWLS

Amid the cloak and dagger, the disinformation, the doubles and defectors, the smoke and mirrors, the cryptonyms and covers, there was a sense of integrity within the CIA that I came to respect, a code of honor that at times triumphed over the chicanery of legends and aliases. Never was this more apparent to me than when two Eastern bloc defectors perished in a plane crash.

The two defectors, both pilots, had been flying covert reconnaissance missions over Tibet for the CIA. Although the work was difficult and extremely dangerous, they had succeeded in completing a number of critical missions. The intelligence they brought back had proved useful on several occasions. Eventually, however, their luck ran out, and they were shot down by the Red Chinese over the Himalayas.

The CIA had previously promised the pilots that their bodies would be returned to their families in their homeland for Christian burial in the event of such a tragedy. With their plane down behind enemy lines, in some of the most rugged terrain on the entire planet, it would have been quite easy to forget the pledge. Who would ever know anyway? The risks seemed to outweigh any obligation.

Against all odds, certainly against today's prevailing wisdom, the promise was kept. Fully understanding the considerable risk, a team was sent in. Not only did the members of the group have to evade Red Chinese patrols and navigate the brutal topography, they had to locate the downed plane—in itself no easy task. They succeeded. They acquired the bodies—what was left of them—and safely brought them out of Tibet.

The job still wasn't over. Complications of a different nature remained. A story had to be developed explaining the horribly mangled state of the corpses. The story would have to be fully backstopped, and then arrangements had to be made to physically return the bodies to the pilots' homeland.

It was decided that a car accident could best explain the defectors' deaths. One was invented—complete with accident reports, autopsies, news coverage, obituaries, insurance claims, the works. Somewhere, in the municipal archives of a small East Coast town, there remains to this day the records of a terrible automobile accident that claimed the lives of two courageous defectors. The fictional story of their deaths is as documented as the true story of their lives is secret.

None of it had to be done. No one would have known one way or the other. The cost in terms of risk, dollars, and manpower had been high, but the promise was kept.

The reconnaissance mission that the two pilots had been flying at the time of their deaths was only one of many covert operations undertaken by the CIA in Tibet. The agency was interested both in gathering intelligence on the Red Chinese occupation forces in the country and in aiding Tibetan freedom fighters.

When the Red Chinese Army invaded Tibet in 1950, long-simmering cultural hatreds erupted. The Chinese perpetrated atrocities of every kind on the civilian population in a campaign of repression that seemed bent on defiling the Tibetan people as much as exterminating them.

Monks were ordered to impregnate prostitutes on the steps of their lamaseries. To refuse was to be executed. The public nature of the spectacle was obviously intended to humiliate the religious leadership and to undermine the population's belief system.

In a variation on the same theme, nuns were rousted from their convents and ordered to copulate with the Chinese soldiers. Again, refusal meant death.

Many women and girls not only suffered the trauma of rape, but were then force marched back to China for imprisonment in labor camps. With the female population so reduced, polyandry, the prevalent Tibetan marital custom that mates an entire family of brothers to one wife, flourished. The scarcity of females also resulted in a widened acceptance of homosexual practices among the remaining male population. One can only speculate if even this development might have been anticipated by the Chinese in their plans to subvert the underlying moral structure of the Tibetan people.

Fleeing into the protection of the rugged Himalayas, many men took up guerrilla tactics against the Chinese. For years they continued their war of resistance against the Chinese invaders and in 1959 mounted a mass revolt that was ruthlessly crushed. The Dalai Lama, the spiritual and temporal leader of Tibet, escaped into neighboring India, where he was granted political asylum.

The CIA had determined that enemies of the Red Chinese were the logical mechanisms through which anti-Chinese political and intelligence operations could be operated. There were no more dedicated and wrathful enemies of the Red Chinese than the Tibetans. The CIA began "exfiltrating" Tibetan nationals from their occupied homeland. A steady exodus of vengeance-seeking Tibetans was transported to Camp Hale, an army base near Leadville, Colorado. There they received eighteen months of intensive training in guerrilla warfare before being reinserted into Tibet. The base, itself, had no other reason for existence. It had been picked because its location high in the Rockies closely resembled the Himalayan terrain of Tibet. The covert operation was code-named the OWL Program.

The OWLs, themselves, were highly motivated—perhaps too much so. Oftentimes their intense hatred for the Chinese caused them to abandon their long-term missions to engage in opportunistic attacks on the Chinese invaders. These reckless free-lance activities often resulted in disaster. In winning a small skirmish, the OWLs sometimes inadvertently tipped off the enemy to the location of their own base. Reprisals were usually swift and thorough.

Twice during 1964, I was assigned to provide security for OWL teams during their transport from Colorado to Tibet. I also participated in the last phases of their training prior to their departure.

The Tibetans were great to work with—tough, fearless, willing, and eager to learn. They demonstrated no reluctance to apply what they had learned. The leader of one of the OWL teams had personally killed eighty-one Red Chinese soldiers and officers. Most groups I've trained resented discipline and were quick to mouth off. By contrast, the Tibetans honorably accepted discipline, turned their backs, gave their prayer wheels a strong spin, and then said a prayer for you—at least I assume they were prayers.

One of the important skills they learned during training was cryptography. After reinsertion, the OWLs were expected to transmit intelligence to us. They were instructed in the use of what was then state-of-the-art encrypting and stored-impulse transmitting equipment. Each of the devices had been miniaturized to about the size of a cigarette pack. The OWLs were taught to poke out a coded message with a needle-like stylus on a cartridge housed in the encryptor. The cartridge was then inserted into the stored-impulse transmitter, which could reduce pages of data to one brief microburst of radio transmission. For the system to work, the transmissions had to occur at precise, prearranged times. Otherwise, the listening posts would not be able to pick up and decode the transmission. Knowing this, the Chinese had begun confiscating watches, clocks, and other timepieces in hopes of sabotaging the timing of the transmissions. We reacted by giving the OWLs a supply of the very finest Rolex wristwatches, which they were instructed to hide and never wear.

The first group I accompanied was shuttled from the training camp to Lowry Air Force Base in nondescript station wagons. Everyone wore civilian clothes. The whole idea was not to attract attention. I had heard that on a previous reinsertion mission, the flight from Lowry had been diverted because of weather or equipment problems to a civilian airport in Texas where the OWLs, in full combat gear, disembarked and fast marched past the windows of the airport coffee shop. The patrons of the restaurant thought it was some sort of terrorist attack. Terrified, they ran for the pay phones and dialed the local authorities. One thing led to another, and before long a National Guard unit was dispatched to quell the "invasion."

We arrived at Lowry without incident. As we boarded our plane,

the maintenance crew was just completing the painting of new identification numbers on the wings and tail. This was a "black flight." It
didn't exist. The ID numbers would be used for one leg of the trip
only. At each refueling stop—Travis, Hawaii, Wake, and Okinawa—
fresh numbers would be painted over the previous ones. The plane
itself was a U.S. Air Force DC6, a four-engine prop-driven transport.
The crew was Air Force, as well—"military assignees" temporarily
working for the CIA. At Okinawa we transferred over to a foreign
chartered aircraft manned by a foreign crew. They took us to our
destination, a staging base in northern India.

Much of what the CIA does is accomplished utilizing *contract
agents* such as the OWLs and the foreign air crew, rather than *staff*
personnel. There are four basic employment designations in the CIA:
staff agents, staff employees, contract agents, and contract employees. An *agent* designation denotes someone operating under a cover
identity. An *employee* is basically an "open," someone openly identified as an employee of the CIA. *Staff* agents and employees have
executive and civil service status. *Contract* agents and employees do
not; they serve under a contractual arrangement, generally with re-
newals every two years.

As ordered, I stayed in India when the OWLs were reinserted. A
foreign crew in a chartered DC6 flew them into Tibetan airspace. The
OWLs parachuted out over the designated drop zone. As was procedure, the DC6 then circled sharply in order to be in position to drop
the heavy military hardware and supplies to land near the men. The
cargo was to be pushed along a track and out of the plane, but unfortunately the mechanism jammed. By the time the cargo parachuted out of the DC6, it was miles from the drop site and
unreachable.

It could have been a catastrophic setback for the mission. The
OWLs were to attack a Red Chinese convoy. Now they would have to
do so using only the light arms they had jumped with. But as I've
said, the OWLs were as tough as they come. They not only decimated
the convoy, but the Tibetan survivors also escaped with two duffel
bags full of sensitive Chinese intelligence materials. Traversing hundreds of miles of rugged terrain heavily patrolled by enemy forces,
they succeeded in bringing the duffel bags safely into India.

I carried the duffel bags back to Washington, where they were
delivered to a brother federal agency involved in national intelligence

and security activities. Some time later we received a letter of appreciation from that agency indicating that the two bags had contained the hardest intelligence yet to come out of Red China. The letter speculated that our acquisition of the material had set the Chinese back ten years. It also noted that the materials had provided insights into the Soviet system, which was the progenitor of the Chinese system. It was a great letter, but it really should have been sent to the OWLs. They deserved it. As it was, they would have to be satisfied with massacring the Chinese convoy. Something tells me that was reward enough for them.

A number of the OWLs were actually lamas, the Tibetan version of Buddhist monks. This is not as strange as it first might seem, when one considers that prior to the Chinese invasion, approximately 20 percent of the Tibetan population belonged to clerical orders. Their hatred seemed to have purged them of any restraint—religious or otherwise—about killing the Chinese invaders. However, their religious beliefs did conflict with other aspects of the OWL Program.

During the preparation for my second mission with the OWLs, I participated in the last phases of their survival exercises at the training base in Colorado. The assignment called for stalking and killing a deer with weapons fashioned from the environment. These mercenaries, who could slaughter Chinese soldiers without blinking an eye, absolutely could not hunt and kill one of the numerous mule deer that populated the area. Finally, a couple of us tracked one down and staked it out for them. We told them that to complete their training, they had to kill the deer. If they didn't, we wouldn't take them back to Tibet. For hours they hovered over the deer, spinning their prayer wheels and mumbling their prayers. For hours they chanted mantras, and the hum of the prayer wheels droned over the mountainside. Finally, all together, so that no single individual was solely responsible for the animal's demise, they stabbed the deer. However much they had resisted dispatching the deer, they sure didn't have any hesitation about eating it when we roasted it later that evening over an open fire. One and all, lama and layman, enjoyed the venison feast. If all that praying was for a tasty dinner, their prayers had been answered.

Making the meal less enjoyable for the Westerners present was the foul odor of yak butter. Somehow the procurement people were getting this Tibetan staple to the OWLs. It was their habit to dissolve it in the tea that they brewed in large cauldrons. If there is a worse smell in this world, I haven't found it yet.

During the last days of training, two big shots flew in from Langley to observe. Over dinner, evidently inspired by the surroundings, they started boasting about their mountain-climbing expertise. The dialogue quickly turned into a "can you top this?" contest.

I climbed Mount This.

Yeah, well, I climbed Mount That.

That ant hill? Hell, I did that one in winter during a blizzard.

And so on it went.

The next morning, to settle the issue, we all headed up to one of the more treacherous peaks in the area. We were accompanied by a few of the OWLs who must have been amused by the whole affair. Inscrutably impassive, they watched from afar as the two supposedly world-class mountain climbers crawled safely on their bellies along the steep ledge that led to the summit. Well back from the peak, they both chickened out and scurried down, again with tummies pressed firmly to Mother Earth. The leader of the OWLs, seeing the ignominious display, whispered something to one of his companions, who then scampered up the ledge with the nimbleness of a mountain goat and stood at the brink of the precipice with the toes of his boots protruding into midair. Like an eagle, he just perched there at eleven thousand feet above sea level! He could have been standing on a street curb or an orange crate for all it seemed to concern him. Over the remaining two days of their visit, I never heard another word about mountain climbing from the two guys from headquarters.

My second black flight with the OWLs was to be the last of the program. It seemed jinxed from the very start. Two of the four engines went out between Hawaii and our landing at Wake Island. It was a crazy scene in that DC6. The OWLs were sure we were about to fall into the sea. They were leaping from their seats, jumping from one side of the plane to the other, pressing their noses against the windows. The prayer wheels were spinning like mad. The mantras were humming, sounding like a swarm of drunken hornets. And in the back of the plane, two of them were going at it.

"Can't you make them stop?" I asked the interpreter.

"They can't help themselves," he replied plaintively.

"I don't care," I answered. "If they don't stop, I'll physically make them stop."

The interpreter did persuade them to uncouple, and for a few minutes the bedlam was at least a bit more tolerable. But just as the box lunches were being passed out, I noticed that the two lovebirds were at it again. I could see I was going to lose this battle. I called for the interpreter and said, "At least have them wait until after lunch." Hunger prevailed over passion, and my request was granted.

Because of the urgency and the highly classified nature of this covert mission, we tried to attract as little attention as possible. After refueling, the pilot chose to push on, and between Wake and Okinawa we lost the third engine, exacerbating the frenzy of the OWLs. By now the scene in the plane resembled something out of a Fellini movie. But we managed to land safely and then completed the final leg to India uneventfully. A couple of days later the OWLs were dropped into Tibet, and I returned home. About a month after that, I read in the *New York Times* that Camp Hale had been closed.

From then on, the OWLs were on their own.

14

JOBS

THE GOLDWATER GAMBIT

During the spring of 1964, the *New York Journal American*, which was part of the Hearst chain, published a series of articles detailing the revelations of a former Eastern Bloc intelligence officer who had defected a few years earlier. According to the defector's account, the Eastern Bloc had penetrated the U.S. diplomatic missions in Moscow and Warsaw via homosexuals employed by the State Department who had been compromised by KGB operations. The hysterical sky-is-falling tone of the articles was in keeping with the arch-conservative editorial policy of the paper. The *Journal American* squarely put the blame for the scandal on the Johnson administration and the Democratic party.

It was campaign season. Former Minnesota Governor Harold Stassen, Maine Senator Margaret Chase Smith, Ambassador Henry Cabot

Lodge, New York Governor Nelson Rockefeller, Pennsylvania Governor William Scranton, former Vice President Richard M. Nixon, and Arizona Senator Barry Goldwater were all either vying for the Republican nomination or being courted to run by hopeful backers. The disclosures offered a dynamite campaign issue.

The defector had been under CIA control for several years and had only been surfaced a few days prior to the publication of the *Journal American* articles. The CIA had provided him with a new name, money, a job, a place to live, identification credentials, a Social Security card, a fully backstopped history, basically everything he needed to integrate safely and prosperously into the American way of life. Such efforts provided the foundation and model for today's more formalized Federal Witness Protection Program. A lot had been done for this guy, and it wasn't part of the bargain that he shoot his mouth off for political purposes.

Making things worse, from the timing of the articles, it appeared that the Republican party—or at least people working for one or more of the Republican candidates—had been in touch with him even while he was still under CIA control. It didn't seem conceivable to us that the defector, immediately upon his integration into society, would be able to proactively make the contacts and set up such a deal. Likewise, it appeared quite obvious that the politicians would not have been able to reach the defector that quickly without the cooperation of somebody inside the agency, probably somebody close to the defector. This last concern definitely brought the incident to the attention of the Office of Security.

I was summoned to headquarters and briefed on the situation. I was also told that agents in New York had already picked the defector up. He was their "guest" in the presidential suite of one of New York's better hotels. I was ordered to immediately go to New York and present to the defector a subpoena from the Senate Subcommittee on Internal Security. The subpoena had been signed by Senator James O. Eastland of Mississippi. I also was handed a letter from CIA Director John Alexander McCone that was to be given to the defector.

The CIA possesses no police power. We couldn't issue subpoenas or make arrests. The only real legal weapon we had was to request the subcommittee to issue a subpoena. Once before the Senate subcommittee, the defector would be placed under oath and sworn to secrecy. Then he would testify in closed session. Thereafter, if he divulged anything he had said to the subcommittee, he could be charged with contempt of the Senate and prosecuted in federal court.

When I arrived at the hotel in New York, I found the defector in a state of great agitation. In the suite with him were several other agents along with a cleared and witting doctor.

"I know my rights," the defector fumed. "I'm a free man. I'm a U.S. citizen."

I asked him and one of the agents who had worked with him since he first came over to accompany me into one of the bedrooms. I presented the documents. He barely read them before ripping them to shreds.

"Fuck you!" he growled. "You can't hold me against my wishes."

I returned to Washington without the defector. I learned later that the defector had "willingly" accompanied the other agents back to Washington, where he had then testified as planned before the subcommittee. Thereafter, he had dropped from sight.

A few days later I was invited to lunch by one of my neighbors, an administrative assistant to a conservative congressman. At lunch, my neighbor, who was under the impression I still worked for the Federal Bureau of Narcotics, asked me if I had any connections with the State Department, the CIA, or the FBI.

"Why?" I asked.

He explained it had to do with the defector who had disappeared.

"The Republican party is pulling out all the stops to locate this guy," he went on. "He has information the American people have a need to know."

"I don't know anyone in particular," I replied, "but I'll ask around."

"We're even willing to provide financial support to fund efforts to locate him," he added.

"Who's behind all this?" I asked.

"Ashbrook and Goldwater," he answered.

John Milan Ashbrook, a congressman from Ohio and a former national chairman of the Young Republican Clubs, was an up-and-comer in the conservative movement. Goldwater, of course, was one of the most vocal members of the conservative wing of the Republican party and was the candidate who would carry the Republican banner, however catastrophically, in the upcoming November election.

I sought guidance from my supervisor, who in turn advised head-quarters. Instructions came down to pursue the matter further.

I made contact with my neighbor and told him there was a chance I might be able to help him locate the defector. Actually, I had no idea where he was. I didn't even know if he was under CIA control. I explained to my neighbor that the information would cost money and that I needed to know the parameters of how much I could spend. We settled on an amount, and I told him I'd get back to him.

Once more I consulted with my supervisor. He told me to try to arrange a personal meeting with Goldwater. He wanted me to receive payment directly from the senator.

The meeting was set up for the very next day, a Tuesday. It would occur at 8:00 A.M. in the Senate Breakfast Room.

Immediately, I put in a request to headquarters for the use of concealed monitoring equipment and surveillance. Surprisingly, the request was denied, and I was instructed to call off the breakfast meeting.

"Forget it," my supervisor explained. "We did it twice over the weekend with the same guy."

I took that to mean that two other operations had already succeeded in getting money from Goldwater, who never got what he paid for.

In this case, compartmentalization worked. I never found out what became of the defector, although I heard some rumors to the effect that he had undergone a "thought reformation" process and had then been set up with a cushy consulting gig. Nor did I ever learn if an investigation had been undertaken to determine who within the agency had put the defector together with Goldwater's people. I have often wondered whether my boss was telling the truth about the agency having sunk Goldwater twice over that weekend. Maybe headquarters had entertained second thoughts about stinging Goldwater, who was really a big ally of the defense and intelligence complex. But if Goldwater had been compromised as I had been told, then there were really only two plausible explanations to account for why the incident never came to light: either the episode had been buried in the archives, or the CIA had struck a deal with him.

WHEN IN DOUBT, SHOOT THE MESSENGER

More than once upon a time . . .

A junior official of a U.S. Embassy behind the iron curtain was grabbed by two sloppily dressed, low-ranking local police officers and hauled off to their station house. The cops were bunglers. Their breath reeked with alcohol. They accused the diplomat of committing a minor currency offense. Since it was obviously a case of mistaken identity, the embassy official acted arrogant and condescending. His detainment at the hands of such incompetents was a most exasperating inconvenience. But nothing he said convinced the officers to release him. The detainment went on for hours. The official—in reality, a CIA agent working under diplomatic cover— only thought of extricating himself and getting back to his home. He struggled to assert his innocence yet preserve his cover. Fatigued, he finally admitted some benign detail concerning his real identity, a harmless shred of information, the true significance of which he considered well beyond the bumbling officers' ability to grasp. The diplomat's captors, however, were not the rubes they appeared to be. They were actually well-trained, highly motivated Eastern Bloc intelligence officers. They had rattled an opposition agent, in the process learning much about the agent's psychological makeup. If the revelations proved significant, they could exploit the "confession" by either deporting the disgraced agent as a persona non grata (PNG) or by extracting promises of future cooperation.

The scene, with slight variation, was played out repeatedly during the mid-1960s. Young, inexperienced agents working under diplomatic cover were placed in captive environments under trumped-up charges by Eastern Bloc intelligence agents posing as local police. All too often, to lessen their own inconvenience, the CIA agents wound up coughing up some morsel of information that should not have been divulged. Often it was something insignificant. But since the opposition well understood the bureaucratic, careerist nature of their targets, they were frequently able to exploit the situation further. They understood that being declared a PNG and being sent home prior to the minimum three-year tour of duty was something the young agents did not want in their personnel files. These were people who enjoyed their desk-bound jobs. They liked rubbing elbows at the embassy receptions. They weren't the type to drive fifty kilometers in the dead of night to service a drop or otherwise take any risks. They would do almost anything to maintain their glamorous lifestyles and their upward career paths.

Diplomatic cover has always been the safest way to insert intelligence officers into denied areas. Because of diplomatic immunity, if a member of a diplomatic mission is caught conducting espionage, the worst thing that can happen is deportation. Knowing this, countries maintain healthy numbers of intelligence agents under diplomatic cover all around the world. And counterintelligence forces in the targeted countries are charged with the task of identifying them, monitoring their activities, and, if appropriate, compromising the would-be diplomats.

The problem had reached worrisome proportions, and the brass decided that better screening had to be done during the training of new agents. The Office of Training under the CIA's Deputy Directorate of Plans (DDP) asked the Office of Security to devise and implement a stimulus-and-response exercise that would determine susceptibility to the Eastern Bloc tactics. Additionally, since some new agents assigned under diplomatic cover were showing reluctance to carry out their intelligence-related assignments, the S&R exercise was also to weed out the more timid trainees.

The trainees involved were relatively few in number. All of them were being considered for diplomatic covers at embassies behind the iron curtain. After completing another phase of their training elsewhere, they were to come to Washington, D.C., for a series of briefings at various government agencies that were intended to help the trainee establish his cover. In between briefings, the trainee would also participate in exercises designed to further the newcomer's trade craft.

After a few meetings, we offered the DDP's Office of Training a program that it accepted. The target trainee would be sent on a trade-craft exercise at a crowded, public place, such as a shopping mall. A typical assignment might be to attach a simulated limpet to the electrical panel. (A limpet, named after a marine mollusk that clings to rocks, is an explosive device that can be attached to a target surface, such as the hull of a ship or the wall of a building.) After he accomplished his mission, he would be stopped by two plainclothes detectives who would "invite" him down to the local police station. The trainee would be told he fit the description of a suspect who had recently molested a thirteen-year-old girl. Female trainees would be accused of shoplifting. At the police station, the trainee would undergo confinement and questioning similar to what the Eastern Bloc intelligence officers were doing. The detectives would be agents from the Office of Security. Other OS agents would surveil all activities outside the police station. The interview room at the police station would be bugged.

We implemented the program. Until word finally got out about our activities, not one trainee passed our test.

Typical was an episode with a middle-aged trainee we stopped at Tysons Corner, a large shopping mall in Vienna, Virginia. Posing as Fairfax County detectives, my partner and I hustled him over to the police station. We were careful not to actually say that he was under arrest. The trainee was pretty cool until we instructed him to empty his pockets onto the table. He started asking questions about the charges, nervously claiming he had not been near the location of the crime. When he finally emptied his pockets, three different entry badges were on the table—Department of Defense, State Department, and CIA.

"So who do you work for?" I asked.

"For Defense," he stammered. "At the Pentagon."

"What are these other badges?"

"They're for liaison," he answered. "I've got to coordinate certain activities with the other two agencies."

It wasn't a bad answer.

"Who's your supervisor at Defense?" I pressed.

"Ah . . . she's a woman . . . I don't remember her name—"

"You don't know your boss's name?"

"I'm new—"

"What about a phone number?"

"I don't know."

Obviously, he hadn't yet mastered his cover legend. I took him back to the beginning—his date of birth, his parents' names, brothers, sisters, where he had grown up, gone to school, part-time college jobs, friends, memberships, travel experiences, details about his marriage. It was all designed just to extend his confinement and make him nervous. After about an hour, he asked if he could call his wife.

"She's at a motel," he explained. "She's pregnant and due any minute."

We allowed him the phone call. Evidently, his wife assured him that the population of the world was not quite yet to be increased by the arrival of his offspring. Returned to the grind of reviewing the inane minutiae of his life, he quickly revealed that he was, in fact, a CIA agent on a training exercise.

"You're police officers," he commented. "I can trust you."

He told us everything about the details of his training and the nature of his planned overseas assignment. I left the room momentarily, ostensibly to confer with another police officer. Upon my return, I told him he was free to go. It had all been a mistake. The real culprit had been apprehended.

On the following day we played the tape of the interview for the Office of Training people. They indicated that the trainee would be disciplined and assigned elsewhere.

On other occasions I participated as a member of the surveillance team. Once, during the dead of winter, in the middle of a blizzard, we trailed a trainee to the Washington Zoo. The geniuses who had conceived his exercise had assigned him to make contact with a training officer in the monkey house. There we were—the trainee, his training officer, the two of us who followed him inside, and the dozens of other monkeys who watched with interest from their cages. Even an inexperienced trainee should have been able to make us. I'm not so sure the monkeys didn't figure out what was going on.

Another time, we stopped a female trainee in a posh department store just after she had completed her training assignment, a brush pass. During a brush pass, two apparent strangers pass each other in a public place, allowing one to inconspicuously "pass" something—an envelope, papers, a small package—to the other, usually dropping it into an open purse or briefcase, or sliding it into a newspaper or coat pocket. She was all decked out in high heels and a fur coat, ready to head over to a cocktail party. Being accused of shoplifting just didn't fit into her plans for the evening.

"Could I see some identification, please," I asked.

"Why?" she demanded.

"We saw you slip something into your purse," I explained. "The management of this store prosecutes shoplifters."

We knew that the papers she had picked up in the brush pass and slipped into her purse were insignificant. We also knew that that they were stamped *TOP SECRET* and that she had been instructed to deny access to the documents. She was in a tough spot. If she showed us the papers, she would be clear of the shoplifting allegation but guilty of violating her training assignment. She stood her ground and refused to let us examine her purse.

We ran her down to the station where we simply took the purse away from her and opened it. She protested, but could do little to stop us. As I reached into the unsealed, unmarked envelope that she had acquired during the brush pass, she began to cry.

"I'm obliged to tell you that I'm employed by the CIA," she sobbed. "That envelope contains classified documents."

"Why didn't you tell us sooner?" I asked. "All this could have been avoided."

"I was afraid of what my supervisors might say," she gushed.

She then proceeded to tell us all about the training exercise we had interrupted. I was tempted to tell her that she was still *in* the exercise, but, of course, I couldn't. We let her go. The following day, as was customary, we reviewed our findings with the DDP's Office of Training. The trainee was declared unsuitable for overseas assignments in denied areas.

And so it went. Trainee after trainee failed in one way or another. It was becoming quite clear that the people responsible for screening new agents just weren't doing an adequate job. The DDP people started getting defensive. Our methods, which they had approved, were suddenly called into question.

The last trainee we confronted was an attorney and a former Marine Corps officer. He was a big guy, every bit as big as myself and my partner, who was also an ex-football player. We had heard that the word was out on us, that the trainees had been tipped off to look for OS agents posing as detectives. It was immediately clear that this trainee knew all about us. When I asked him for identification, he refused, telling me that unless I was placing him under arrest, he was not required to provide any information whatsoever. When I put my arm on his and told him he was going back to the station with us, he hauled off and punched me. My head was half turned, and I didn't see it coming. It was a sucker punch, and it really pissed me off. My partner didn't like it any better than I did. He tuned that marine's clock up but good. Before I knew what happened, the smart-ass was on his back. He offered no further resistance when we cuffed him, but he stood up to us at the station, refusing to say a word and demanding to see an attorney. We gave up after about two hours and cut him loose.

A week later, the program was axed. Those of us who had participated in the counterprobe were criticized. We had sorely embarrassed those who had done the recruiting and the training. The trainees we had confronted would have been putty in the hands of an opposition intelligence officer. It was just that simple. That's what our work told them. They didn't like the message, so they shot the messenger.

ACCIDENT-PRONE

In January 1965, the Maryland State Police notified the CIA that two suspicious men had been spotted in the woods along the Potomac River opposite the entrance to the agency's Langley, Virginia, headquarters. At the time, besides my regular duties for the Office of Security, I was running a covert "can-do" squad for the SRS's Col. Paul Gaynor. Gaynor suggested that I look into the situation.

Quickly I organized a surveillance and determined that the two men were using high-powered optics to watch the activity at Langley's George Washington Parkway entrance. The trees in the heavy woods along the Potomac River were devoid of foliage at that time of year, and they had a clear, unobstructed view. I assumed that they were recording vehicle tag numbers that they would later trace back through Department of Motor Vehicle records. Doing so would give them valuable information on the comings and goings at headquarters. Even the tags on rented vehicles could, with a bit more effort, be traced back. Somebody was obviously very interested in Langley's traffic pattern.

When the two men packed up and left, we followed them. They headed straight for the Soviet Embassy on 16th Street. I reported back to Gaynor, and he encouraged me to continue the surveillance.

I decided to focus on the younger of the two men, a bachelor. By following him around for a few nights, we learned that he spent most of his free time at an Irish-style pub on 11th Street. There, he kept to himself and genuinely seemed to enjoy watching other people. The antics and cavorting of the tavern's heavy-drinking patrons apparently amused him.

I told Gaynor what we had learned. His eyes lit up when I mentioned the pub.

"You know," he mused, "I wouldn't be surprised if one night he didn't get punched out in a rough joint like that. Stuff like that happens all the time."

Sure enough, it happened just as Gaynor predicted. Not more than a couple of nights later, our boy was sitting at the end of the bar peacefully sipping his schnapps when in walked a big guy with a pretty girl on his arm. The couple cozied up to the bar right beside the Russian and ordered two drinks. Then, without warning, the big guy was all over the Russian.

"Hey!" he shouted. "What are you, a fuckin' wise guy?"

The Russian, who had done nothing to provoke such an outburst, cowered against the bar. Obviously, he wanted no part of the angry young man who towered over him. But the man was irate, acting as if the Russian had just made a pass at his woman. He hauled off and smashed a right cross in the Russian's face. The Russian flew off his stool onto the floor, clutching his broken, bleeding nose. Of course, he didn't want a scene, so he just took off and bolted out the door.

Two weeks later, however, the Russian was out barhopping again. His nose was heavily bandaged. One eye was still swollen. He didn't dare go back to the Irish pub. Instead, he went to a place on Maine Avenue near the old Flagship Restaurant. As luck would have it, when he came out and headed for his car, two guys were waiting for him. They beat the shit out of the poor bastard.

Soon after that, the Russian disappeared from sight. I guess after he kept coming to work all banged up, his comrades decided to get rid of him before he made a scene for them. Obviously, the guy was accident-prone. Apparently they shipped his unlucky ass back to Mother Russia.

As far as I know, nobody else ever tried spying on Langley's George Washington Parkway gate from the woods across the Potomac River.

That's the way things got done.

OVER EASY

One of the primary objectives of counterintelligence operations is to flip the opposition, to get the other side's guy to work for you. That part of my job was somewhat similar to much of what I had done for the Federal Bureau of Narcotics. Only now, spies had replaced drug dealers as the targets. The means were still pretty much the same, however. Simply stated, the idea was to get something incriminating on the target and then use it as leverage to switch the target's allegiance. Obviously, other complications and considerations often presented themselves, rendering the process a bit more complex.

One such case I worked involved a graduate student who was just about to complete his work for a doctorate in aeronautical engineering at a major U.S. university. The student was a foreign national who had received his master's degree from a university in Moscow. His homeland was a Middle-Eastern country then in the Soviet sphere of influence. As was required in that country, the student's family had posted a large cash bond with their government ensuring their son's eventual return. I was brought in after intelligence had been developed indicating that the Soviets had approached the student, encouraging him to procure a university research job that would position him to penetrate a sensitive U.S. government aerospace project. If he did so, he would be allowed to remain in the United States without forfeit of the bond. I devised a plan wherein the student would be offered just such a job at a prestigious northeastern university.

University personnel cooperated, making the initial contact and inviting the student to visit the campus. Once the appointment was finalized, we made arrangements with a local hotel, ensuring that the student would be assigned to a specific room. My unit then planted surveillance equipment in the preselected room. We also bugged the lobby pay phone, anticipating that the student's handlers might have instructed him not to use the room telephone.

In this instance, bugging the room was quite easy since we had full access to it prior to the subject's arrival. We simply placed a Shure button microphone in the room and tucked the wire under the carpet next to the baseboard. We opened up the phone and popped alligator clips on the appropriate contacts, again running the lead along the floor trim. Since we were set up in the next room, it was quite easy to run the concealed wires under the adjoining doors. We had two reel-to-reel tape recorders hooked up to each input. All together we had six in the room, including two that were hooked up to the pay telephone in the lobby. This way, as a tape ran out, we could switch over to the back-up recorder without missing a word.

In cases where we didn't have preliminary access to the area, we would be forced to drill a hole through an adjoining wall. In hotel or apartment situations, we'd usually go in behind a wall hanging. The trick was to drill as far as possible without penetrating the last layer of paper on the Sheetrock in the subject's room. A straw containing the microphone would then be inserted into the hole.

At one East Coast hotel that cooperated with us, we had an entire floor bugged, with the leads all tied into the central switchboard. Careful subjects would be relieved at check-in to find many available rooms to choose from. No way could they all be wired!

The student was under intensive surveillance from the moment he arrived at the local airport. He went directly to the chosen hotel, registered, and brought his bags to his rooms. He then returned to the lobby and made a call from the pay phone we had bugged. The man he called was his homeland's local resident agent, whose identity had not been previously known to us. Information was exchanged, instructions were imparted, a meeting was set. Now we had the goods on two of their people.

Unlike my work for the FBN, intelligence operations tended to be extremely fragmented due to the security-driven discipline of compartmentalization. This could be extremely frustrating. Just when a case was developing into something hot, it could be taken away from you. This was one of those times. I had placed my piece of the puzzle. I was done. It was somebody else's job to take the case further. I did learn, however, that my successors easily flipped the student, turning him into a double agent. I assume that surveillance was established on the local resident agent and that he was flipped as well.

15

JMWAVE

THE SECRET WAR WITH CUBA

Early in 1960, a big-time mafioso by the name of Giuseppe ("Bayonne Joe") Ziccarelli walked into Service Armaments, a sporting and military surplus firearms merchandiser in Ridgefield, New Jersey, and attempted to purchase a thousand M-1 rifles. His stated purpose was to donate the arms to Cuban exiles in Miami for their inevitable counterrevolution. It's doubtful that Bayonne Joe's motives were rooted in patriotism. His inspiration much more likely sprang from greed—or perhaps even from that most basic of human instincts, self-preservation.

Prior to Fidel Castro's takeover, the mob enjoyed a cozy business relationship with Cuban President Fulgencio Batista y Zaldívar. It had invested millions in the island's "recreation industry," and it was raking in huge profits from the hotels, casinos, loansharking, and prostitution. The Mafia's Cuban interests also provided a much-needed means of laundering money from its nefarious stateside operations. The proceeds from the Cuban rackets were split 50-50 with Batista. It was a small price to pay for what amounted to partnership with a sovereign government.

When it became apparent that Castro's rebellion had a chance of succeeding and unseating Batista, the mob sent emissaries to meet with the bearded, cigar-smoking revolutionary. Castro assured his visitors that the basic arrangement would remain intact under his leadership, although the split would be adjusted to 60-40 in Cuba's favor. The mob negotiators left Castro convinced they could do business with him.

Ironically, a U.S. government contingent had also met with Castro and had come away with similar assurances. Gravely concerned about the spread of communism in the Western Hemisphere, no less to an island but ninety short miles from the Florida coast, it was necessary to ascertain Castro's intentions. Castro was diplomatically vague, but the delegation came away convinced that he would play ball.

Within weeks of the New Year's coup of 1959, it became apparent that Castro had no intentions of honoring previous commitments. The panic that surged through the myriad offices, chambers, and briefing rooms of the government was mirrored in the private social clubs, restaurant back rooms, and guarded residences where the mob bosses plotted their enterprises. The overlords of organized crime saw untold millions going up in smoke. Their most promising venture had been obliterated by an enigmatic bearded man in combat fatigues.

Castro threw all the U.S. crime figures out of Cuba. He seized more than $1 billion in U.S.-owned assets, including virtually all of the mob's interests. The only criminal who got out with anything of value was Jack Lansky (brother of the more notorious Meyer Lansky), who escaped in a private plane with $1 million in cash just minutes ahead of Castro's militia. Bayonne Joe Ziccarelli's attempt to arm a counterrevolution was a bit flamboyant and not the kind of attention-attracting enterprise normally favored by his peers, but it did perfectly reflect the frustration and anger that he and many of his fellow mobsters must have been feeling.

The CIA's reaction to Castro's takeover was to establish JMWAVE, its primary base of operations for all activities in the Western Hemisphere. JMWAVE operated clandestinely out of the University of Miami's South Campus in Perrine, Florida. The campus had formerly been the Richmond Naval Air Station. During World War II, it had been used as a dirigible antisubmarine base. Dormant since the end of the war, it was reactivated to deal with the Cuban situation.

JMWAVE's original focus, under President Eisenhower, was to marshal the Cuban refugees in south Florida and prepare them for covert operations in Cuba. Borrowing heavily on principles of guerrilla warfare established during World War II, the operation was launched, with the Everglades providing natural camouflage. The plan called for the establishment of a communication system with an external base, the creation of a reliable means of supply, and the institution of strong security within the unit, including a reliance on compartmentalized assignments and the use of safe sites and routes of travel. The primary objective was to organize a viable underground in Cuba and to instigate a revolution from within.

When the Kennedy administration took the reins in 1961, the charter for JMWAVE changed. Kennedy favored a more overtly military campaign. "Executive actions" were sanctioned: bridges were blown up; sugar cane and tobacco fields were burned; communications installations were sabotaged. Kennedy's so-called secret war went on for several months, with training, planning, and supply orchestrated by JMWAVE. The campaign was weakened—but not ended, as many think—by the disastrous Bay of Pigs invasion in 1961. It was actually the Cuban Missile Crisis of 1962 that finally restricted the military aspect of the operation. As part of the negotiated understanding with Moscow, Kennedy agreed to forgo executive actions. At our own risk, we would continue infiltration and exfiltration activities, as we would continue to recruit in Cuba. We would plan for sabotage and demolition, but we wouldn't actually engage in such missions. Basically, we were back to the Eisenhower plan.

I was transferred to JMWAVE during 1965 to be a security officer for the base. Since JMWAVE was basically considered to be our base in Havana—albeit in exile—it was regarded as an overseas posting. I received a housing allowance and a car, as well as other benefits reserved for nondomestic assignments. If anything started in Cuba, we were expected to be there within hours.

Our legend in Perrine was that the property was owned by the U.S. government and leased back to the University of Miami. My cover was that I was a civilian working as a security consultant for a federal agency in conjunction with classified research that the University of Miami was conducting for the government. According to the cover legend, I was the head of a seventy-five–man police force.

In actuality, there was no research going on there, and I was one of four agents assigned to counterintelligence for the Office of Security. I had two principal agents working for me, both cleared and witting contract agents. All in all, there were probably about two hundred CIA personnel at JMWAVE.

One of my principal duties was to maintain a close working relationship with the local police departments and other law enforcement agencies in the area. We really took care to stay close to the Florida Department of Conservation people down in Monroe County in the Keys. We were running a lot of operations down there, and we needed their cooperation. Since they had a bird's-eye view of our activities, we also had to make sure that their people were trustworthy. Almost without exception, I found the law enforcement officers in the area to be extremely cooperative and enthusiastically patriotic. Of course, it didn't hurt our cause that on occasion we supplied them with expensive ammunition for hunting and target practice. We also earned some goodwill when, after a devastating hurricane wracked the coast, the agency supplied blankets, food, and other essentials.

While I was at JMWAVE, I used a cryptonym when signing internal correspondence. A cryptonym differs from an alias in that it is utilized only within an intelligence organization. It can denote a person or a place. JMWAVE, itself, is actually a cryptonym. For reasons known only to the CIA, the cryptonym I used at Perrine is still classified and therefore cannot be revealed here.

An alias was used in contacts with people outside the agency. As usual, it was fully backstopped. I had a driver's license, a Social Security number, and credit cards, all under the alias name. There was an address, an employment record, and other supporting documentation.

Besides JMWAVE, there were a number of other CIA facilities spread throughout south Florida, most of which I knew about only through rumor or observation. One of the more critical installations was situated in Miami. It was equipped with all the latest electronic monitoring devices then known. I had the feeling that if Castro sneezed in Havana, someone was saying, *"Salud!"* in Miami.

One of the more curious outgrowths of the agreement that resolved the Cuban Missile Crisis was that it became known that all Cuban radar would shut down along a particular stretch of beach from 7:00 P.M. each Friday night until 7:00 A.M. the following Monday morning. Our people were free to enter virtually without risk during those periods. Many of the Cuban exiles took the opportunity to visit friends and family. Many more exploited the breach of security by smuggling in automobile parts, which was exactly what Castro wanted them to do. Since the United States had shut off trade with Cuba, it had become impossible for the Cubans to keep their American cars running. Castro acquiesced to a black market supply controlled by his avowed enemies as an economic necessity. From an intelligence point of view, it also made the infiltrators more visible to his own G2 (the Cuban intelligence service) and, thus, more trackable. He had already won the concession from Kennedy banning executive actions, but the black market car-parts trade further ensured that any would-be heroes, inclined on violating the ban, would be kept in tow by their companions who were prospering from the lucrative business. The CIA was happy because the smuggling gave a sense of purpose and a means of funding to a group it had trained for a counterrevolution that every day appeared less likely to occur.

We continued to run people in and out of Cuba. Bridges, airports, military bases, communications installations, government buildings, and other targets of interest were repeatedly photographed. Troop movements were scrutinized, radio traffic was monitored, human assets were recruited. Plans and contingency plans were constantly updated. Every couple of months or so, we floated a barge loaded with fireworks into Havana harbor and detonated it. The full-alert response of the Cuban military establishment was observed and analyzed, giving us insights into Castro's capabilities and revealing the details of the Cuban order-of-battle plan.

Surveillance of Castro, himself, was also a priority. Over time, through our assets on the island and those we inserted, we developed a good understanding of his habits and routine. Of special interest were the frequent cocaine and sex orgies he hosted for a group of generals and their mistresses. Our intelligence reports indicated that Castro and his generals both snorted the cocaine and used it as an aphrodisiac by rubbing it over their sexual organs prior to intercourse, a practice that was in vogue among Cuban drug abusers. I'm sure it must have occurred to one of our analysts that any action against Cuba might be well timed to coincide with one of Castro's parties.

As for actually attempting to take out Castro, I can say only that we had the ability and chose not to pursue it. The persisting allegations that the CIA enlisted the Mafia to assassinate Castro strike me as ludicrous. However motivated the mob may have been, what sense would it have made to employ mob hit men—who would have been out of their element and totally outclassed compared with the forces and resources deployed to protect Castro—when we had an asset in place who had access to Castro and who was begging for permission to kill him? That permission was routinely denied even though it was thought that the asset had tremendous probability of succeeding. And whether the proposed assassination resulted in success or failure, the asset's connection to the CIA was quite easily deniable. If the CIA had the inclination to assassinate Castro, it certainly had the means without resorting to an unreliable and entangling liaison with organized crime. We simply didn't need the likes of Miami's Santo Trafficante, Jr., or Chicago's Sam Giancana or any of the other names that have surfaced over the years.

One of the more pressing problems facing us at JMWAVE was just how to keep the now not-so-secret army of Cuban exiles under control. Here was this rough-and-ready group whom we had trained in all the black arts sitting in the Everglades waiting for the thumbs-up for an invasion that wasn't to be. Their sense of distrust had increased dramatically since the Bay of Pigs, and some were becoming more and more tempted to use the skills we had taught them to embark on criminal careers here in the States. Now that we had also instructed them in the fine art of smuggling, some of them applied their newly learned expertise to drug trafficking. But since the Mafia controlled the heroin business, there really wasn't another hard drug available in sufficient quantity to support a major entry into the narcotics trade.

In South America, however, steps were already being taken to organize the mass production of another hard drug. Cocaine was not a new drug. It was known to the Cubans, and it was known elsewhere primarily in jet-set and bohemian circles. But it had never been available in large quantities, nor had there ever been a consistently reliable means of supply.

But that was changing—and one of the key people responsible was Fidel Castro's right-hand man, Ernesto ("Che") Guevara.

CHE

When Castro took power in Cuba, he was welcomed into the world community of Communist countries. Both the USSR and Red China jumped in to support his fledgling regime. But eventually the rift between the two Communist superpowers became manifest even in Cuba. One of the big differences between Russia's and China's ideology was how each handled revolution. The Soviets preferred a peaceful process of revolution through the electorate, through subversion, through penetration and control of the educational system, the factories, and the media. The Chinese, on the other hand, advocated violent revolution—strangulation of the cities, organization of the countryside, terrorism, shock. Each was vying for Castro's exclusive favor. I can almost imagine the Soviet foreign minister whispering into Fidel's ear, saying with typical Russian bluntness, "Look, comrade, either they go or we go"—or something along those lines. Since the Russians were pouring more money into Cuba than the Chinese were, Castro did, indeed, kick the Chinese off the island.

Somewhat problematic in this development was the relationship that Che Guevara had with the Chinese. Che, a popular hero of the Cuban revolution, was a vocal supporter of the Chinese brand of communism. He had authored a book on guerrilla warfare that read much more like Mao than Moscow.

Che's official postrevolution titles included president of Cuba's National Bank, a position that mandated that his signature appear on all Cuban currency. He chose to sign simply as "Che," a word that meant "pal" in his Argentine homeland. He also had the dubious distinction of being Castro's minister of industry and along with it the impossible responsibility for rebuilding Cuba's industrial infrastructure. His real mission, however, involved the exportation of the Cuban revolutionary experience to the other underdeveloped countries of the world, especially those in the Western Hemisphere. Castro was already being heralded as *Lider de los Americas* (Leader of the Americas), and it was Che's job to train and motivate the would-be Communist rebels of the Third World. Thousands of them came to Cuba for this purpose.

Che's activities did not fit neatly into the Kremlin's agenda. The Russians knew he was backed by the Red Chinese, and there was a concern that his operations would succeed in spreading Beijing's sphere of influence. The Soviets continued to pressure Castro to get rid of his friend. Although there has been speculation that Castro betrayed his longtime *compañero*, it's more likely that, as a political necessity, he convinced Che that his talents could be better employed elsewhere. It's also conceivable that Castro, having mollified the Russians, continued to utilize Che as a conduit to the Chinese.

In December 1964, Che left Cuba to address the United Nations and to visit Africa. He returned to Cuba on March 14, 1965. It was the last time he was seen publicly on the island.

According to our intelligence, one of the operations that the Chinese had implemented through Che was the organization of a network of cocaine laboratories in Chile, where there was a sizable Chinese population. The work had started while Che was still based in Cuba, and it continued after he departed. From Chile, the network spread into Peru and Bolivia. It was a classic case of a covert intelligence operation utilizing drug trafficking as a double-barreled weapon. Not only did the drugs, themselves, work to undermine the moral fiber of the target country, but the *business* of drugs produced a lucrative means of discretionary funding for other, more overtly revolutionary activities. Ironically, in the target country, the United States, a disenchanted subgroup of Cuban exiles, superbly trained in smuggling and the black arts as a result of another covert intelligence operation, was waiting impatiently, along with others, for their chance to import and distribute this new hard drug.

Prior to Che's involvement, cocaine was barely known inside the United States. According to the Federal Bureau of Narcotics *Annual Report for 1961*, the first year the report even listed statistics on the drug, "the total quantity of cocaine seized throughout the United States during 1961 was 4 kilograms, 62 grams, compared with 2 kilograms, 680 grams seized in 1960." The 1962 report listed annual seizures of 10 kilograms, 646 grams, going on to cite Cuba, Bolivia, and Peru as the principal source countries. By 1964, the numbers had more than doubled, at 23 kilograms, 564 grams. The quantities of cocaine seized have continued steadily upward ever since to the present day, when annual seizures can now be measured in the hundreds of *tons*. Today, it is not uncommon for one good-sized raid to net more cocaine than was seized in the entire year of 1961.

Throughout the mid- and late sixties, at a time when tens of thousands of American young people were deifying Che Guevara, hanging his bereted and belligerent poster image on their walls as a symbol of their own rebellion against the establishment, Che, himself, was pioneering the cocaine trade, setting the stage for the addiction of the generation to follow. Much like Hollywood, the counterculture of the era produced heroes whose public personas were altogether disconnected from reality.

During 1966 and 1967, I spent much of my time tracking Che's movements through South America. Along with another agent, a case officer from the psychological warfare unit, I underwent survival training in preparation for a planned mission to insert us into South America to act as advisers to the Bolivian military, which was hunting him down. I was chosen specifically because of my background in federal narcotics law enforcement, but I had to back out at the last minute due to the arrival of my third child. My partner did go to South America and was with the Bolivians on March 8, 1967, when they cornered and wounded Che in a canyon outside of La Higuera. The CIA advisers present argued for Che's evacuation to medical facilities. The Bolivians ignored them, taking him instead to the village schoolhouse. On the following day, one of the Bolivians, probably acting on the direct orders of Bolivian President Barrientos, executed Che.

According to the information that filtered back to me, Che was set up by his girlfriend, who was actually an undercover KGB agent. Like Che, Tamara Bunke Bider had been born in Argentina. However, she was of German descent, and her contact with the KGB may, indeed, have been through the East Germans. Operating under the code name Tania, she is thought to have passed on key intelligence that ultimately resulted in the discovery and takeover of Che's base camp at Nancahuazu, a blow from which Che's Bolivian campaign never recovered. Tania, suffering from terminal cancer, was killed in an ambush during August 1967.

Although it was the Bolivians who actually killed Ernesto ("Che")

Guevara de la Serna, America took the blame after news quickly leaked out that CIA advisers were at the scene. The Soviets set him up, and we wound up looking like the heavies. If that was their plan, it sure worked. Perhaps the operation was designed as a move against the Chinese or an attempt to keep Che from returning to Cuba, but the by-product was the creation of a world-class Marxist martyr.

We took the rap, and Che's picture went up in another ten thousand college dorm rooms.

TILL DEATH DO YOU PART

One of my duties at JMWAVE was to screen incoming CIA transferees. I'd brief them on security procedures and debrief them regarding their previous assignment.

One agent who transferred in had just returned from a hot area in Southeast Asia. He was in his mid-twenties. His career looked promising. Tragically, his young wife had died abroad, and he was engaged in a legal battle with his wife's family over custody of his two children. During the interview, I sensed a problem, something spooky, something beyond grief and the preoccupations that would normally come from such troubled circumstances.

As was my habit during interrogations, when I wasn't satisfied with the information I was getting, I started focusing in on little details, idle tidbits, the seemingly insignificant minutiae of everyday life. Eventually the discussion covered a description of his house overseas. We went through it room by room, finally getting to the bedroom. I had him go over every piece of furniture, what was in it, what was on it. When he described the nightstand, he mentioned that there was a can of rat poison and a glass of milk on it.

"What does anyone do with rat poison in the bedroom?" I asked.

"We had rats," he answered.

"In the bedroom?"

"All over."

"But you kept the poison on the nightstand?"

"Yes."

"Next to a glass of milk?"

"Yes."

"Why?"

"I don't know."

"Why there? Why not in a cabinet or under the sink? Something like that."

"I don't know. . . ."

I kept it up, grinding away, and before long, although he never categorically admitted it, it became clear he had poisoned his wife. I think he was looking to get it off his chest, that he was haunted by what he had done. He had to tell someone, and I gave him that chance. He certainly didn't have to tell me about the rat poison and the glass of milk—unless he needed to.

Immediately I prepared a cable and sent it off to Langley. Word came back that headquarters was sending Director Richard Helms's private plane down to pick him up. Helms was the last real pro to hold that job, and we all loved him. I personally respected him because he had withstood the pressure from J. Edgar Hoover and had steadfastly supported our position in the Nosenko controversy.

I accompanied the young agent on the flight up to National Airport and handed him over. That was the end of my involvement with the case, although I did hear back through the grapevine that he was sent for "thought-reformation" at a medical facility. I had no actual first-hand knowledge of such activities, but there was a general consensus among CIA agents that the agency had the resources for what is commonly called "brainwashing," as well as the resources and desire to offer more traditional forms of rehabilitation to employees with problems. As we understood it, the focus of "thought-reformation" efforts centered on attitude adjustment. Electric shock, drugs, and indoctrination were rumored to be the principal means by which attitudes were "turned around." Evidently, intellectual capabilities were not impaired by such treatments—or at least that was the intent. In fact, I later heard that the possible wife-killer went on to pursue advanced degrees in mathematics at a major university.

The inherent problem with a case of this nature, besides the agency's obvious desire to keep it quiet, was the legal situation. Our courts, as the result of a case springing from a murder that had occurred in Italy during World War II, had jurisdiction even though the crime had occurred on foreign soil. The publicity that would have accompanied such a trial would have been disastrous. Additionally, the case could have been tried in the country where the crime had been committed. The CIA was not about to allow its agent either to go to court here or to be extradited and tried overseas.

I knew a bit about the legal aspect because of a story that had been previously told to me by Henry Manfredi, my old friend at the Federal Bureau of Narcotics. Manfredi had headed the investigation in postwar Italy that eventually led to the clarification of jurisdiction for criminal cases involving Americans on foreign soil. As we flew to Langley, I recalled Manfredi's story and wished that I had been given the charter and resources to pursue my investigation like Manfredi had been given to pursue his.

As Manfredi told it, just before the end of the Allied campaign in Italy during World War II, two OSS officers—Maj. William Holohan and Lt. Aldo Icardi—parachuted in behind enemy lines. Their drop zone was in the mountains about fifty miles outside of Milan. Holohan was a forty-year-old, Harvard-educated attorney for the Securities and Exchange Commission. Icardi, who had previous experience working with the Italian underground, was a twenty-three-year-old graduate of the University of Pittsburgh. Among Icardi's other duties, he was to act as Holohan's interpreter. Parachuting in from a second plane was Icardi's radio technician, Sgt. Carl LoDolce.

After a few months, Holohan was criticized by the leader of one of the partisan groups that had Communist leanings. He felt that the major was favoring the more conservative guerrillas when he distributed arms and funds. On December 2, 1944, Vincenzo Moscatelli, commander of the Communist Garibaldini Partisans, complained that his group wasn't getting its fair share. Holohan had heard that Moscatelli had been using OSS-supplied munitions against rival partisan groups, as well as against the Germans. Holohan demanded that Moscatelli assure him that any weapons provided to him would be used only against the Germans. Moscatelli refused to agree to Holohan's terms. When a shipment of forty-four automatic weapons arrived later that very day, Holohan gave the guns to the conservative Christian Democratic party.

Holohan disappeared four days later. Icardi radioed OSS headquarters in Siena and told command that Holohan had been killed in an ambush. Icardi distributed subsequent arms shipments almost exclusively to Moscatelli.

After the war, a partisan who knew more about Holohan's disappearance suffered pangs of conscience and confessed to a local priest. As Manfredi later pieced it together, the partisan evidently told the priest that Icardi had ordered the killing of Holohan and then dumped his body into the waters of icy Lake Orta. Deeply troubled by the horrible secret he carried, yet not wanting to violate the sanctity of the confessional, the priest turned to the craft of divination. Wandering about the village with a forked branch, he proclaimed the presence of gold, oil, and precious stones at various locations. Upset over the odd behavior of their priest, the parishioners wrote angry letters of complaint to the bishop. They were sure their priest had gone mad. But the divinations continued, and one day, while the priest was sailing out on Lake Orta, he announced that gold could be found in the depths directly under the boat. When divers finally investigated the priest's claim, they discovered the corpse of Major Holohan, well preserved by the glacial waters.

Henry Manfredi, then the head of the army's Criminal Investigation Division (CID) for the occupation forces in Italy, had already started his investigation of Holohan's disappearance at the time the penitent Garibaldini made his confession. Manfredi had found it curious that Holohan's body had never been found. He had also heard about the major's falling out with Moscatelli. He concentrated his efforts on two former partisans, having his investigators constantly surveil the men and interrogate everyone they had contact with. When one of them suddenly sought out a priest for confession, Manfredi felt that the case was about to break.

Once Holohan's body had been found, Manfredi succeeded in flipping both of his suspects. They told him that Icardi and Georgi Aminta Migliari, another partisan, had been planning to go into business together. After the fateful meeting of December 2, Holohan had assumed tighter control of the OSS operating funds that had been entrusted to the mission, much of which Icardi and his partner had earmarked for postwar entrepreneurism. Icardi and LoDolce, who was also in on the deal, then poisoned Holohan by lacing his soup with cyanide. The poison made Holohan gravely ill, but it didn't kill him. The two conspirators flipped a coin, and it was thus determined that LoDolce would finish the job, which he did with two shots into Holohan's head.

Charges were brought against Icardi and LoDolce, who by that time were back in the States. The complicated legal proceedings that followed over the next several years involved extradition hearings, a congressional investigation conducted by the House Armed Services Committee, a perjury trial, and an appeal. Icardi retained the noted barrister Edward Bennett Williams as his counsel. Williams hired Robert Maheu, a former FBI agent with purported CIA connections, as his assistant. The defendants were eventually acquitted.

The Holohan murder case caused quite a stir, bringing to public attention the realization that U.S. laws didn't apply to events occurring on foreign soil. Over time, the laws were changed to vastly extend the reach of American justice, as we've seen quite recently in the arrest and trial of Panamanian President Manuel Noriega. I debated relating the whole story to my prisoner, but decided not to. I suspected that headquarters had its own plans for handling him. Whatever legalities had evolved, with a bit of indirect help from a clever village priest, probably would never be applied to him. No one was going to hear about this guy—least of all the court system.

A MOLE

It's become popular in books and movies to refer to the CIA as "the company." In my experience, CIA insiders seldom used this term. As far as I can tell, it was the Cuban exiles in south Florida who first coined the nickname. In Spanish, *Cía.* is the abbreviation for *compañía*, which literally translates as *company*.

It's also become popular to portray the CIA as an omnipotent force that knows all. We certainly didn't know all in the case of a Cuban G2 intelligence agent who had penetrated our operation at JMWAVE. And our supposed all-encompassing power boiled down to the initiative of individual agents driving around Miami looking to bag the G2 man before he had the chance to make good on his threat to murder eight people. No cadres of ninja-like assassins. No James Bond electronics. No think tanks plotting strategy. Just flesh-and-blood human beings speeding around Dade County and hoping to spot him before he had the chance to hurt somebody.

Although executive actions had been deescalated, we continued to run heavily armed teams of Cuban exiles into the island. Almost since the very onset of the Cuban ops, significant amounts of weapons and explosives were being lost during the missions. Upon their return, some of the teams told harrowing tales of escape. Increasingly, to evade Castro's forces, they were being forced to jettison their munitions overboard in an effort to make their boats lighter and faster. Unfortunately, many of the supposedly jettisoned weapons—everything from hand grenades to submachine guns—were resurfacing in the hands of criminals on the streets of Miami.

In 1967 we decided to do something about the growing problem. We traced weapons that the police had confiscated to one of our teams that operated under the cryptonym HANGMAN. (HANGMAN is not the actual cryptonym; the actual cryptonym is still classified.) I ordered that the entire HANGMAN team be called into the Perrine facility for polygraph examinations.

Without tipping them off to what was going on, we investigated each member of the team, completing our work on one before moving on to the next. We referred to them by their numeric designations— HANGMAN 1, HANGMAN 2, and so on. We never used their actual names.

Gradually we pieced together what they had been doing. On their return trips from Cuba, they'd simply detour to one of the little keys and stash their armaments and munitions. Later in the week, they'd head back down to the cache, pick the guns up, boat them back to Miami, and sell them to street criminals.

One day in late spring of 1967, we polygraphed HANGMAN 22. The session went routinely, and when it concluded, he, like the others before him, was allowed to leave. I organized my notes in preparation for the follow-up conference with Fred Evans, the polygraph technician. I had concluded that HANGMAN 22 had diverted a case of hand grenades and a Swedish K. Adolph Gustapson 9mm machine gun.

Later, as Evans reviewed HANGMAN 22's tape, he suddenly exclaimed, "Holy shit! We missed a big thing here."

"What?" I asked.

"This guy is G2!"

We were so locked into solving our security problem with the weapons that we entirely missed seeing that HANGMAN 22 was working as a double agent for Castro's intelligence agency. The polygraph technician had discovered a pattern in HANGMAN 22's responses that all but screamed that he was a mole.

The worst fear of any intelligence organization—and the CIA in particular—is penetration by a mole, a double agent working for the opposition. Most of the paranoia is reserved for high-level moles capable of making or influencing policy. But penetration, even at the level of a HANGMAN 22, is deadly serious business.

I jumped on the phone and called HANGMAN 22's case officer, the veteran CIA agent responsible for his handling.

"Bring him in!" I ordered.

A few minutes later, the case officer called me back. "I reached him," he said. "HANGMAN 22 told me he had killed eight people in Cuba before coming over here and before the day's out he's going to kill eight people here."

I mobilized the agency resources that were available to me. Basically it came down to a handful of security officers and case officers hopping into their vehicles and cruising around Dade County on the slim chance they'd spot this guy driving around. Some of them were detailed to surveil his home and favorite hangouts. Time was of the essence. If we were to take the mole's threat seriously, we needed to get him under wraps immediately.

Then I called my contacts in the surrounding local police departments and briefed them on the situation, giving them HANGMAN 22's description and a description of the car he might be driving. I told them to consider HANGMAN 22 as armed and dangerous.

Having done what little I could to coordinate the manhunt, I jumped into my car and joined the effort. I couldn't just sit on my hands waiting for the phone to ring. I started driving south down Route 1. I hadn't gone very far when I spotted HANGMAN 22 driving northbound. I made a U-turn and followed him. When I passed a cop, I flagged him down, flashed my cover credentials, and told him to stop HANGMAN 22's car. The cop turned on his lights and siren and raced after HANGMAN 22. I followed in my car.

HANGMAN 22 pulled off into the parking lot of a shopping center where a Jefferson's Department Store was located. Incredibly, the cop just took off. I guess he felt he had done his part and now it was up to me to take over.

I pulled up alongside him, about twenty yards away. I was out of the car as soon as it stopped rolling. HANGMAN 22 jumped out of his car with a gun in his hand. He leveled it at me, but I already had the drop on him.

"Move and you fucking die," I shouted.

He believed me. He dropped his gun.

I didn't have any cuffs with me, so I decided to make him drive my car to the City of South Miami Police Station. I slid into the passenger seat, stuck my gun into his ribs, and made him drive himself to jail.

My superiors recommended me for the Intelligence Medal, a coveted decoration awarded to intelligence agents. The recommendation was denied. Giving me a medal for bagging HANGMAN 22 would have meant acknowledging that the CIA was involved in domestic activities.

That wasn't going to happen.

16

SOB

DOMESTIC ACTIVITIES

The CIA's charter gives it responsibility for foreign intelligence operations just as the FBI's gives it responsibility domestically. Neither is to trespass on the other's turf. All other government entities are to filter their intelligence requirements through the appropriate authorized channel. In the sixties, if the Department of Agriculture officials wanted to know what kind of wheat the Soviets were growing on the steppes of Russia, they were precluded by law from developing their own covert mechanism to go out and collect that intelligence. They brought their request before the Security Council, which then levied a requirement upon the CIA. The agency activated its appropriate apparatus, which went out and collected the intelligence covertly. I suppose it was just too easy to walk down 16th Street, knock on the door of the Russian Embassy, and simply ask.

However, the line that separated foreign intelligence operations from domestic *counterintelligence* operations, which were also considered within the CIA's purview, was growing faint, sometimes with the help of those who were promoting special interests. In the late sixties, the CIA found itself drawn increasingly into domestic involvements.

In August 1967, I transferred back to the Washington, D.C., area. This time I was assigned to headquarters at Langley. I became chief of the Special Operations Branch of a division (the name of which is still classified) responsible for extralegal domestic covert activities. The plaque over my office door read *C/SOB*, initials that gave my detractors ample ammunition.

The SOB was an outgrowth of counterintelligence efforts that had been implemented during the construction of the Langley headquarters complex. To protect against the covert installation of monitoring equipment and remotely controlled explosive devices, workers in the building trades had been recruited to keep an eye on things. When the construction of Langley was completed and these assets drifted off to other jobs, many were kept on retainer. They could be called upon at any time to aid with counterintelligence surveillances from within the cover of their real jobs. In addition to construction workers, the agency also retained those engaged in other professions, such as taxi drivers and trash-removal services.

I inherited the apparatus of tradesmen and other blue-collar workers that was already in place. I also was given the task of putting together a new nationwide apparatus of college students, professors, and administrators to deal with the growing wave of anti-Vietnam War and anti-Johnson administration demonstrations. Our primary mission was to protect the agency's on-campus recruiting efforts, many of which had been compromised. It was also felt that penetrations of certain dissident groups would provide an early warning signal to alert us to planned actions targeted against our recruitment activities. Additionally, if the protest movements were financed, directed, or manipulated as part of a foreign covert intelligence operation, we wanted to know about it.

We also understood that we couldn't always control what fish was going to take the bait. It was quite possible to go out looking for one thing, yet find something else entirely. Oftentimes we discovered illegal activities that didn't fall under our jurisdiction, but which we couldn't ignore. Ways were found—overtly or covertly—to pass such intelligence on to the appropriate local or federal authorities.

One of the groups that we penetrated was the Washington, D.C., chapter of the Black Panthers. We were able to determine its plans for operations during the civil rights riots of 1967 and 1968, giving us the ability to advise local and brother federal authorities prior to their implementation. We also learned that the Panthers were stockpiling a large cache of weapons and explosives at a house on 16th Street, N.W. This information was also turned over to the appropriate agencies that had the authority to take the required action.

We also penetrated the Women's Strike for Peace, an organization that, despite its ennobling name, had drawn our interest. Our insert there was the wife of one of the primary assets in our apparatus. She became an officer of the organization and supplied us with copies of the membership rolls, donation records, confidential correspondence, and general mailings. Even more valuable were her reports of conversations she had with leaders and members of the group. She also reported that the cultural attaché of the Soviet Embassy had contributed to the group, clearly in violation of her diplomatic status, which prevented involvement in U.S. internal affairs. We used the information to have the attaché declared persona non grata.

In our division, there was also a branch that handled covert domestic investigations. To augment their activities, the branch's staff actually set up a national network of private investigating offices as a cover for their work. They ran into problems, however, when walk-in customers, totally unaware of their true purpose, retained their services. Beyond the dilemma of dealing with non-CIA cases, there was the question of what to do with the fees received. Not only did the CIA not want to compete with legitimate private investigators, but the whole idea of making money off the venture was actually repugnant to the agents involved.

The situation stands in stark contrast to some in the Iran-Contra bunch who have been accused of having a clear interest in making money. Unfortunately, that's how much attitudes have changed over the years. Not only does it appear that Ollie North and some of his gang profited personally, but they rationalized running their supposedly *covert* operation from the White House, *the* single most visible building on the entire planet. Running a covert program out of the White House is a bit like landing a Stealth bomber in Red Square during the May Day Parade. It might not produce any blips on the radar screen, but chances are, someone is going to spot it.

Suddenly it's okay for a covert agent to have a $200,000 college fund set up for his kids by his "business associates." Or to have an elaborate personal residence security system installed, compliments of "patriotic benefactors." No one gave my kids any tuition money. No one was worried about the safety of my home. I received a paycheck from the government for what I did. That was enough for me and for the thousands of others who participated in covert activities solely because they thought they were doing what was required of them by their country.

While I was chief of the Special Operations Branch, some of the guys who later would be bagged in the Watergate affair worked for me. I understand that when I left the agency, most of the functions of the SOB were transferred to a unit supervised by E. Howard Hunt, another Watergate figure.

Prior to Hunt, there was no formal arrangement for special endeavors on behalf of the White House. What generally occurred was that an agent was instructed by some very senior officer to proceed to the White House or to the Executive Office Building for a meeting. The senior officer would make it clear that he did not know anything else about the scheduled meeting. During the meeting, the agent would be briefed: "The president wants. . . ."

Hunt took the operation and tried to institutionalize it at a very high level. He tried to make it permanent. He sold it to the people at the Nixon White House, and he managed to create an empire for himself. The problem with empires is that once they're established they have to justify themselves. Here were all these hotshots sitting at their desks, scratching their heads, and saying, "Now what are we going to do?" So they went out and tackled some psychiatrist out in San Diego on the basis that he was the shrink for Daniel Ellsworth, the guy who had leaked the "Pentagon Papers." The whole operation was to prove their capability. But they screwed it up—just like they would screw up at the Watergate Hotel.

BOOTSIE

In checking through the membership register of the Women's Strike for Peace (WSP), we were surprised to find the name of one of our senior analysts. Since it was a very common name, we had to make sure that the person listed on the register and our analyst were one and the same. We instituted surveillance on the analyst, and, sure enough, we managed to follow her to a WSP meeting.

Advancing our interest was the discovery that the analyst, a divorcée, had previously been married to one of the CIA's senior operations officials. She was from a blue-blood, old-money family. Attractive and stylish, she appeared years younger than her actual age. She was a chic dresser who favored the go-go boots that were then fashionable. When we escalated our operation, we couldn't help but give in to the obvious temptation: We named the investigation Operation Bootsie.

Surveillance proved difficult. Bootsie was well schooled in trade craft and liked to use wigs and other disguises. Whether she was on to us or she was just being careful to mask her activities, we weren't sure. Oftentimes we'd pick her up on foot outside her fancy Georgetown townhouse. It was common for her to duck into bars or restaurants or into the boutiques along M Street and Wisconsin Avenue. When she resurfaced, she'd be wearing a different outfit. Often she would change her boots, as well, making sure to alter the heel height. Heels greatly affect overall walking characteristics, an important "signature" that we focus on when maintaining an ambulatory surveillance. More than once, she managed to lose us.

One afternoon, after several evasive moves, she walked to her car and drove to an impoverished area in southeast Washington, D.C. We followed her to an apartment building but couldn't determine exactly which apartment she had entered. About a week later, after gaining entry to her parked car, we dusted the steering wheel and floor mats with a phosphorescent powder that can be seen only under ultraviolet light. When she returned to the same apartment building, we were able to follow her trail of glowing footprints under the beams of a black light. Later, we determined that the apartment she visited had been leased by her.

At the apartment, Bootsie was joined by a man whom we subsequently discovered was a chauffeur employed by one of the African diplomatic delegations. At the time, that particular African country was aligned with the Soviets. The liaisons were repeated frequently over the next several weeks.

We brought our findings to James Angleton, chief of the Counterintelligence Staff. Since Bootsie was involved in some sensitive work, Angleton was very concerned about the situation. It was critical that we find out if Bootsie's companion was an asset of the opposition's intelligence apparatus. If that was the case, it was possible that a penetration of the CIA had occurred. He ordered a full investigation.

We persuaded Bootsie's next-door neighbor in Georgetown to go on an extended vacation. An agent was brought in from Chicago. Along with his wife, he moved into the vacated townhouse. Bootsie's home and office phone lines were tapped. Plans were made for the covert installation of monitoring equipment in her townhouse. Surreptitious searches would also be conducted.

One night, with a colleague, I searched Bootsie's office safe at the agency. In the bottom drawer, buried beneath a pile of innocuous paperwork, was a series of classified cables reporting the movements of the *José Valdez,* one of the CIA's top secret ELINT (electronic intelligence) ships. It was not unusual for such cables to cross her desk, but there was no reason for her to have squirreled these away in her safe. Even more suspicious was that this particular ELINT vessel happened to be the sister ship of the U.S.S. *Pueblo,* which had recently been captured by the North Koreans, a situation that had embarrassed the government and created quite a scandal. Furthermore, the ELINT ship was operating off the coast of Africa in the vicinity of the country that employed the chauffeur she was meeting.

Before the conclusion of Operation Bootsie, I transferred out of the CIA. Influenced by my good friend Henry Manfredi, and somewhat disenchanted with the "spy business," I decided to go back into federal drug law enforcement. I suppose a few of my contemporaries at the agency were disenchanted with me, as well. More than once, I had been referred to as a loose cannon. And those guys who wrote blue memorandums sure weren't going to shed a tear over my leaving.

A brand new bureau was being put together by merging the old Federal Bureau of Narcotics from the Treasury Department and the Bureau of Drug Abuse Control (BDAC), which had been set up under the Food and Drug Administration to deal with the emerging problem of hallucinogenics and synthetics. The new Bureau of Narcotics and Dangerous Drugs (BNDD) was to be under the Justice Department. I had the opportunity to get in on something new, and I took it.

I heard later that Bootsie was forced to leave the agency. I don't believe that she was ever prosecuted or that her former husband was ever implicated in any way.

I may have been done with Bootsie, but she wasn't done with me. Seven years later, Senator Frank Church and his Senate Select Committee on Intelligence would drag the case out as an example of the CIA meddling in domestic affairs, and I would be forced to testify about it in executive session.

Years later, I have reflected upon those hectic years when the United States was fighting a bloody war in Vietnam, the Soviet Union seriously threatened freedom, and U.S. streets, cities, and universities were filled with controversy, demonstrations, and violence. I can understand why high-level U.S. government officials wanted to investigate groups that were creating disorder and threatening the activities of government. But, in the quieter 1990s, I can also understand now that the surveillance tasks given to me would be resented by American citizens and that these tasks were on the very fringes of CIA responsibility, as defined by the fuzzy legislation that established the agency. In perhaps the greatest irony, some of our surveillance in the 1960s might have crossed the path of then antiwar protester Joe DeSario, my newfound friend who helped me develop this book. In our own way, Joe and I have personally reconciled some of the bitter differences that divided our nation during those difficult times.

17

THE PURGE OF '68

"A disposizione, Commendatore!"

Italian law enforcement officials—high government authorities down to the lowliest Carabinieri—always showed Henry Manfredi the utmost respect. They'd snap to attention as soon as he entered a room.

"At your disposal, Commandant. What can we do for you?"

Manfredi spent twenty-four remarkable years in Italy earning that respect. From the Federal Bureau of Narcotics, he first came to Italy during World War II as an officer in the OSS. After VE-Day, he stayed on with the occupation forces to head the army's Criminal Investigation Division in the country. He remained in Italy, eventually going back to work for the Federal Bureau of Narcotics. His assignment required close liaison with the CIA, and he developed, over the years, an excellent relationship with the agency as well as a keen understanding for intelligence operations.

In 1967 Manfredi returned to the States. Knowing of my dissatisfaction with the CIA, he suggested that I transfer over to the new
Bureau of Narcotics and Dangerous Drugs (BNDD).

"Today you work against a Czech," he contended, "and tomorrow
he's your friend. Then you work on a Finn, and later he's your buddy,
too. But who likes a dope peddler?"

It was a persuasive argument—and coming, as it did, from a man
who was a veritable legend both in the arenas of drug law enforcement and intelligence, it had to be taken seriously. It's even possible
that factions within the agency had asked Manfredi to pitch the Bureau of Narcotics and Dangerous Drugs to me. With strong contacts
in both organizations, he was in a perfect position to try to help both
the CIA and the new BNDD.

The CIA was sophisticated. The agency had the best equipment
and seemingly limitless funding, but the gray shadow world of intelligence work wasn't all that I had expected it to be. The one job that
I really wanted, the DDP's Italian Desk, was not available. That was
the position that I thought would have allowed me to achieve my
potential and best serve the agency, but it was not open to me. The
DDP was organized into geographical divisions—Western Hemisphere, Western Europe, Eastern Bloc, Asia, etc. Each division was
further subdivided into "desks." One of the most desirable was the
Italian one, and like other sought-after desks, it was a closed shop.
The same elite group of officers changed positions every three years
between Rome and Langley. No one really left the desk, and no one
entered. When someone retired, the replacement was selected from
among the DDP's inner circle of favorites.

The agency had little restraint in sending me off on extralegal
operations when it suited its purposes, but it also had those blue
memorandums ready and waiting at the most inappropriate moments.
The action guys were losing out to the do-nothing ass-coverers. The
OSS mentality was being supplanted by the FBI's more sedate way of
doing—or in many cases, *not* doing—things. The first order of business seemed to be: *Don't rock the boat.* The likes of James Angleton
were on the decline. The politicians, bureaucrats, and wimps were
looming on the horizon.

I was a bull in their china shop. A cowboy. *The loose cannon.* It was
time to go.

On April 15, 1968, the BNDD was created by an act of Congress.

I transferred over from the CIA on that very day, becoming the first inspector recruited by the new bureau. Swearing in shortly after I did were Tom Taylor, Ike Wurms, and Ira Greenfeld, all seasoned law enforcement pros. I was immediately assigned to the Office of Inspection to work under Andrew C. Tartaglino, an experienced FBN veteran who was the new director of security.

Tartaglino's previous job was as assistant to the enforcement coordinator for the Department of the Treasury. He had also been successful as a supervisor in the FBN's New York office, where he had headed up an intensive investigation focused on the entry permits of several diplomats. His work had resulted in the arrest of Maurice Rosal, the Guatemalan ambassador to the Benelux nations (Belgium, the Netherlands, and Luxembourg). Based on information supplied by Tartaglino's team, Guatemala revoked Rosal's diplomatic immunity, paving the way for his arrest. When Rosal was bagged in New York, Tartaglino's agents found fifty kilograms of pure heroin concealed in his diplomatic luggage.

Tartaglino's reputation was beyond reproach. It had to be. The Office of Inspection, which he headed, was charged with cleaning house. The old problem of corruption had already found its way to the new BNDD.

One of the law enforcement entities that was consolidated into the BNDD was the Bureau of Drug Abuse Control (BDAC). Under the control of the Food and Drug Administration (FDA) since its inception in 1965, BDAC was a hodgepodge of paper pushers, bureaucrats, and former chicken inspectors. It also served as the destination for an underground railroad that shuttled over agents who were under suspicion for corruption and integrity violations at the FBN. A few individuals within the FBN, contrary to policy, concealed negative information in the personnel files of the transferring agents. On the receiving end, I'm sure there were those within BDAC who closed their eyes to what may have already been known about the transferees. BDAC needed professional drug-busters, and the FBN seemed able to provide a ready, if somewhat questionable, supply.

However, the underground railroad was about the extent of the two bureaus' cooperation, unofficial as it was. If FBN agents came across LSD or mescaline—or any of the other hallucinogenics or synthetic drugs that were the domain of BDAC—they simply ignored them. When BDAC inspectors encountered heroin, cocaine, or morphine, they worked the case, contrary to their charter, and then turned them over to the state police, local authorities, or even the U.S. Customs Service. By 1968, Congress had had enough of the jurisdictional warfare and decided to dissolve both organizations. Drug law enforcement was yanked away from the Treasury Department and the FDA. For better or for worse, the drug problem was now the responsibility of the Justice Department.

The top man at Justice, Attorney General Ramsey Clark, knew the history of corruption within the FBN and BDAC. He also knew that all those agents under suspicion, whom the FBN had allowed to transfer over to BDAC, would now be absorbed into the new BNDD. His orders to Tartaglino were clear: "Clean it up, or I'll put it all under the FBI!"

Tartaglino was the perfect choice for the difficult—some would say, *impossible*—job of fighting corruption within the ranks of federal drug law enforcement. In his previous job at the Treasury Department, he had maintained files on all the personnel with "investigative tails." Already, he knew where to start looking for trouble.

Corruption had not abated since the days when Wayland Speer had conducted his one-man probe into irregularities at the FBN's New York City office. But Speer hadn't had the support or the resources to carry on the fight. Furthermore, Treasury Department regulations mandated that corruption and integrity investigations be conducted by the Internal Revenue Service. However, the IRS often delegated the assignment back to another Treasury Department bureau. The hot potato–passing made for lots of paperwork and little actual reform.

One dedicated group in New York, led by Tom Taylor of the IRS, did take up Speer's banner, however. Taylor succeeded in bringing about several prosecutions of narcotics agents, including a case against two FBN agents who had left the bureau under a cloud of suspicion. Taylor investigated the two men after they had secured jobs as detectives with the Nassau County Police Department. He bagged them for selling dope they had previously seized.

The Office of Inspection (OOI) was not my first choice of assignments at the BNDD. I had been offered an assignment in Rome, basically to take up the work so ably handled up to that point by Henry Manfredi. I was quite enthralled with the idea of working in my ancestral homeland, as well as with the various perks and benefits that came with a foreign posting. The responsibilities of raising a family, complicated by a failing marriage, however, convinced me not to take the overseas assignment. We had just moved up to the Washington area from Florida, and I didn't think the added strain of a foreign posting, along with a job that required a great deal of travel, would be good for my family situation. Resigning myself to a domestic assignment, I was proud that Tartaglino wanted me in the OOI. His trust told me that the hotshots in Washington considered me to be honest and incorruptible.

The first case I worked on was actually an extension of a case I had started back in 1962 at Charlie Siragusa's request. Following Siragusa's instructions, I interviewed a Washington, D.C., banker who had just received a cash deposit of $9,000 from one of the FBN's New York agents, Charlie McDonnell. Besides being interested in the size of the transaction, I was suspicious that all but $200 of the cash was in denominations of $20 or less. I analyzed the serialization of the bills and determined that most of it had been distributed in New York City. We interviewed McDonnell and asked him about the money. He explained that it was a loan from his brother, who lived in the Washington, D.C., area, a story that didn't square with what we knew about the origin of the bills.

It was not the first time McDonnell had mentioned his brother. Just about every weekend he would leave New York to return to Washington, where he had grown up and where he still maintained a residence. Prior to his trips, he'd go around the New York office taking orders for booze. He had told his co-workers that his brother owned a liquor store in Washington and that he was able to purchase liquor at dealer cost. In fact, there was no store. The bottles he brought to his co-workers on Monday mornings had been purchased at retail, the only price advantage being the capital's lack of taxes on liquor at the time. But the scam ingratiated him to his peers and perhaps distracted them from questioning the frequency of his travels.

Nothing came out of that investigation, but interest in McDonnell had continued throughout the years I was with the CIA. Now I was entrusted with the case that had already progressed with Manfredi's help and under Tartaglino's supervision.

At the time I joined the BNDD, the investigation of McDonnell had concentrated on one of his informants, a colorful character named

Joe ("Joe Louis") Miles with whom McDonnell now shared an apartment in Baltimore. A former heavyweight prizefighter, Miles was well known in sports circles. He enjoyed a flamboyant lifestyle supported by drug operations in New Orleans, Baltimore, and New York. In New Orleans, he also ran a house of prostitution. Manfredi, working with senior investigators Joe Arpaio and Frank Pappas, had succeeded in making two buys from Miles. When they arrested him, he flipped, immediately coughing up McDonnell as his source of heroin supply.

By 1968, Charlie McDonnell had ascended to the position of deputy regional director for the Baltimore region of the BNDD. In that capacity he was the chief operations officer for the BNDD in a region that included the nation's capital. Using Miles, we decided to make the required two buys from McDonnell. The first was accomplished on April 15, my first day on the job. The second was done shortly thereafter. I wired Miles so that we could monitor and record their conversation. As soon as the second purchase was completed, we arrested McDonnell.

Like Miles before him, McDonnell flipped and cooperated with our investigation. He fingered a number of people within the BNDD, including some senior officials with grades as high as GS-18. The targets of his allegations ran the gamut from low-level personnel all the way up to the bureau's highest echelons. We would have preferred to have kept McDonnell in place at his job so that he could set up some of the personnel he had implicated, but we found it impossible to keep his arrest quiet. The politicians needed the PR. Anyway, most of the targets knew we had busted him. They thought he would protect them. He didn't.

All in all, with McDonnell's help and with the help of other cases that were being developed, we fired thirty-two agents in the first six months of the BNDD's existence. Another eight agents were charged and prosecuted for criminal offenses. The BNDD rank and file called it "the Purge of '68" or "the Corruption Circus," depending on their point of view.

Going after a corrupt agent's informant, as we did in the McDonnell case, became our modus operandi at the Office of Inspection. The tactic was based on the limited options available to a crooked agent. Whether he had stolen money or dope, which had to be converted into money, it required working with the underworld. A law enforcement officer's primary link to the underworld is his informant. We targeted an agent by looking for patterns in the agent's work history—complaints from prosecutors, defense attorneys, defendants, informants; allegations of stealing, lying, concealing, or manufacturing evidence. Then we usually started our investigation by focusing on the agent's informant. If the informant put the agent in the trick bag, we'd wire the agent and get him talking to any other agents he had implicated.

The scams we uncovered were varied and clever, but usually, sooner or later, they involved an informant. For instance . . .

■ Two agents have just raided an apartment, made an arrest, and seized six kilograms of heroin. Afterwards, they go to a bar and start crying in their beer about all the bills they have to pay. One of them has to pop for his wife's varicose-veins operation. The other one is marrying off a daughter. Suddenly a 200-watt bulb lights up over their heads: *Why not turn in only three kilograms as evidence and sell the other three?* That way the bills get paid, and everyone lives happily ever after. The guy who's in jail sure isn't going to complain that he's being charged for possession of three kilograms instead of six. It's a clean deal except for one slight problem: How do they sell the three kilograms of heroin? They can't take out an ad in the *New York Daily News*, and they can't peddle it at a garage sale. So they wind up calling one of their informants. Who else could get this done for them? Who else can they turn to?

. . . or . . .

■ A tight-knit group of crooked agents convinces one of their informants to set up a $25,000 heroin buy. But the informant is not provided with real heroin to complete the transaction. Instead, he's given turkey, a bag of flour that only looks like heroin. The time and place of the buy are arranged, a parking lot after sundown. Surveillance is established. The buyer arrives and enters the informant's car. The informant asks to see the cash. The buyer wants to see the heroin. The informant reaches under his seat and shows the package of turkey to the buyer, who, convinced he's looking at the real McCoy, hands over the money. The informant starts counting it, his signal to the watching agents, who then swoop down and bust both of them. The agents slap the informant around a bit to make the whole thing look convincing, an Oscar-worthy performance by one and all. They take the buyer aside and say, "Look you scumbag, you're one lucky son of a bitch. We didn't find any dope or money in your possession, so we've got no choice but to cut you loose." The buyer takes off thinking he's the luckiest guy alive—and the agents and the informant divvy up his $25,000. *Five thousand for you, and five thousand for you,* and so on.

One common scam that didn't involve informants was based on a manipulation of regulations and perceptions:

■ A seasoned undercover vet looking to make some extra spending money might approach two unsuspecting, uninvolved agents to surveil a buy he is setting up. Typically the two surveillance men were the least active guys in the office, preferably green newcomers from another team.

The vet signs out for the purchase money and proceeds to the prearranged meeting site, usually a bar. The surveillance agents position themselves outside the bar because they've been told that the buy will occur on the street. Sure enough, after the veteran agent has been in the bar for a while, sipping drinks that he will later voucher as operational expenses, he appears outside the door of the bar with another individual—no doubt, the dope peddler. The suspect hands something to the undercover agent and then walks off.

The agents reconvene at the office where the undercover veteran produces a small package of heroin he claims he just bought from the suspect. The surveillance agents are happy because they'll receive credit on the monthly report for a case initiation. However, the case belongs to the veteran undercover man. He controls it. He's responsible for making the required second buy, which proves impossible. After a year has elapsed, regulations dictate that the investigation be dropped—and it is.

What actually happened was that the veteran simply struck up a conversation with a stranger in the bar. Leaving together, outside the door, the vet asked for a match. From a distance, the surveillance agents saw something being passed from hand to hand and concluded it was heroin. At the office, the veteran produced real heroin he had withheld from a previous seizure. The government's money, which supposedly bought the evidence, never left the undercover agent's pocket.

When corruption involved senior people, it often reflected the misuse of power:

■ Honest agents make a buy from a guy who turns out to be a big-time mafioso. Excitedly, they report their penetration into the mob and kick off the appropriate flurry of investigative activity—mail coverage, tolls, passport checks, vehicle records, surveillance, the whole nine yards. But before they're able to make a second buy, the suspect drops from sight. His phone is disconnected, and his house is vacated with no forwarding address. After some time passes, the senior operations officer tells the investigating agents that intelligence has crossed his desk placing the suspect in Montreal. Again the machinery jumps into high gear. The memo mill churns out correspondence to headquarters, to the Canadian Embassy, to the Mounties. More time passes before replies from Canada indicate that the subject cannot be located. After a few more months, the senior operations officer has new intelligence, this time placing the suspect in Miami—and again the ensuing investigation comes up empty-handed. By the time another false lead has taken the investigation to Italy, a year has elapsed, and the case is dropped. "Close this dog out!" says the senior operations officer, and the file is shut for good.

Of course, the senior operations officer had, probably through a bagman, cut a deal with the mafioso: "You screwed up. You sold dope to one of our people. But for $50,000 I can absolutely guarantee you won't go to jail." Once the bribe had been received, it was simply a matter of keeping the honest agents off on one wild goose chase after another.

As the purge continued, the group of agents under suspicion began calling themselves "the mob." One of them was a former FBN agent who had since become a security officer for the National Security Agency (NSA). He began boasting that he could find out "everything that Inspection is doing" through Tom Tripodi. There was no truth to what he was saying, but it was still damaging to my reputation. I wired myself and arranged a meeting with him. During our conversation, which occurred under the surveillance of other inspectors, he actually implicated himself in a number of corrupt practices. We presented the evidence to the NSA people and eventually they fired him—although they never admitted that the termination was based on the information we had provided.

Our investigations often led to suspects outside of the BNDD. One of the more notorious names we investigated was Bob Leuci, a New York City narcotics detective who would be later glamorized in a book and a film as "The Prince of the City." The work we did on Leuci back in 1968 and 1969 would pay off later during the Knapp Commission hearings into corruption within the New York Police Department.

Leuci, feeling the pressure of our ongoing investigation and knowing that we were getting ready to indict him, approached Rudy Giuliani, then chief of the Official Corruption Unit under the U.S. attorney in New York, and basically said, "Let's make a deal."

Giuliani talked to me about it. "No way," I said. "Let's not make a deal. Let's indict him and then talk to him." Over my objections, Giuliani cut a deal with Leuci.

Unfortunately, much of Leuci's testimony proved useless. As it turned out, he hadn't told us half the shit he had done. Defense attorneys found it quite easy to discredit him.

One of Leuci's coconspirators was a New York cop by the name of Joseph Nunziata. Andy Tartaglino wound up taking a lot of heat when Nunziata committed suicide. It came out that Tartaglino had told Nunziata, "You can do one of three things: You can work with us, you can go to jail, or you can blow your brains out." It was a pitch commonly used by law enforcement and intelligence people, but the BNDD's critics came after Tartaglino as if he had invented it. The detractors ignored the fact that Tartaglino had gone on to advise Nunziata that jail and suicide were not viable options. Evidently, Nunziata wasn't convinced. Although he was too vain to put a gun to his head, he did shoot himself in the heart.

Nunziata had good reason to fear death less than a jail cell. Prison for drug offenders is bad enough. Prison for ex-narcotics cops is hell inside of another hell. Convicts have long memories, and they love to dole out their version of justice on dirty cops. Two undercover agents we prosecuted, Joseph Mordecai and Edward Bell, found this out the hard way.

Mordecai and Bell had tried to shake down a dope seller, in the process compromising an undercover agent. I arrested them, and they flipped. I cut them a deal: If they would agree to tour the various BNDD offices and lecture the personnel on the evils of sin, we'd move for suspended sentences. They agreed. Unfortunately, they drew a real hard-ass judge when they went to trial in New York. She broke bad when she heard they had jeopardized the life of an undercover agent. She sentenced them to two years each. That very night they rode the U.S. marshal's bus to the federal penitentiary at Lewisburg, Pennsylvania. Before they ever even made it to the prison, they were severely beaten and raped. I spent the next day starting proceedings to get them moved to a safer facility.

There are those who say that the corruption work we started in 1968 actually saved the BNDD and its successor, the federal Drug Enforcement Administration (DEA). But at the time, we made more enemies than friends.

Retaliation was coming.

The wheels were already in motion.

18

SPECIAL AGENT IN CHARGE

In addition to corruption cases, the Office of Inspection was also responsible for investigating malfeasance and misfeasance incidents. It was our job to determine if BNDD agents had failed to perform their duty or if they had wrongfully acted in the performance of their duty. One such case took me to the Deep South, where I investigated an incident in which an agent had shot and killed a suspect trying to escape arrest.

As I was able to reconstruct the events that led to the shooting, it became clear to me that the agent had actually conducted himself in exemplary fashion. If anything, he had shown restraint. My final report, rather than criticizing him, recommended that he be considered for a commendation.

The shooting incident had occurred on a street during a surveillance. A signal had gone out to all agents in the vicinity to close in on the suspect for the purpose of making an arrest. The agent under investigation rushed to the scene and attempted to arrest the suspect, who then tried to run him over with his car. The agent fired twice. Both shots hit home, and the suspect was killed. In similar situations, many agents I knew would have emptied their guns, adding to the danger of stray shots and increasing the risk of damaging property and injuring bystanders. But the agent had exercised restraint, as well as keen marksmanship under pressure.

However, my investigation also discovered that the regional director for that enforcement area was also at the scene. In fact, he was armed and sitting in a car parked only thirty feet away from the suspect's. Yet, when the arrest was attempted, the regional director never made a move. In my report I faulted the regional director for not aiding a fellow agent who was at risk during an incident that wound up claiming a human life.

By this time, Andy Tartaglino had been kicked upstairs to a better job. His replacement as chief inspector was Pat Fuller, a friend of the regional director I had blasted in my report. Both of them had come over from BDAC. When Fuller saw my report, he summoned me to his office.

"I want you to change your report," he said. "Delete the criticism of the regional director."

"If you want to change things, write your own report," I shot back.

"As long as I'm chief inspector," he bristled, "don't expect any promotions." Then, for good measure, he added, "You better start looking for another job."

I did just that.

In January 1970 I landed in Newark, New Jersey, only about twenty-five miles from where I had grown up.

I was between a rock and a hard place. Fuller had pressured me out of Inspection. Now I was vulnerable to the people whom I had previously investigated, as well as their friends. It was open season for anybody who wanted a piece of Tom Tripodi. To make matters worse, my wife announced that she would not accompany me to Newark. Our marriage had been failing for years, and she refused to relocate from the Washington, D.C., area. I had passed up the job in Italy to spend more time with my family, but now I would only be able to see my wife and children on weekends anyway.

My new position was special agent in charge of the Newark District Office. Basically, I was the chief federal narcotics law enforcement officer for the entire state of New Jersey—or at least that's what it said on the job description. Unfortunately, the position, however big it may have sounded, was totally at the mercy of the BNDD's bureaucracy, which was considerably bigger. *Effectiveness,* the long suit of the old FBN, was held hostage by a dedicated pursuit of *efficiency,* the perceived strength of BDAC. In reality, the administrative procedures and organization of the BNDD were anything but efficient.

In merging with BDAC, we had absorbed most of its considerable bureaucracy. The organization chart was top-heavy, with multiple layers of supervision. The New Jersey office was under the umbrella of the New York regional office. I reported to the assistant regional director in New York, who reported to the deputy regional director, who reported to the regional director, who reported to headquarters in Washington. God only knows how many assistants, deputies, adjutants, and supervisors were sitting on their asses back in the capital, all reporting to each other and making sure appropriate derrieres were covered at all times. One can only imagine how many hundreds of paper cuts must have been suffered in the line of duty—not to mention the cauliflower ears inflicted by telephone receivers held for durations above and beyond the call of duty.

If the old FBN got things done because of minimal supervision—which many criticized as fueling the corruption problem—then BDAC, followed by the BNDD, had gone to the opposite extreme. You needed a ream of memos and a stack of approval signatures to do anything. It often felt like I was the special agent in charge of waiting for permission.

When the governor of the state of New Jersey called me on a Friday to ask me to testify the following Monday before the state legislature on proposed narcotics legislation, all I could say was, "I'll get back to you."

"Why?" he asked.

"I have to check with New York."

"Why should I care about the state of New York?" he asked logically enough. "You're the senior BNDD man in New Jersey, right?"

A good question. I was starting to wonder myself. There I was, sitting in my office taking incoming rounds from a governor because the BNDD had an org chart that made the Pentagon look like a model of efficiency. I got off the phone and called my supervisor in New York. He said exactly what I knew he was going to say: *"I'll get back to you.*" I'm sure at that point, he called his supervisor who told him, "*I'll get back to you.*" And on and on all the way back to Washington. Hell, I could have called headquarters myself and saved the government a lot of time and long-distance phone bills—but that wasn't SOP (standard operating procedure). The governor would have to wait for his answer, just as did our ambassador to Italy—*a presidential appointee*—when, later in my career, he was misguided enough to ask for assistance. I was the top guy in Italy at the time, but still I had to check with our Paris office.

"Why should I care what's going on in France?" the ambassador would ask in utter astonishment.

"I'll get back to you," I'd reply.

And so on until you wanted to puke.

By 1970, the MBO (management by objective) style of management had infected the brass at the BNDD with a vengeance. Basically, we organized, planned, and prioritized on the basis of predetermined goals. Supposedly this concept works in business and industry, but as the underlying philosophy of a law enforcement agency, it left much to be desired.

To make things fit neatly into the MBO mold, the whole intertwined jungle of illegal drug activity was subdivided into ten "systems"—heroin, cocaine, marijuana, hashish, and six others that included the hallucinogenics and synthetics. The most active traffickers in each of the individual systems were then identified and targeted. That was the *O* in *MBO*—the objective, to get these guys off the streets. But the traffickers who were being targeted were the guys that were vulnerable. They were not necessarily the guys who were the worst offenders within any particular "system." But what good is an objective if it can't be attained? Promotions, fatter paychecks, and grade increases didn't go to people who failed to achieve the *O* in *MBO*.

The whole thing reminded me of the FBI's old "Ten Most Wanted" list. It was common knowledge in law enforcement circles that some criminals had been put on the list only after their whereabouts had been determined by the FBI. Then, on a slow news day, when the PR people figured the bureau needed a shot in the arm, the SWAT teams would be called out, and the felon would be bagged. It was an early version of MBO, and it was considered a huge success. No one seemed to care that the objectives were being determined after they had already been achieved.

Although I was one of the biggest critics of the systems approach, the successes achieved by the Newark office during my tenure as special agent in charge ironically were cited as a justification of the method's efficiency. In the year and a half I was there, with a contingent of only eight BNDD agents and perhaps twenty law enforcement officers from various state and local task forces, the Newark office had achieved so many of its MBO goals that the bureau decided to expand its office space and quadruple its personnel.

One of the cases I supervised in New Jersey was Operation Eagle. A group of Cuban exiles had been identified as top targets in the cocaine system. Several of them had ties to the former "secret army" CIA covert operation in south Florida and were well schooled in the black arts. At least a couple of the Operation Eagle targets had participated in the Bay of Pigs invasion. I personally recognized two of the suspects as men I had seen while I was working for the agency at JMWAVE in Perrine, Florida. Of course, at that time I knew them only by their cryptonyms.

The suspects were retailing mass quantities of cocaine that they were buying from other Cuban exiles in Miami. They'd buy in kilo quantities and sell it on the streets of Newark an ounce at a time. We ran the investigation for about six months. During that time, undercover agents working for me managed to make several buys.

The operation was fairly sophisticated for the era. The suspects employed many of the intelligence and security techniques they had learned from the CIA, making our job that much more difficult. They were among the first dope traffickers to use two-way radios and to monitor government frequencies on electronic scanners. We were careful to always utilize codes in our transmissions. In the event our messages were intercepted, it was hoped they would prove meaningless to the subjects. The suspects were also adept at countersurveillance. Our watchers had to be constantly aware of who might be watching them.

Once sufficient evidence had been accumulated, we arrested more than a dozen of the Operation Eagle targets. The arrests were coordinated to occur as simultaneously as possible. I participated with a group of agents that was to arrest a perpetrator known in the local Cuban community as *El Brujo*—the witch doctor.

El Brujo lived above a poultry shop he owned. It seemed logical enough that he'd want to be close to a supply of chickens for his occult rituals. However, when we hit the place, we found all the coops empty. Two rather large and angry German shepherds were on the premises, and we had no choice but to shoot them. As we progressed further into *El Brujo*'s living quarters, we found ourselves surrounded by ritualistic claptrap. There were dozens of large jars and beakers containing unrecognizable substances and artifacts. We came upon one glass container, at least four feet high, that held an upside-down crucifix stuck into a layer of sand. Statues were all over the place, a weird mix of Catholic and pagan icons.

A large crate caught my eye. It was bigger than a coffin, and it reeked with an animal odor I couldn't identify. I reached inside, then thought better of it, and retracted my hand quickly. I took a broom and poked into the crate with the inch-thick wooden handle. The head of an enormous snapping turtle shot out and bit the broom handle in two. I can't imagine what it would have done to my hand.

There are some situations that all the training and experience in the world just can't prepare you for, and this was certainly one of them. George Gaffney had never mentioned in my initial interview that a decade later I'd be standing in a witch doctor's inner sanctum staring down at a killer turtle. *All in a day's work,* I told myself. Then I shot it.

As an adjunct to Operation Eagle, we also made what was then the largest marijuana seizure in the state of New Jersey. By today's standards, the four hundred to five hundred pounds we confiscated seems paltry, but at the time it was considered one hell of a haul.

The Newark office also made a significant contribution to Operation Flanker, a regional operation targeted against Italian heroin traffickers. The guys we bagged in Flanker were heavy hitters who were sourcing their heroin directly from manufacturers in Europe. As in Operation Eagle, undercover agents made a number of buys before the arrests were made. The coordinated multitarget raid, an enforcement action that was gaining popularity at the BNDD both for reasons of effectiveness and PR value, extended beyond Newark. Simultaneous to our raid, other offices along the East Coast launched raids against their Italian heroin system targets. When the newspapers came out the next day, the headlines told of dozens of arrests in several cities. Since all the arrests came as the result of one BNDD operation and because all the suspects were from one ethnic group, it appeared as if the government had crushed one huge cartel. In fact, there was little evidence to suggest that the factions in different locales even knew each other, let alone did business together.

It didn't take long for the fiction of ten separate and distinct drug systems to collapse under its own weight. The criminals just didn't cooperate. Evidently, they didn't realize that trafficking in one drug had to be mutually exclusive of any other. Eventually, the geniuses in Washington replaced the *systems* system with a *class* system called G-DEP that categorized targets according to their station in the traffic. A Class One target dealt in quantities of at least one kilogram. Class Two dealers handled less. The lowest designation, Class Fours, were users and small-time dealers.

The problem with the new system was that transaction quantities varied over time. A guy might have dealt in kilograms only once in his life, but if we heard about it, he was pegged a Class One. And if we bagged him four years later—four years during which he's been nothing but a low, street-level user/dealer—you can be sure someone in Washington was breaking his arm patting himself on the back for apprehending a notorious Class One offender. The headlines would read, "Feds Bust International Dope Ring." In Peoria, the good citizens would go to bed secure in the knowledge that their government had taken a major dope peddler off the streets.

About eighteen months after my arrival in Newark, the regional director whom I had criticized in the shooting incident down south transferred up to New York to take the deputy regional director's job. He was now my boss.

"Tripodi, don't expect any promotions," he told me.

Gee, where had I heard that before?

19

"JUST SHOW ME X'S ON THE MAP"

On the very day in mid-1971 that the Newark office was expanded, I transferred back to BNDD headquarters in Washington, D.C. The deputy regional director in New York, my old nemesis, had made an issue of my weekend commutes back to Washington to be with my family. His boss, the New York regional director, who was actually a decent guy, had no choice but to confront me about the trips.

"You can't be a part-time SAIC," he said. "Stuff happens on weekends. You've got to be here, or you've got to find another job."

He was right. Stuff *did* happen on weekends. But my weekend trips home probably would never have become an issue if the deputy regional director hadn't made it one. He had a score to settle for the bad write-up I'd given him on the shooting incident down south, and he used my family situation to force me out of the Newark job.

Probably because of my CIA intelligence experience and my familiarity with covert operations, I was appointed chief of operations for the Office of Strategic Intelligence. My responsibilities included liaison with the CIA on matters of mutual interest and the covert collection of narcotics intelligence outside of routine BNDD channels.

With CIA support, we decided to direct the covert intelligence-gathering effort at locating heroin laboratories, primarily in southern France. As is the case with most drugs, the international traffic pattern for heroin basically resembled an hourglass. From its growing and harvesting as a raw material, the product moved over an ever-decreasing number of routes to the relatively few processing laboratories—the slender midpoint of the hourglass. From the laboratories, the finished product then moved over a steadily increasing number of distribution channels to its final destination in the veins of an addict. The laboratories represented one central constricted point where the amount of contraband present was extremely high and where the number of targets was relatively low.

The agency transferred over three experienced case officers and agreed to provide trade-craft training and other support. I recruited an additional agent, Alessandro ("Sandy") Bario, a special investigator for the Senate Rackets Committee. Bario, a native of Bari, Italy, and a former Carabinieri officer, had a great undercover appearance. Furthermore, he was fluent in several languages. Bario was to be dispatched under deep cover to Marseille, France. Compartmentalized from him would be the three CIA transferees—one in Marseille, one in Paris, one in Turkey.

Before we ever got the operation off the ground, it fell victim to bureaucratic infighting. The entrenched enforcement people within the BNDD didn't like the idea of Intelligence running such a high-profile operation. Their position was that they should run *all* operations. But since they had neither the inclination nor the covert intelligence acumen for what we had devised, they simply let the whole thing die on the vine after they wrested control away from the Office of Strategic Intelligence.

Bario was taken away from me and sent up to New York to work on the Knapp Commission corruption probe. He played a part in bagging Joseph Nunziata as well as a big-shot Brooklyn politician and a few more New York City cops. We remained close friends until about 1974, when Senator Henry ("Scoop") Jackson's Permanent Subcommittee on Investigations started poking into corruption in federal narcotics law enforcement. When people started choosing sides, Bario distanced himself from me and aligned with those who would come after me. In 1979, Bario was arrested for diverting a large amount of cocaine from a seizure and selling it to an informant. At the time, he was supervisor of the DEA's Mexico City office.

Bario's brother, a colonel in the Carabinieri, and his father-in-law came over to intercede on his behalf with DEA Administrator Peter Bensinger. Knowing of my previous friendship with Bario, they stopped in my office and asked me to act as their translator. I was willing, but Bensinger didn't want me involved. Although a decade had passed since Charlie McDonnell had first implicated federal narcotics officers in wrongdoings, many of the people he had named still retained their jobs. Associate Attorney General Rudy Giuliani was leading the charge from the Justice Department to get them bounced. Bensinger had dug in to resist another purge. He was no fan of mine because I supported Giuliani.

Not long afterward, while incarcerated without bail in a Texas jail, Bario died under mysterious circumstances. The official autopsy stated that he had choked to death while eating a peanut butter sandwich. There were also traces of a tranquilizer in his system at the time of death. The prescription medication may have contributed to the suffocation, but the whole episode struck me as odd. After all, who ever heard of an Italian eating a peanut butter sandwich?

My most challenging assignment while with the Office of Strategic Intelligence was to draw up a secret, extralegal plan designed to apply significant "risk factors" to trafficking in narcotics. The so-called risk factors that I was to develop were ones not present in traditional law enforcement methodology. Once the plan was devised and approved, I was to implement it—or at the very least, supervise its implementation. Basically, we were going to throw out the rule book and make life very tough on those who chose to sell drugs for a living.

The plan that I conceived was broken down into four phases, although, in reality, each of the four phases was actually a stand-alone operation. Each was targeted separately. Not only were the phases differentiated geographically, but they involved divergent aspects of the drug trade.

The first phase was targeted against the mushrooming drug traffic that was emanating from or traveling through South and Central America. The cocaine problem had grown astronomically since the days of Che Guevara's involvement. More and more marijuana was being grown in the region for shipment to the United States. The area was also serving as an important transit point for the international heroin traffic. I traveled extensively through the region as the advance man for a later trip by BNDD Director John Ingersoll. The trip also served to cover my other activities: developing local support for covert operations and identifying a target that would provide the greatest repressive yield.

In Brazil, I recruited a major in the Brazilian Army. He specialized in narcotics enforcement and counterinsurrection. He agreed to support our operations.

Collateral intelligence developed in the States brought to our attention a team of bush pilots out of New Orleans who were routinely flying in large quantities of cocaine from Chile. They'd stuff their plane full of blue jeans, transistor radios, and whatever else they thought they could peddle and then hedgehop their way down to Chile, where they'd sell off their cargo. Once the plane was empty, they'd on-load fifty to one hundred kilograms of cocaine, turn the plane north, and head back to the States.

On the return trip, they'd puddle-jump along the Brazilian border—a vast international boundary that touches just about every other South American country—landing and refueling at various rural airstrips. Their route allowed the pilots to come in contact with narcotics suppliers from a number of South American countries. Hitting these two guys would send a strong message to several South American traffickers.

In order to demonstrate the integrity and seriousness of the plan, I insisted on handling this particular phase personally. The Brazilian major I had previously recruited agreed to guide me to one of the clandestine airstrips. He'd transport me in a helicopter leased through an appropriate proprietary of the U.S. government. We knew from previous surveillance that while their plane was being refueled, the two pilots would leave the aircraft, walk about two hundred yards to a nearby shack, and down a few beers. While they were wetting their whistles, the helicopter would land me about two miles away. I'd hike through the jungle with a shoulder-held rocket launcher, find the plane, and do a number on it before the two pilots knew what happened.

The plan was simple, cheap, and thought to be potentially effective as a means of slowing down the growing South American cocaine supply. We felt strongly that the pilots would attribute the demolition to rival narcotics factions. Therefore, there was the chance that some internecine hostilities among the South American traffickers might erupt, a possibility that wouldn't have caused any of us to lose any sleep.

Phase Two was targeted on the Golden Triangle of Southeast Asia. The region, located near the point where the borders of Burma, Thailand, and Laos converged, had emerged as a major supplier of heroin. Coming at a time when we were pulling our people out of nearby Vietnam, I felt that the BNDD was in an ideal position to exploit the unique talents of some of the CIA covert types who were still in the area. I knew from my liaison work with the agency that it would be quite happy if we could find a way to employ any part of the extensive apparatus it had established in the region. Although the agency did not suggest how we might use its people, it was clear the CIA felt a strong loyalty to its assets and would appreciate their use by a brother federal agency.

I proposed that we go in and adopt a number of CIA assets, using the BNDD's funding and targeting. Not only were the CIA people already in place, but they also had the knowledge and training I was looking for. The hardware I needed was also on hand in great abundance. If we were no longer going to employ it against the Viet Cong, why not put it to good use against drug producers?

The plan was simple. Our adopted assets would go in, locate a targeted heroin lab, and mark it with a transmitter they'd plant surreptitiously. Then they'd call in an air strike. The Air Force would scramble two jets. Within a couple of hours, they'd dive in out of the sun, home in on the transmitter, and drop their payloads. The labs would be sitting ducks. I figured nothing would discourage the mass production of heroin better than a little well-placed napalm.

We had a bit of a problem in determining the optimum time to hit the labs. We didn't want to kill a lot of people unnecessarily, but unfortunately the only time that there are significant amounts of dope present in a laboratory is when the site is staffed and manufacturing heroin. Finally, we resolved that there was no point in demolishing a dope factory that had no dope in it. We rationalized that there are no innocent bystanders in a heroin laboratory.

The third phase of the plan was specifically targeted against two traffickers who made a monthly drug run between Washington and

New York. An informant for our Washington, D.C., district office had indicated that the pair traveled in a new Lincoln. They'd leave on a midweek morning and drive at legal speed to New York via a set route. In the car would be $25,000 in cash belonging to a group that monthly invested in a one-kilogram purchase of heroin. In uptown Harlem they'd drop off the cash. Then they'd kill a couple of hours before driving to another location where they'd pick up the dope in a gift-wrapped package.

The idea was simply to hold them up at gunpoint either on their way into or out of the city. It wasn't like they were going to complain to the police or file an insurance claim. Whoever was backing these two guys would be sucking wind for the money or the heroin. Chances were they'd figure the heist for a scam and put some heavy heat on the drivers.

The legal types in the BNDD had all kinds of problems with this one. The extraterritorial ops didn't bother them too much, but this one did. It was, after all, a criminal act. And what were we to do with the heroin? Or the money? We couldn't enter it as evidence because it derived from an illegal seizure. The law also stipulated that we had to arrest the two drivers once we found them with contraband.

The Black Panthers were the focus of Phase Four. However, they were not the targets. Instead, we planned to use them as our means of implementation—albeit without their knowledge.

At that particular time, the Panthers in New York were dead set against drugs. They had rightly identified illegal drugs as one of the major threats to the overall welfare of black urban communities. Not interested in working within the structure of the established legal system—a system they felt had disenfranchised blacks—they had adopted a vigilante stance toward drug traffickers on the streets of New York City. Never shy about converting their rhetoric into action, the Panthers had identified and beaten up a number of dope peddlers.

We planned to have two black undercover agents approach the Panthers and offer them some money. They'd say that they represented a group of wealthy Midwest industrialists who had heard about the Panthers' antidrug activities. The industrialists wanted to help financially, but of course, they also wanted to remain completely anonymous. The industrialists were even in a position, via their two representatives, to point out likely targets.

The four-phase plan was ready, but the bureaucracy was not. Once we had secured White House funding and Justice Department approval for the plan, Director Ingersoll asked me to brief a group of about fourteen division heads at a staff meeting. I knew then and there that the plan was dead. The BNDD was fairly new, but it had its share of old-line guys who had come over from the FBN. They were damned if anybody besides them was going to do something like this. They certainly weren't going to permit someone out of Intelligence to implement such a plan. They put pressure on me to go into Enforcement. That would have fit better on the organization chart. The petty jealousies and protectionist attitudes gradually eviscerated the original plan to the point where it wasn't worth implementing. We had to abort before we ever began.

Prior to this, I never committed any of the operational details of the plan to paper. I did put together a sanitized proposal to request funding. We had been told that the White House had discretionary money available. To tap the White House funds, we needed the attorney general's approval. Before the infighting had scuttled the plan, I went with Ingersoll and Director of Strategic Intelligence John Warner to pitch the plan to Attorney General John Mitchell. As I started to brief Mitchell on what we wanted to do, he stood up and covered his ears.

"I don't want to hear it," he said. "All I want is for you to just show me X's on the map."

Those were his exact words.

20

SDECE

Back in 1960 when Andy Tartaglino made his case against Guatemalan Ambassador Maurice Rosal, no one really saw it as anything more than an aberration in the drug trade, a dirty diplomat who had sold out. Later, when I was with the CIA and realized that drug trafficking could be an extension of an intelligence operation, as it was in the case of Che Guevara, I began to think that the Rosal case wasn't an aberration at all. Over the years, I became familiar with more narcotics cases that involved diplomats or figures with connections to the intelligence services of foreign states. In particular, I noticed that a significant percentage of the heroin traffickers that we were busting were linked in one way or another to *Service de Documentation Extérieure et de Contre-Espionnage* (SDECE), the intelligence arm of the French government. (In recent years SDECE has been transformed into DGSE, *Direction Général de Sécurité Extérieure*.)

It was not considered unusual that the BNDD and the Customs

Service were arresting significant numbers of French nationals (especially Corsicans) for violations of the narcotics laws. With the French port city of Marseille at that time being the main heroin-processing and transshipment point for morphine base originating in Turkey, it followed that many of the couriers, those engaged in the most vulnerable phases of narcotics distribution, would be French or Corsican. However, what struck me as odd was that upon continuing investigation, many of these traffickers were found to have ties to SDECE or one of its covert-operation fronts.

Heroin starts out as a poppy flower. The residue collected from the plant is known as opium, a drug that is smoked and favored in the Far East. Close to the poppy fields, that part of the opium harvest that is earmarked to become heroin is converted into morphine base, a process that reduces the volume of the product by approximately a seven-to-one ratio. The morphine base is then transported to a processing laboratory, where it is transformed into heroin. I found it curious that although most French-processed heroin originated in the poppy fields of Turkey, an increasing amount was being traced back to Southeast Asia.

Although by the early seventies French colonial ambitions in Indochina had all but evaporated, a number of law enforcement experts familiar with the heroin problem were beginning to revise their ideas as to exactly where all the heroin-destined poppies had been grown over the previous twenty-five years. As they reviewed the available historical data, it became clear that less of the heroin base had originated in Turkey than previously thought. Conversely, more had come from Southeast Asia than anyone had thought during the fifties and sixties. The rapid growth of Asian product had really begun during the period that coincided with the French colonization effort, a time during which significant numbers of French intelligence types were operating in Indochina.

I decided to do further research. Over the course of 1971, while working in the Office of Strategic Intelligence, I reviewed as many cases as I could involving French nationals. I drew on my liaison capacity with the CIA to augment my research. I also reviewed Customs Service cases and investigations that dated back to the old Federal Bureau of Narcotics. As I suspected, a pattern emerged. The conclusion was inescapable: SDECE was in the drug business.

In February of 1972, I published my findings in a report entitled

"Intelligence Aspects of International Traffic in Narcotics." The report was reviewed by the brass at the BNDD and sent on to the CIA and the FBI.

In considering the relationship between state intelligence operations and drug trafficking, the first question to consider was *why*. What was the reason that led one state to engage in narcotics trade targeted at another state?

My report attempted to get at the issue of motivation and contained the following analysis:

> The occasion and opportunity for the exploitation of a drug problem sooner or later will be recognized. An intelligence operation directed at such an accessible target has appeal in that it is more "humane" in contrast with the classical forms of extreme executive actions such as sabotage, assassination and terrorism. Yet, the tangible results upon the population's potential and mobility could be approximated. Through the exploitation of the drug problem, the overall effectiveness and readiness of the work force would be diminished. In terms of wartime, the effects upon the military and defense industries are obvious. At peacetime, labor costs would rise as a consequence of the drug problem and would place the victim country at an economic disadvantage on the competitive world market. Through the covert encouragement of a drug problem, a heavy burden is placed on the target country by compelling it to divert large manpower commitments and expenditures in servicing the problem. The costs, for instance, of narcotic law enforcement, medical and rehabilitative services are staggering. Finally, the exploitation of a drug problem in a target country would provide an unending lucrative source of revenue.

On the surface, it might appear that the passage cited above explains why an *enemy* state might engage in drug trafficking as an extension of its intelligence effort, but not fully explain why a supposedly *friendly* nation—such as France—might choose to do so. After all, France is an ally and a strong trading partner. Outside of the universal need for funding to support intelligence operations, there would not appear to be an ideological basis for France to engage in such an activity—*unless the French intelligence services had been compromised by an enemy state.*

During the fifties and sixties, a goodly number of KGB defectors came over to the West—among them such notables as Peter Deriabin, Michael Goloniewski, and Anatoli Golitsin. Many of the defectors told of KGB penetrations into French, West German, British, Canadian, and U.S. intelligence and diplomatic services. Each of the countries involved initiated investigations into the allegations. There followed many vigorous prosecutions and convictions in all the affected countries—that is, all except for France, where only one significant prosecution occurred. The situation became a bone of contention between France and its allies. Within the U.S. intelligence community, many felt that the French were covering up the scandal, in itself a possible indication of the depth of the KGB penetration.

So accepted was the premise that SDECE had been thoroughly infiltrated by the Soviets or sympathizers that when one of its agents came over to the United States to cooperate with the CIA, he was listed on official government press releases as "a defector." Who ever heard of a defector from an allied country? What the press releases were recognizing, and what had strained CIA-SDECE relations for the previous twenty years, was that SDECE was sometimes being manipulated by the Soviets. The SDECE officer was "a defector" because those in the know considered SDECE to be a sometime instrument of the KGB. Through SDECE, the Soviet agenda was also being served by the French drug trade with America.

A close look at post-1940 French history provided key insights as to how the trade had developed. The historical basis for the French/Corsican involvement in drug trafficking probably has its roots in the resistance movement during World War II. Prior to the war, the heroin trade with America was principally controlled by Sicilian and other Italian groups with product originating primarily in Turkey. While there was significant cultivation of Asian opium, its consumption was limited mostly to the Far East. During the war, the traffic originating in Turkey and Asia was curtailed for obvious reasons, not the least of which were the controls imposed upon shipping and transportation.

In Marseille, France, two resistance groups emerged—the Gaullist, Corsican-dominated *Forces Françaises de l'Intérieur* (FFI) and the Communist *Franc-Tireurs et Partisans* (FTP). Prior to 1944, the two groups operated essentially independently of one another. During the last years of the conflict, however, with Socialist factions acting as a unifying force, the two resistance groups cooperated. It's probable that during this brief period of solidarity each group accelerated its attempt to infiltrate the other, with several successful penetrations occurring on both sides.

When the war ended, the FFI and the FTP parted company once again. Each group fought for political control of Marseille, a port city known even before the war as a processing point for heroin. The FTP received considerable support from the Soviets and gained control of the Municipal Council. In 1947, a physical confrontation between Corsican elements and the Municipal Council occurred. Rioting broke out. The *Compagnies Républicaines de Sécurité* (CRS), a national police unit that was heavily populated with former FTP members, was called out to quell the violence. The CRS did little to restore peace, and the FTP called for a general strike—both developments being agreeable to the Soviets. The United States then provided support to the FFI, by then a Corsican-Gaullist-Socialist conglomerate, and the strike was broken. The FFI wound up with control over the docks and police force, powers that enhanced their drug-trafficking ambitions.

In 1948, the French Expeditionary Force landed in Southeast Asia. SDECE was an important part of the French campaign to hold Indochina. A senior SDECE officer, Gen. Maurice Belleaux, was quoted in published statements in 1971 as saying that one of the missions of SDECE in Southeast Asia was to purchase and sell opium for the purpose of "raising funds for discretionary purposes." One of the mechanisms used for this activity was *Groupement de Commandos Mixtes Aéroportés* (GCMA), a guerrilla force sometimes referred to as the "Red Berets." Former GCMA commanding officer Col. Roger Trinquier corroborated Belleaux's allegations, also in published statements. Trinquier elaborated on GCMA's involvement in the drug trade and also indicated that units of the French Air Force were responsible to SDECE for the local and long-range flight movements of opium. An investigation undertaken in 1960 by American Gen. E. G. Lansdale had also concluded that elements of the French government were engaged in the heroin traffic.

While there has never been any substantive proof that French President de Gaulle knew about or approved SDECE's involvement with narcotics, there were those within our own intelligence services who had speculated that de Gaulle's anger over U.S. President Eisenhower's refusal to support the French adventure in Indochina may have led de Gaulle to turn his head to what he already must have known, a de facto acquiescence that could have been interpreted by some as tacit approval. By the time the French finally pulled out of Southeast Asia, the associations with the local drug lords were firmly in place. The military pulled out, but the relationships with those who supplied the raw product remained.

Beyond Belleaux's and Trinquier's damning published statements, and the corroborating testimony of mules and brokers, it was the long list of SDECE-connected arrests and seizures that really convinced me that the drug business had become institutionalized within the French intelligence services.

Andy Tartaglino's case against Guatemalan Ambassador Rosal in 1960 determined that Rosal had been recruited as a narcotics smuggler by Étienne Tarditti. Following his arrest, Tarditti told his interrogators that he had been a "big man" in the resistance in Marseille during World War II and that he had highly placed friends in the French government. He mentioned belonging to Gaullist anti-Communist political groups and intimated that he was involved in intelligence work beneficial to American interests. With Tarditti, a man with connections to SDECE front groups, now identified as Rosal's recruiter, it was easier to understand why previous requests to French authorities for information on Rosal had been unproductive. In fact, FBN investigators had been told repeatedly that there was no record of Rosal in French law enforcement files. Tartaglino learned later that the Paris Provincial Police Subversive Branch had an extensive file on Rosal that reflected coordination with SDECE. French police surveillance of Rosal had documented a history of homosexual encounters with young boys. That the French authorities failed to arrest Rosal for these transgressions suggests strongly that intelligence interests took priority—or that these surveillances were considered useful as "motivation" for services yet to be rendered.

In 1962, the New York City Police Department in cooperation with the FBN made a sizable seizure of heroin in the famous case that would be portrayed in the movie *The French Connection*. Many of the suspects were French nationals. One of the defendants, who was convicted and incarcerated at the New York State Prison in Attica, was François Scaglia. While serving time at Attica, Scaglia was frequently visited by Corsican Maurice Castellani, another former resistance fighter with connections to SDECE front groups.

At Columbus, Georgia, in 1965, FBN agents arrested U.S. Army Chief Warrant Officer Herman Condor in possession of ninety-six kilograms of heroin. Condor had just transferred back to the States from France. The heroin was found in a freezer that had been shipped with his household goods from France. Condor's apprehension led to the arrest of several others involved in the trafficking, among them, Jean Nebbia. Examining Nebbia's personal effects, investigators came upon the name of Blaise Gherardi, who was a prominent figure in other narcotics investigations. Also in Nebbia's effects were papers related to a Corsican association in New York. The president of the association was Albert Dion. A scrutiny of telephone call patterns determined frequent communications between Gherardi and Dion, and also between Gherardi and known SDECE agent Philippe Thyraud Devosjoli, who had previously provided American officials with details regarding the KGB's compromise of SDECE. In fact, Devosjoli was the very same SDECE agent who had been repeatedly referred to as a "defector" in official U.S. government press releases.

Continuation of the Nebbia investigation eventually implicated Jacques Jean Douheret. Under interrogation, Douheret revealed that the organization he was part of had introduced approximately 1,500 kilograms of French heroin into the United States. He also disclosed that former French Army Capt. Michel Victor Mertz was the control point for the operation. Douheret confessed to having accepted packages containing heroin in the past from Mertz while Mertz was still on active duty with the French Army and "in uniform." Efforts to determine if Mertz had affiliations with SDECE were stonewalled by French authorities. However, Nonce Luccarotti, a Corsican whom Douheret named as his initial recruiter into the drug trade, had, according to Douheret, compared drug trafficking with intelligence work. Both Douheret and Luccarotti had been involved with the resistance movement during World War II.

In 1970, French authorities arrested Serge Constant on conspiracy charges emanating from an investigation conducted in the United States. Constant was a member of the *Service d'Action Civique* (SAC), a political group started by Corsicans and former FFI members that acted as SDECE's covert operations mechanism. He was charged with carrying drugs into the United States. Constant claimed that he had been told by his SAC superiors that the sealed packages he brought into the United States contained secret documents. In actuality, they contained heroin. Constant told his interrogators that SAC enjoyed protection in high places and that he had been acting under the direct orders of the Chief of SAC in Marseille, Marcel Galvani.

Also in 1970, French authorities arrested a Madame Bonnet after finding 105 kilograms of heroin in her car. Mme. Bonnet was the widow of Mathieu Bonnet, who had died the previous year. Mathieu Bonnet had been the chief of SAC in Grenoble.

In April of the same year, BNDD agents in New York arrested three suspects after they had delivered seven kilograms of heroin to a BNDD-controlled informant. The case was expanded into a conspiracy investigation. Seven members of SAC were indicted, including Marseille SAC chief Galvani.

A year later, federal agents arrested Roger Leon Delouette at Newark, New Jersey. Delouette was in possession of forty-four kilograms of heroin secreted in his Volkswagen minibus, which had been transported from France via ship. Delouette stated that he was employed by SDECE. He claimed he worked for Colonel Fournier, who was also a member of SAC. Fournier had previously served, then a major, under GCMA Colonel Trinquier during the Indochina campaign.

In Delouette's possession at the time of his arrest was an address book containing an entry under the name *Des Clers*. Delouette stated that Des Clers was an old friend who owned an air cargo company. The BNDD believed that Des Clers was actually Renaud Desclers, an individual regarded as a prominent trafficker. In Ban Me Thout, Vietnam, in 1959, three hundred kilograms of opium were seized in a small cargo plane piloted by Corsicans and owned by Renaud Desclers's company. In that covert intelligence operations routinely employ air cargo proprietaries as a cover for clandestine activities, it was considered quite possible that Desclers also had connections to SDECE.

Also in 1971, an automobile was seized in New York containing ninety-three kilograms of heroin. Richard Berdin, the principal defendant in the case, implicated, among others, André Lebay, a former SDECE officer. Lebay was arrested by French authorities in possession of 106 kilograms of heroin. At one time Lebay served as chief of security for President Moise Tshombe of the Congo, a position that was considered by U.S. intelligence to be a cover for an SDECE operation. While Lebay was in the Congo, Colonel Trinquier made several trips to and from the country. Upon each and every return to French soil, he was debriefed by SDECE officers.

Berdin also implicated Raymond Moulin, who had been first recruited by Lebay while the SDECE officer was serving in the Congo. It was also Lebay who later introduced Moulin to drug trafficking. Berdin further revealed that he once met with a man known to him only as Dominique to discuss a future narcotics delivery. The meeting occurred shortly after the Delouette seizure, and, according to Berdin, Dominique mentioned that he had recently "lost" a shipment of fifty kilograms of heroin in a Volkswagen in New Jersey. Dominique was later identified as Dominique Mariani, whose brother-in-law Jean Claude Marchiani was a former SDECE officer. (Marchiani was severed from SDECE after he was implicated in an SAC disinformation campaign involving doctored photographs of French President Pompidou's wife.)

Relationships with the French were strained as it was. My report, which I had identified as "essentially provocative," was a hot potato that nobody within the BNDD wanted to catch. The CIA basically dismissed it as "not being consistent with its understanding of the situation," but neglected to comment on any of the details. As far as I know, the FBI never offered an opinion.

My report went on the shelf.

SDECE's involvement with heroin just went on.

21

EXILE MINOR

On November 25, 1971, the French newspaper *L'Aurore* ran an article written by its "special envoy" Christian d'Epenoux under a headline that translates as "When the Americans Severely Judge French Justice." The piece dealt with what it called "the Fournier-Delouette affair," the scandal that had begun the previous April when the U.S. Customs Service seized forty-four kilograms of heroin hidden in Delouette's Volkswagen minibus.

Delouette's disclosures regarding Colonel Fournier and SDECE's involvement in the heroin trade had caused ripples on both sides of the Atlantic. The French press seemed ready to adopt a scenario suggesting that the seizure was something more than the result of an entry inspection by a vigilant customs agent. Innuendoes that the seizure had really resulted from an ongoing BNDD investigation, one aimed at impugning the integrity of the French intelligence service, abounded.

The episode prompted John Cusack, the BNDD's regional director for Europe, then stationed in Paris, to make some statements that were evidently critical of SDECE. Comments attributed to Cusack were widely reported in the French press, and the episode soon became a cause célèbre. In the *L'Aurore* article, Cusack's remarks were referred to as "shattering statements."

As the controversy raged, Cusack returned to the United States. Reporter d'Epenoux from *L'Aurore* came to the States in late 1971, looking for Cusack and for information about the Delouette case. He interviewed Commissioner of Customs Miles Ambrose and was told what he had heard before, namely that the seizure was the isolated enforcement action of an alert official. During Thanksgiving week, d'Epenoux arrived at BNDD headquarters. He had been promised an interview with George Oakey, an analyst in the Office of Strategic Intelligence. At the last minute, Oakey bowed out, and I was instructed to take his place.

As usual, my big mouth got me in trouble. D'Epenoux also spoke with others at the bureau. Brave souls that they were, they all insisted on anonymity, a luxury unavailable to me since I had been appointed as the official mouthpiece. In the *L'Aurore* article, I was the only named source for a composite of information d'Epenoux had gleaned from an assortment of BNDD personnel.

The French reporter asked me about Cusack. According to SIO Contact Report No. 054, which I wrote immediately after the interview, I told d'Epenoux "that I have known Cusack for twelve years and that I consider Cusack among the most honest and intelligent among my acquaintances. I stated that Cusack was a hard-working, tough Irish cop with the highest dedication to the principles of narcotic enforcement."

L'Aurore took some editorial license with my comments about Cusack: "He is an Irishman, therefore somewhat impulsive."

Needless to say, Cusack didn't appreciate the quote, nor did Director Ingersoll. I got called on the carpet for that one. And Ingersoll also made an issue of a quote concerning an experimental "very delicate detection system which will be placed on a helicopter in order to locate the clandestine laboratories." I had not said a word to d'Epenoux about the system. In fact, I didn't even know of its existence. Information about the secret project, which ultimately proved to be a colossal failure, could have leaked only from one of the propeller-heads in the Science and Technology Division or from someone highly placed who knew about the development project. But no one seemed interested in my version of the interview. Once again, I was in the doghouse.

Not long after the *L'Aurore* fiasco, Ingersoll asked me to process a security clearance for a Berkeley professor who just happened to be a personal friend of his. Ingersoll wanted to set the professor up with funding to do a study on the Mexican-U.S. heroin traffic. As was customary, I checked with other federal agencies and learned that at one time the professor had been granted a liaison clearance from an agency in the intelligence community. That clearance had subsequently been revoked. Federal regulations at the time clearly mandated that denial of clearance by one federal agency automatically disallowed clearance by another. I told Ingersoll the bad news. It was my swan song at Strategic Intelligence.

Ingersoll reassigned the case to another officer, who had a more flexible interpretation of the clearance regulations. The professor somehow received his clearance and was given $150,000 in BNDD money to conduct his study. He went to Mexico City and managed to piss off enough high-ranking Mexican officials that they threatened to declare him persona non grata. To avoid that embarrassment, the BNDD yanked the professor out of Mexico. Some time later, the Government Accounting Office (GAO) poked its nose into the BNDD's books and asked for an accounting of the $150,000. The money had been expended, but no study had ever been delivered. GAO contacted the professor and demanded that he return the money. He stated that he was unable to finish the study because the BNDD had pulled him out of Mexico. Therefore the money was his, he insisted.

Ingersoll's friend kept the $150,000.

I got exiled to the Baltimore Regional Office, which was purgatory for those who had fallen from grace at BNDD headquarters. That's where the bureau sent you when it wanted to knock you down a peg. If the bureau had been really pissed off at me, it would have shipped me off to California or Texas or some other faraway location that would have necessitated a physical move. I was assigned two jobs in Baltimore, Organized Crime Strike Force representative and supervisor of Intelligence.

The Organized Crime Strike Force (OCSF) was a division of the Department of Justice. OCSFs were structured apart from U.S. attorney's offices across the country. They were autonomous with their own staffs, premises, and funding. OCSF investigators came from all the various federal agencies that were interested in organized crime. In essence, the OCSF was an attempt to bring together and coordinate the efforts of the entire federal law enforcement apparatus for the purpose of wiping out organized crime. On paper, it looked like a great idea.

The OCSF in Baltimore didn't really turn up anything significant. In the Italian community, which by 1972 was mostly second and third generation, we found no connection between local crime elements and organized crime in New York. There didn't appear to be an international connection either. The Italian crooks in Baltimore had been smart enough to turn to politics. About the biggest organized-crime target we had was some hamburger who was selling hot clothes and boots out of the trunk of an old Cadillac.

The Intelligence position proved far more interesting. Ironically, my activities as Intelligence supervisor would actually set the foundation for what would become my most significant effort in the area of organized crime—namely, my work in Palermo against the Mafia in 1978.

In 1972, when Red Brigades terrorists gunned down thirty-six Puerto Rican Catholics on a religious pilgrimage at the airport in Rome, the Italian authorities asked for help from U.S. experts. In the aftermath of their investigation of the terrorist incident, they had discovered that the Red Brigades (*La Brigate Rosse*) was in the drug business. BNDD agents Mike Antonelli, Norman Jerseny, and I were sent to Italy to assist.

The relationship between the Italian and American intelligence communities had, like so much else, originated during World War II. First there was our support of the resistance effort and later, after the war had ended, our assistance to the Italians as they established their own intelligence and enforcement services. Although we influenced the development of those services, they evolved according to a methodology uniquely Italian. The differences between their system and ours were significant and little understood by Americans.

We arrived in Rome on a Saturday morning and decided to see the sites at the Vatican. We happened to get to St. Peter's Square as the local police were dragging off a lunatic who had just attacked Michelangelo's *Pietà* with a hammer. A few minutes later, I was approached by a souvenir vendor. He showed me his collection of lacquered postcards. As he flipped through the stack and came to the one that pictured the *Pietà*, we saw that the shiny finish was peeling off the card. Since it was the only postcard in his inventory to be so defaced, the vendor, in true Italian style, took it to be evidence of a miracle, God's way of mourning the damage to His beloved *Pietà*. The vendor dropped to his knees and clasped his hands in fervent prayer. His piety, however, did not prevent him from accepting my payment for the "miracle" postcard, which I still possess.

While in Italy, Antonelli covered the ports in the northern part of the peninsula, looking for evidence of drug smuggling. Jerseny concentrated on Naples. I took Bari, Brindisi, Ancona, and Pescara. None of us went to Sicily. The island of the Mafia's origins was considered *terra proibita*. No one from federal drug law enforcement had ever spent more than token time on Sicily. It was simply too dangerous. Sicily was off-limits as far as the BNDD was concerned.

We remained in Italy for about seven weeks. Prior to our trip we had scoured our files for all actionable data to provide to the Italian authorities. We worked with them to develop profiles on narcotics traffickers and couriers. We completed dossiers on those involved in drug traffic and terrorism. Although no significant seizures were made while we were in Italy, critical relationships were established. We succeeded in demonstrating in no uncertain terms that the United States was ready to help the Italians with the sharing of information and the deployment of personnel.

In 1978 I would return to Italy. In a precedent-setting operation, I would work in Palermo, Sicily, the heartland of Mafia dominance. Were it not for the groundwork done in 1972—the establishment of mutual trust and the enhancement of my knowledge of the Italian enforcement system—I don't believe the later trip would have been the success that it ultimately was.

22

TREADING WATER

During 1973, the federal alphabet soup was stirred again. The BNDD was transformed into the DEA, the Drug Enforcement Administration. The Justice Department's Office of Narcotics Intelligence was incorporated into the new DEA, as were a number of former Customs Service agents who were specializing in drug law enforcement. For many of us in the trenches, however, the event constituted little more than a name change.

Earlier that year, before the reorganization, I had been repatriated to the capital. I transferred to the Washington, D.C., District Office where I took over as supervisor of the Intelligence Group. For a while, I worked under Special Agent in Charge Abe Azzam, a great guy and a good friend. I was fairly comfortable for a while. My exile was over, and I was sheltered by Azzam from the attacks of those I had investigated during the 1968 probe.

The period of relative security didn't last long, however. Azzam was replaced by one of the very guys I had previously investigated, a spineless bureaucrat whom others soon nicknamed "the Lizard"—a reference to the Giant Komodo dragon of Indonesia, a monitor lizard reputed to eat its own young as well as its own feces. Career survival now required watching my back at all times. Working at the Washington District Office soon became the law enforcement equivalent of treading water in a shark tank.

During the summer of 1974, David Weiser, a DEA agent in Albuquerque, New Mexico, called and asked if I would participate in an undercover operation he was putting together. I was to play an Italian heavy from New York looking to score some cocaine. The target was Eddie Barboa, a New Mexico state senator who enjoyed a reputation as a champion of the poor man's causes.

I flew to Albuquerque and met with Weiser and his informant. Soon thereafter, the informant cut me into Barboa. I established my legend with Barboa, and he gave me a sample of his merchandise, a small quantity of very-high-quality cocaine. He agreed to call me the next time he had a good-sized shipment to sell. I gave Barboa a New York phone number that was rigged to forward to me in Washington.

Barboa called me a number of times, each time indicating that he had anywhere from one to ten kilograms of pure cocaine to sell me. After each contact, I flew to Albuquerque only to find that the cocaine did not exist. Usually, Barboa claimed that his partner had already sold the drugs. When, after several such dead ends, Barboa once again indicated that he couldn't come up with the promised drugs during a meeting in a hotel bar, I exploded.

"Look, my money man is upstairs in a room with the cash," I told Barboa. "He's going to be really pissed if he has to go back to New York empty-handed. You're going to at least have to pay for his travel expenses."

I knew that if Barboa agreed, we could sink him. If he paid me to reimburse the travel expenses of a drug courier, we could use the conversation and the money as evidence.

Barboa went for it.

"How much?" he asked.

"Five hundred," I replied.

He dug into his pocket. "Here's a little over four hundred. It's all I've got on me."

I took the money. Then I grabbed his hand and pulled off his big turquoise ring. "That'll go toward the difference," I said.

He left. I returned to the hotel room where other agents had monitored the entire conversation. I turned over the ring and the cash as evidence.

The deputy regional director had flown in from Denver in anticipation of a big seizure and the attendant PR circus that would go with it. Disappointed that things had not worked out as planned, he came to my room the next morning.

"You've got to return the money and the ring to Barboa," he said.

"Why?" I asked, not believing what I had just heard.

"It's going to mess up the accounting system."

That was a new one!

I argued that it had had nothing to do whatsoever with the accounting system.

"Seal it, and process it as evidence," I insisted.

"Give it back to Barboa!" he commanded.

"At least contact Don Svet," I pleaded. Don Svet was the local assistant U.S. attorney. I felt he should have been consulted regarding the release of the evidence.

"*Give it back!*" the deputy regional director ordered.

I did as I was told. An agent from the Albuquerque office arrived shortly thereafter with the cash and the ring. I put the evidence in a hotel envelope, sealed it, and made arrangements for the hotel staff to return it to Barboa.

When Barboa was indicted later that year, I was dragged down to Albuquerque as the government's "star witness." The trial resulted in a hung jury.

A few weeks later, the government tried again in Las Cruces—and again the trial ended in a hung jury. There was some question of jury tampering, but the case was not pursued. Assistant U.S. Attorney Don Svet, who tried the case, indicated to me that there was no doubt in his mind that if the money and ring had been retained, Barboa would have gone down.

Barboa did eventually go to jail, but it was years later and on another charge. His sentence was five years.

While I was in Albuquerque for one of the Barboa trials, a professor from the University of New Mexico contacted the local police and asked to speak with me. He had learned of me through newspaper and television reports of the legal proceedings. His last name also happened to be Tripodi. We arranged a meeting.

Professor Tripodi was an elderly, distinguished gentleman. He was distraught over the recent suicide of his grandson. At the funeral, he had heard that his grandson, a Georgetown Law School student, had had dealings with the DEA. Professor Tripodi wanted to know if I knew anything about it.

As it turned out, I did. Some time previous, I had been asked if I had any relatives in North Carolina. It was explained that agents had busted a Georgetown student named Tripodi who hailed from North Carolina. The student was in possession of synthetic drugs at the time of his arrest—either PCP or LSD, as I recall. The agents indicated that the suspect had flipped and was willing to cooperate. Although I didn't think I had any relatives in the area under question, I took all the required steps to dissociate myself from the case. I wrote memos articulating procedures that would prevent any related files from crossing my desk. Not long afterward, the agent handling the case told me that the student, distraught over his girlfriend's death (from natural causes), went to her grave and killed himself with a shotgun.

I could see that Professor Tripodi had been very close to his grandson. I could also see that he didn't have many years left himself. I wasn't going to add to his grief. I told him that we had recruited his grandson for the position of special agent within the DEA. That seemed to make the old man's burden a little lighter.

During 1973 and 1974, I also assisted in several corruption cases in New York. The assignments were TDYs—temporary duty. The rampant corruption of the past decades had suddenly become *the* front-page issue. Serious attempts at reform were being made.

The Knapp Commission had convened under the supervision of Whitman Knapp to look into corruption within the New York City Police Department. It was actually an outgrowth of the BNDD's corruption investigations that began in 1968. Since there was a close working relationship between NYPD narcotics detectives and BNDD agents working out of the New York Regional Office, it was not unusual for BNDD inspectors, in the course of investigations, to also uncover evidence of wrongdoing within the ranks of the city police force. Such cases were remanded to what was known as "the Wurms file," so named for BNDD Inspector Ike Wurms, who maintained the confidential dossier. Eventually, the file was turned over to NYPD's Internal Affairs Division, but little action was taken. When news leaked that Internal Affairs was ignoring evidence of widespread corruption within the NYPD rank and file, the Knapp Commission was put together.

Even prior to the creation of the Knapp Commission, Whitney North Seymour, Jr., U.S. attorney for the Southern District of New York, had initiated his own corruption probe. With Justice Department support, Seymour's Official Corruption Unit was investigating attorneys, prosecutors, judges, and politicians.

Assistant U.S. Attorney Rudy Giuliani, who in 1989 would run for mayor of New York, was appointed chief of the Official Corruption Unit. He succeeded Richard Ben Veniste, who had been very effective before being transferred to Washington, D.C., to be a prosecutor in one of the Watergate trials. On several occasions, I traveled to New York to assist Giuliani. I participated in the surveillances of "Prince of the City" Bob Leuci and other dirty New York cops. Although Leuci wound up implicating a number of cops, his stated motivation for cooperating with the probe was to nail corrupt prosecutors and judges. After Leuci flipped, I helped with his debriefing.

I got on fairly well with Leuci. He was a fast-talker. He came off as a glib, New York wise guy, but when it suited his purpose, he could suddenly go quiet and thoughtful. In the debriefings I attended, which were conducted in Giuliani's office, I got the distinct impression that Leuci was very well organized. He was not about to discuss any subject he hadn't previously thought out thoroughly. If he didn't have the time to formulate an appropriate response, he was likely to say, "I have to think about that," or "I'll have to give that one some thought." He wasn't about to be pressured into making a mistake.

About two blocks away from where we conducted the debriefings in the Federal Courthouse, there was a watering hole that was a big hangout for NYPD cops. I was there one day having a beer at the bar when Leuci walked in with his two NYPD bodyguards. You could see immediately that the bodyguards hated their assignment, as you could see that the patrons in the bar hated Leuci. They saw him as a former brother who had betrayed them. He was a cop stool pigeon, and he was to be shunned. That was the unwritten code of the NYPD. Leuci saw me and approached. I set my bottle down and turned toward Leuci to converse with him. From the corner of my eye, I spotted the bartender as he plucked my full bottle of beer off the bar and dumped it into the sink. I had talked to Leuci. I was guilty by association. I'd have to find another watering hole.

On one of the TDYs I participated in the bust of a group of NYPD narcotics detectives who were basically running a variation of one of the ops plans I had pitched to Attorney General Mitchell. They were ripping off Colombian mules, taking their drug money, just like I wanted to rip off the couriers who were transporting dope between New York and Washington—only these guys were keeping the money for themselves. The detectives used illegal wiretaps to determine where the mules were staying prior to their return to Colombia so they could hit the couriers at the most advantageous times. I gained a modicum of respect for one of the detectives when I learned that he had used the money he'd stolen to buy a house for his father. I convinced him to cooperate with us and then helped him enter the Federal Witness Protection Program.

Back in Washington, one of the cases my Intelligence Group put together involved members of the Redskins football team. An undercover agent working for me penetrated a ring of drug traffickers. He was with them when they sold cocaine to two Redskins. The case was cut-and-dried. We had the two Redskins cold—red-handed, so to speak. We were getting ready to arrest the football players when the Lizard started interfering with the investigation. It became clear to me that my superiors didn't want to embarrass the National Football League. The Lizard took the case away from me and assigned it to agents he could control. When I protested, he pushed to get me reassigned.

The football stars were never indicted.

I wound up with a new assignment in New York City.

Several high-ranking DEA officials wound up with season's tickets to the Redskins' games.

23

THE FRENCH CORRECTION

In 1971, moviegoers flocked to see a gritty new police thriller called *The French Connection*. The Oscar-winning movie was based—ever so loosely—on the 1962 seizure of forty-four kilograms of heroin found secreted in the automobile of French television industry figure Jacques Angelvin. Gene Hackman played the leading role of New York City Police Department Detective Jimmy ("Popeye") Doyle, a character supposedly based on real-life NYPD Detective Eddie Egan. In the movie version, Popeye is clearly the hero; he's the dogged gumshoe who cracks the case. Coattailing Popeye's efforts is "Fed" (federal agent) Bill Mulderig, a minor supporting role played by a little-known character actor. The Mulderig character doesn't appear until a full half-hour of the film has elapsed, and then only in brief snippets where he's usually pictured carping at Popeye. Many who were familiar with the actual French Connection case assumed that Mulderig's character was based, however erroneously, on FBN Agent

Frankie Waters, who had worked on the investigation and who—prior to the movie, at least—was a close friend of Egan's. The blatant inaccuracies portrayed in the film, as well as its unflattering rendering of the Mulderig character, reportedly caused a rift between the two former buddies.

In actuality, it was Waters—not Egan—who initiated the so-called French Connection case. Waters was working a fugitive investigation when he noticed a Citroën automobile pull up at the residence of a relative of the suspect. His experience and instincts evidently told him that something was amiss. His follow-up work concentrated on the Citroën, leading him eventually to the hidden dope and to the French nationals who were behind the smuggling ring. It was only when Waters required a "gypsy wire"—a phone tap—that Egan and the New York police were called in.

Waters and Egan had been pals for years. Both were headstrong, colorful characters of Damon Runyon proportions. Their notoriety in law enforcement circles was already established well before *The French Connection* hit the nation's movie screens. As with all figures whose reputations approach legendary status, it's sometimes difficult to separate fact from fiction, but it's nonetheless clear that these two New Yorkers were not your average, everyday, garden-variety cops.

One of the stories making the rounds in the sixties placed Waters and Egan in the old Nassau Bar shortly after one of them had taken pistol practice at a shooting range. As the tale came to me, each began bragging about what a great shot he was. They continued their boasts and their drinking for some time. The claims of marksmanship would have put the likes of Wild Bill Hickok and Buffalo Bill Cody to shame. Finally, one of them pulled out his gun and put six shots into the wall clock. Not to be outdone, the other emptied his gun into the television. As bullets whistled over their heads, terrified patrons dove for cover under tables. Having killed time and the TV, the two cops slapped a few hundred bucks on the bar and split. At five o'clock in the morning, they were finally supposedly picked up by New York police as they were shooting out streetlights on Fifth Avenue in an effort to resolve their argument.

Apart from his street reputation, however apocryphal it may or may not have been, Frankie Waters was considered to be a very effective agent within the Federal Bureau of Narcotics. He worked hard and wasn't afraid to take chances. As he had demonstrated in the

French Connection case, he had a keen deductive instinct—that innate sixth sense that tells a good cop that things just aren't quite what they appear to be. However, like many other effective agents of his era, Waters's career had been plagued by allegations of wrongdoing. When some heroin and a significant amount of money were found in his car, his superiors cut the papers to transfer him to the Texas District Office. Waters had been able to explain the dope and cash, but his story was evidently not entirely satisfactory to the brass.

If the Baltimore office was purgatory, then Texas was hell itself. You sent an agent to Baltimore for "rehabilitation"; you sent an agent to Texas strictly to get rid of him. The district supervisor in Texas really gave a tough time to subordinates who were sent to him for disciplinary reasons. People who worked for him under normal circumstances thought him to be a capable and fair supervisor. Those who were thrust upon him because of problems elsewhere generally considered the Texas district supervisor to be the premier son of a bitch in federal narcotics law enforcement. No out-of-favor agent could work for the guy—not for long, at least. After a few weeks or months in Texas, an out-of-favor agent usually quit, which is exactly what the brass intended. New Yorkers were doubly vulnerable. Not only did they have to contend with an impossible superior, but they also had to attempt the equally impossible assimilation to what was, to them, a hick environment. Waters didn't disappoint the brass. Before he ever even ventured deep into the heart of Texas, he turned in his resignation.

When former BNDD Regional Director Charlie McDonnell started making allegations about other federal agents in 1968, one of those he named was Frankie Waters. McDonnell even claimed that the heroin he had sold to us, as well as the heroin that informant Joe Miles had sold to us, actually had come from the French Connection seizure.

I became involved with the investigation of Waters from the moment McDonnell fingered him. Over the next seven years, even while in positions not directly concerned with internal corruption, I was drawn repeatedly back into the Waters case. On the day before the statute of limitations would have run out, Waters was indicted. When I was pushed out of Washington in 1974, I was assigned to Paul J. Curran, Seymour's successor as the U.S. attorney for the Southern District of New York, who was preparing to prosecute Waters. For the rest of 1974, until the trial ended in February of 1975, I worked almost exclusively on the Waters investigation.

There was a faction within the DEA that clearly hoped I'd blow the Waters case. I suspect some of them actually worked behind the scenes to undermine my efforts. They were frightened that if Frankie Waters was convicted, he might flip. That possibility made a whole bunch of people very nervous. The Waters case was the DEA's can of worms, and I had the dubious distinction of being cast as the opener.

The original French Connection had produced two heroin seizures—one weighing eleven kilograms and another weighing thirty-three kilograms. However, upon continuing investigation, we came to believe that the eleven-kilogram quantity was actually from a previous shipment. Since the car had been weighed upon entry into the United States and found to have an unexplained discrepancy of fifty kilograms, we started to think that as much as seventeen kilograms had never made it to the evidence room.

After McDonnell had flipped and was under the control of the Office of Inspection, he made several calls to Waters, all of which we monitored. In December 1968, McDonnell met with Waters at a bar at La Guardia Airport, a location Waters had specified. I surveilled the meeting along with a number of other agents from the Office of Inspection. I noticed that while McDonnell and Waters were conversing, another individual, not known to us, was eyeballing McDonnell from the end of the bar. After the meeting concluded, McDonnell took the shuttle back to Washington. Once he was out of sight, Waters and the mystery man at the end of the bar got together and held a long conversation.

Later we identified Waters's companion as Robert Williams. As it turned out, Williams's file was long and interesting. He had a history for organized-crime involvement and dope trafficking. Intelligence reports speculated that he was a hit man for the mob. We immediately theorized that Williams had "made" McDonnell for a contract he was to fulfill at a later date.

We researched Williams's criminal history and determined that he had violated the terms of his probation from a previous conviction. He had left the country without informing his probation officer—an action that, although a technicality, was a verifiable violation of his probation. We threatened to press the issue in an effort to renew the old prosecution. Williams didn't want any part of it. He flipped.

We took his sworn statement and recorded him on video. He confirmed our suspicions and agreed to testify against Waters. Shortly before the trial, however, Williams called me and said, "If I do what you're asking me to do, it's the same as putting a gun to my head." At my insistence, and with the full support of U.S. Attorney Curran, who was personally handling the case, around-the-clock surveillance of Williams's girlfriend, Barbara Jacquette, was ordered.

At the time, Williams was sharing an elegant house on New York's Upper West Side with Jacquette. DEA agents leased a house across the street. However, the agents on the surveillance were not under my direct control or the control of the U.S. attorney's office. Their efforts were token, at best. Either they were doing the bidding of those who felt threatened by the ongoing anticorruption work or, reading between the lines, they just decided not to rock the boat.

Every day, the surveillance team watched as Williams's roommate drove off. *No one ever followed her!* Had they tailed her, she would have led them to Williams's true location, a motel in Connecticut. As it was, when the trial convened, nobody knew the whereabouts of key government witness Robert Williams. The trial had to proceed without his testimony.

Another key witness who never testified was the same Joe ("Joe Louis") Miles, the New Orleans dope trafficker and former boxer, who had originally led us to McDonnell. Miles was prepared to testify that on occasions when he received heroin from McDonnell, the name "Frankie Black" had been mentioned by McDonnell as his source for the drugs. McDonnell had since claimed that Frankie Black was an alias for Frankie Waters. Furthermore, we had some of the McDonnell-Miles conversations on tape.

The month before the trial, four hit men burst into Miles's house. Quickly, they put two .22 caliber slugs in each of his knees. Miles was one big, tough son of a gun. If they hadn't crippled him, those four torpedoes wouldn't have walked out of there themselves. But with his legs useless, the four hit men were able to handle Miles. They dragged him to his girlfriend's apartment where they tortured both of them. Sometime during the grisly proceedings, a neighbor happened on the scene. When the cops finally got there, they found three bodies—Miles, his girlfriend, and an innocent bystander who happened to be in the wrong place at the wrong time.

We had hoped to produce still another witness whom we thought might implicate Waters. Joe Gurney was a New York organized-crime figure. He had been involved in illegal dealings with "Prince of the City" Bob Leuci, and we had reason to think he might be connected to Waters. But shortly before the trial, Gurney's body was found in the trunk of a car. Whoever had killed him had done it in very old-fashioned Mafia style. A rope had been tied around his ankles. Then, the killers forced Gurney to bend his legs into a kneeling position. They looped the other end of the rope around his neck and threw him in the car trunk. As Gurney's muscles tightened from fatigue, they caused his legs to straighten, thereby drawing the noose tighter around his neck. Gurney died a slow, horrible death, strangled by his own uncontrollable muscle contractions.

No one was ever able to determine the reasons behind the murders of Miles or Gurney.

McDonnell wound up being the only witness testifying at the trial who could claim firsthand knowledge that Waters was selling heroin. Without corroborating testimony, the jury was forced to decide whether to believe McDonnell, the admitted dope peddler, or Waters, the hero of the French Connection.

On February 26, 1975, they found for the defense.

Frankie Waters was acquitted.

When the jury was dismissed, Waters ran to the jury box to shake hands with those who had pronounced him innocent. I watched as most of the jury members turned away and refused his hand.

In April 1975, U.S. Attorney Curran was kind enough to write a letter to DEA Director John Bartels, Jr., commending my work on *United States* v. *Francis E. Waters*. In part, he wrote:

Because the defendant was a former Federal Narcotics Agent and due to other factors of which you are aware any agent assigned to this case, in addition to being competent, had to have and use good judgment and had to be able to deal effectively with individuals of disparate backgrounds and attitudes. Agent Tripodi demonstrated that he possesses all of these attributes in large measure.

I may have possessed those attributes, but I sure didn't possess the attribute of knowing how to climb the career ladder. Those individuals of disparate attitudes within the DEA didn't much care for what we had done in the Waters investigation—even though we had failed. They weren't exactly planning my next promotion.

In 1976, Assistant U.S. Attorney Jeffrey Harris, who had assisted
Curran on the case, wrote the following:

> During the course of [the Waters] trial preparation I became famil-
> iar with all of McDonnell's allegations. As of late 1974 many of those
> allegations were still unresolved. There were constant rumors that
> many DEA officials mentioned by McDonnell were concerned that if
> Waters were convicted he might cooperate.
>
> In the midst of this atmosphere Agent Tripodi was assigned the task
> to single-handedly act as the case agent. In my opinion he received
> grudging support. Nevertheless he performed all his duties in a highly
> professional manner.

What Jeffrey Harris tactfully referred to as "grudging support" was
really more like outright obstructionism. There were more than a few
DEA heavyweights who had a vested interest in the outcome of the
Waters case. Even though they had gotten the verdict they wanted,
my work for Curran, Giuliani, and Harris once again identified me as
their enemy. Furthermore, now that the Waters prosecution had
failed, there were those who saw me—and the corruption work of the
previous several years—as somehow discredited. Once more, I was a
marked man.

The Waters trial was considered so critical that Senator Jackson's
Permanent Subcommittee on Investigations suspended its probe of
DEA corruption pending its outcome. Now that it was over, the
hearings recommenced. I was subpoenaed and spent many hours in
closed executive sessions.

While I was behind closed doors telling the Senate investigators
what I knew about corruption in the DEA, those who had reason to
fear my testimony were busy planning their revenge.

This time they wouldn't be satisfied with a job change.

This time they wanted me gone.

24

EXILE MAJOR

After the Waters trial, I returned to my Intelligence Unit job in Washington, where once again, I had to work under the Lizard. Almost immediately, I was deluged with harassing memorandums. Every petty issue that my boss could exaggerate or fabricate was fodder for the memo mill. Standards that were overlooked for others were rigidly enforced when doing so worked to my disadvantage. If traffic made me five minutes late for work, I received a memo about it. If one of my men made an incidental mistake on some paperwork, I'd get written up for the error. If some arcane point of operating procedure was transgressed, it would be documented.

In the meantime, I continued to testify under subpoena to the Jackson committee. Demands were constantly made by DEA management that I reveal exactly what I was telling the Senate investigators. That information was critical of many of those who now wanted to know what I had said. At first I refused to comply. Under increased pressure, I did give them a bullshit memo just to get them off my back, innocuous crap that didn't amount to anything. When they asked for more information, I gave them more bullshit. I didn't particularly enjoy the subterfuge, but there was no way I could cooperate with those who were trying to do me in. Had I come clean with them, they would have twisted my words to suit their own purpose.

During the hearings, a group from the Washington Regional Office, who referred to themselves as "Concerned Agents," wrote to the Jackson committee and to the press expressing grievances and concerns about the state of federal narcotics law enforcement. They also cited evidence of wrongdoing they had witnessed. The whole episode, of course, proved extremely embarrassing to management. Unable to determine just which agents were sending the correspondence, the deputy regional director—who just happened to be the Lizard's prime benefactor—decided to come after me. In March 1975, he issued a memorandum demanding that I supply him the names of the so-called Concerned Agents. I had previously approached him on behalf and at the request of two agents who were preparing a class action against the DEA. He conveniently confused that group with those who were sending letters to the Jackson committee. I told him that I had no idea who was in the latter group and that since I was considered as part of management, it was highly unlikely that I'd be taken into their confidence. Needless to say, I was reprimanded for failure to comply with his directive.

Eventually, the Jackson committee got around to calling in DEA Administrator John Bartels. He testified for several days in open session before the panel of senators. When he finished, I was scheduled to be the next witness. My previous appearances had been conducted in closed-door executive sessions. Now the whole mess was going public. My testimony was to be followed by U.S. Attorney Paul Curran, the man who had prosecuted Frankie Waters. Curran's testimony was considered critical because, as U.S. attorney for the Southern District of New York, he was the premier federal prosecutor in the United States. After Curran would come Assistant U.S. Attorneys Jeffrey Harris and Rudy Giuliani. Then, after the stage was set by the three Justice Department heavyweights, Charlie McDonnell was to come in and drop his bombshells. Based on what I knew McDonnell was going to say, at least seven very high-ranking DEA officials had much to worry about.

A few days before I was to testify, Curran called and asked me to pick him up at the airport. We drove directly from the airport to a restaurant. Over lunch he asked me what I thought about our scheduled appearances before the senators.

"We should do everything we can to avoid a circus," I told him.

As much as I wanted to see justice done, I didn't want to see the DEA get slammed just so some fat-cat politicians could make names for themselves. If there was a way to clean our laundry in-house, I was all for it. Curran seemed to be of similar mind.

"Drop me at the White House," Curran said, after lunch was finished.

At about 2:00 P.M. I let him off in front of the White House. I didn't think much of it. Curran's father and Vice President Rockefeller were old buddies, both of them being prominent in the moderate wing of the Republican party. It didn't strike me as unusual that Curran would have business on Pennsylvania Avenue.

I understand that at about 4:15 P.M., Administrator Bartels was summoned to the White House. By that evening, he had resigned.

That was it.

The scapegoat had been chosen and sacrificed.

Bartels wasn't guilty of any wrongdoing as far as I knew. My problem with him was that he created a safe haven for those who had investigative tails dating back to the "Purge of '68" and before—and he had let those very guys assume positions of dominance over those of us who had tried to clean things up.

I never testified. Neither did Curran, Harris, Giuliani, or McDonnell. You could hear sighs of relief throughout the DEA. Guys who had been consumed for months with sanitizing files and rehearsing rebuttal testimony drifted back to business as usual.

Now, more than ever, I was at the mercy of those I had previously investigated and the others who protected them. The agent from the South whom I had written up in the shooting incident had risen to the lofty position of deputy administrator. The Lizard was my immediate superior. He had the full support of the deputy regional director. They were smelling blood in the shark tank, and I was running out of room to maneuver.

The paper attack intensified, memo after memo, petty complaint after petty complaint. Finally, in December of 1975, their campaign culminated in a "notice of adverse action."

I was charged with "failure or delay in carrying out orders, work assignments, required reports, and instructions of superiors." Effective in thirty days, I was to be reduced from "supervisory" to "non-supervisory" status. I was to be once again transferred from Washington to Baltimore, that dark place of recurring banishment.

The charge included thirteen specifications. One of them involved my refusal to identify the "Concerned Agents," whose names were not known to me in the first place. I had complained about my last annual performance evaluation; now that complaint surfaced in no less than three of the specifications. I also hadn't written a job description to the satisfaction of my boss. And I had let a rookie agent, who was a former police officer, but who had not as yet been to DEA training school, drive a government automobile.

Nine of the specifications were initiated by the Lizard. There was no consideration given to his being a former subject of one of my internal security and integrity investigations when I was an inspector. Among the Lizard's specifications, my heinous crimes included deficient report-writing and the acquisition of too many parking tickets—both attributed not to me, but to my subordinates. Also included were two citations of perceived attendance problems, which basically boiled down to my inability to satisfactorily account to the Lizard for my whereabouts at every second of every day.

Each and every one of thirteen specifications was false, contrived, or trivial. I was entitled to a hearing, and I was certain that the adverse notice would be recognized for what it was—blatant retribution for past anticorruption work. But I had underestimated my adversaries. Through bureaucratic maneuvering of Machiavellian complexity, the gutless wimp bastards were able to prolong the process far beyond what I imagined could be possible. Faceless and nameless, working always behind the scenes, not one of them had the guts or the decency to come forward and end the charade. They knew it was a pack of lies, but they let the red tape choke off my career, hoping all along that I'd get frustrated and quit.

In April 1976 I was refused my right to a hearing. My appeal of that ruling was not heard until June 1979, at which time my appeal was dismissed. I went to court in October 1980 and won the right to be heard. The hearing finally took place in July 1981—five and a half years after the notice was effective.

During the hearing, a commotion rippled through the courthouse when a limousine pulled up. In strode Rudy Giuliani and Jeffrey Harris. At the time, Giuliani was associate attorney general and Harris was executive director of the attorney general's Task Force on Violent Crime. Both testified on my behalf. Giuliani, who through the course of his long and distinguished career had worked with hundreds of law enforcement people, stated that I was one of the best agents he had ever met. To the credit of the two attorneys, neither one ever attempted to use the influence of his high office to intercede for me. In contrast to the actions of my enemies, who preferred the anonymity of bureaucratic manipulation, these two high-ranking Justice Department officials contributed to my case solely through their testimony in open court. Of course, they had nothing to hide.

Ten of the specifications were summarily dismissed. Three were upheld. More than two more years passed before the appeal process finally resulted in full vindication.

From December 1975 until September 1983—for almost eight years—my career was stymied under the cloud of false allegations. Each time a supervisor recommended me for a promotion, the silent contingent, working in the comfortable shadows of their protective bureaucracy, was able to get it blocked. And even after the charge was completely laid to rest in 1983, I still couldn't get the DEA to reinstate my supervisory status for the previous eight years. That fight continued until shortly before I retired in 1985, at which time I was restored to my supervisory ranking.

Needless to say, the struggle to clear my name cost me a small fortune in legal fees. It also cost me any chance to further my career. But it did not cost me the opportunity to continue my work as a federal agent.

I refused to let them win.

I refused to quit.

25

PALERMO

They were the dark years—1976 and 1977.

My time of laying low.

I was enduring my second Baltimore exile. I was off the main track. Derailed. Out of the way.

Some time was spent with my attorney, Axel Kleiboemer, as we researched and prepared for my administrative hearing and appeal. I was also preoccupied with personal affairs. Although I had been separated from my wife since 1970 and the finalization of an actual divorce was considered to be an inevitable formality, there continued to be one major point of controversy. I had never been able to get enough of my kids. A protracted dispute over visitation and custody finally was resolved in a series of separate court actions. Custody of all four of my children eventually transferred to me.

The DEA assignments I was given in no way allowed me to work up to my full potential, but I did what was asked of me, biding my time, waiting for vindication. I ran the Intelligence Unit in the Baltimore office. For a couple of months, I conducted a survey in Los Angeles. I did a feasibility study related to the possible opening of a new office on the East Coast and completed security surveys for the Middle Atlantic region. During slow periods, I was able to attend various schools and acquire some special training.

Toward the end of 1977, Mike Antonelli, who had participated with me on the 1972 trip to Italy, asked if I'd be interested in running some ops for him in Italy on a task force basis. Antonelli had risen in the ranks to head of the Italian Desk at headquarters.

At the time of Antonelli's request, I was still heavily involved with my preparation for the administrative hearing. I told him I was interested, but that unfortunately I couldn't make the trip just then. I asked him to keep me in mind for future opportunities.

By the summer of 1978, although I had still not been granted a hearing, I had the preparatory work pretty much squared away. Antonelli had been promoted to a significant position in Rome. He was the country narcotics attaché for Italy. As a veteran narcotics agent with an unparalleled knowledge and understanding of the drug and organized crime situation in Italy, he was eminently qualified for the job. He was essentially running the show on the U.S.-Italian bilateral operations in Italy.

Antonelli happened to be back in the States on R&R. He asked again. This time I was ready.

The preparation for the task force assignment was intense. Back at headquarters in Washington, I worked with the Intelligence people over a period of several weeks. Our research effort mandated frequent communications with our Rome office as well as other stations. We fine-tuned our target analysis and selection. Soon, we were in a position to formulate our ops plan. Daily, Antonelli was consulted and apprised of our progress.

The final plan, named Operation Caesar at my suggestion, was multifaceted. The task force would pursue intelligence reports of clandestine laboratories in Sicily and elsewhere in Italy, and it would explore the feasibility of establishing a permanent DEA presence in Palermo. It would develop actionable prosecutorial cases on major violators. We planned to go right after Mafia leaders in Palermo, thereby striking at the traditional safe haven of the international Mafia in an area previously considered to be off-limits to U.S. law enforcement personnel. We wanted to make a case quickly for shock value, to put the mafiosi on notice and let them know we weren't afraid of them, that we were willing to battle them on their own turf. We wanted the Italian police, who believed we were afraid to work in the Mafia's backyard, to get the same message. We felt that relationships with the Italian law enforcement community could be furthered dramatically once we demonstrated our willingness to work with them side by side.

Later on, the task force objectives were expanded to include an investigative focus on terrorism and the P2 (*Propaganda Due*)—a supersecret, right-wing Italian consortium of businessmen, bankers, politicians, military men, clergy, and mafiosi.

In September of 1978 I flew to Rome. My first day in Italy was taken up by conferences with Antonelli, Special Agent James Porten—one of the hardest-working agents it's ever been my pleasure to know—and John Costanza, the resident agent in charge of the Milan office. Over the next few days, there followed a series of meetings with the Director Provenza of the *Direzione Anti-Droga* (DAD) and some of his key people. Then I was off to Sicily, where I would operate as a singleton agent for the better part of a year. Although Porten, Costanza, and Special Agent Joseph Sullivan would come into Sicily to assist me at times, their visits would be brief, each one lasting no more than a few days. Basically, I was to be the DEA as far as the island of Sicily was concerned.

It had never been done before. Because of the danger, no one from American law enforcement had ever spent a protracted period of time on the Mafia's home turf. The challenge was immense. Palermo was to the Mafia what the Vatican was to the Catholic Church. It was the very root of the Mafia's power, its capital city. It was time for me to lay it on the line and see if the DEA, working with the Italian authorities, could put a serious dent in the Sicilian heroin trade.

I arrived at Punta Raisi International Airport, about ten miles west of Palermo, and took a taxi to the former castle that was the Villa Igeia Hotel. Surrounded by thick stone walls, the Villa Igeia afforded classic European elegance in a fortress-like setting. One could easily develop a siege mentality in such a place.

Upon settling in, I called Giorgio Boris Giuliano, the vice questore (deputy commissioner) of the Italian National Police (INP). ("INP" represents DEA terminology for an amalgam of Italian law enforcement entities; there is no single agency under the name of Italian National Police.) Within an hour, he met me at my hotel accompanied by his assistant, Ignazio D'Antone, and INP Officer Vasquez. I presented the many documents I had carried from Washington and Rome.

Boris Giuliano was internationally respected in law enforcement circles. He had been the only foreigner ever to have gone through the FBI Training Academy at Quantico, Virginia. He was fluent in several languages, and his English was excellent. He was a sharp dresser and sported a handlebar mustache. Smallish, slight of build, he nonetheless effected a commanding presence. A devoted family man, he frequently interrupted meetings to call home and speak with his wife, Maria. He doted on his three children—son Alessandro and daughters Emanuela and Gabriella. Those who became close to him, as I did, were allowed to call him by his middle name, Boris. His father, a professor, had given all his sons the names of famous Russians; he had named Boris after Boris Pasternak. As vice questore, Boris was the second in command within the INP. The position of questore being mainly political, Boris was, for all intents and purposes, running the INP in Sicily.

During that first meeting, Boris and I discussed several active investigations that were in progress both in the States and in Sicily. We explored the relationships between U.S. and Italian crime factions, each helping to fill in the blanks in the other's understanding of the multinational drug network. We outlined operational plans and schedules, concentrating on the goal of locating clandestine heroin labs. Boris was enthusiastic in his support, but he demanded to be personally apprised of all my activities. I agreed, but both of us had been around long enough to know that security considerations made it impossible for me to tell him everything.

"I want to carry my Colt automatic," I informed him.

"I can't give you a permit for that," Boris replied.

"I wasn't asking for a permit," I clarified.

Boris reflected momentarily, then responded: "Well, if you use it, we'll worry about it then."

Before Boris left, he handed me a voluminous investigative report he had completed on the murder of Giuseppe Di Cristina, a notorious Mafia figure who had been gunned down in broad daylight the previous May.

I spent most of the night reading the huge report, translating from Italian as I went along. Essentially, it was one of the first comprehensive looks at the laundering of proceeds from the Sicilian-American drug trade. It outlined the network of transfers that guided money from the sale of heroin in the United States back into "legitimate" investments throughout the world. The conspiracy involved several major banks and other financial institutions. Some of the principals in the Di Cristina case would later emerge in the headline-making Vatican Bank scandal—among them, Michele Sindona. Although I didn't see it then, that report was really a probe into the ultrasecret P2.

The P2 probably had its origins in the first days following World War II. With Eastern Europe ceded to the Soviets, there were those who feared that communism would soon prevail in Italy, as well. The emergence of Communist political parties and sympathetic labor groups only exacerbated their fears. A secret society was formed, perhaps with the help of Western intelligience agencies, under the cover of Masonic lodges. Captains of industry and finance, political leaders, and members of the Catholic Church hierarchy banded together and laid plans for the counterrevolution they would lead if ever the dreaded Communists came into power.

Expedience probably paved the way for the Mafia's entry into the P2. It dominated certain unions, it possessed muscle, and it had cash. Mafiosi had the ability to get things done outside of the normal channels of law and commerce. Their own secret society predated the P2's by several decades. They had survived Mussolini and the Nazi occupation. They were experienced at this sort of thing.

The Communists tried via the electorate but never took control of the Italian government. The counterrevolution had never been needed. Nonetheless, the P2 continued to exist and grow. Many believed it comprised a shadow government, the true seat of Italian political power. Some envisioned it as an underground military-industrial complex, legitimized by the church but made viable by the Mafia. Theories abounded, but few researchers had really been able to penetrate the veil of secrecy that cloaked the P2's activities. Some that tried were killed or just disappeared. Boris had been able to document relationships via telephonic intercepts, bank records, surveillances, and informant disclosures. He saw the P2's role in money laundering, the sleight of hand practiced by bankers, businessmen, and lawyers that converted heroin profits into shopping centers, hotels, and skyscrapers. Through the Di Cristina investigation and other probes, he was quietly assembling a comprehensive dossier on the P2—a risky endeavor, indeed.

My initial target in Palermo was Gaetano Badalamenti, whom we had identified as the dominant Sicilian mafioso with interests in the Sicilian-American heroin trade. Carlo Dondalo, who had worked for us in New York on the Knapp Commission cases and who was descended from a prominent Venetian family that traced its lineage to before the Renaissance, worked as my undercover informant. He had been in jail with Giuseppe Giuliano (no relation to Boris), a mafioso who had contacts within Badalamenti's organization. Dondalo introduced me to Giuseppe Giuliano, who cut me into Rosario DiMaggio, a Badalamenti lieutenant.

Giuseppe Giuliano and Rosario DiMaggio knew me as Tom Tarantino, an Italian-American from New York, a fugitive from U.S. justice, guilty of a minor commercial crime. If anyone checked, he'd find my criminal history in the NYPD's Bureau of Criminal Information. If he checked in Sicily, he'd find that a Tom Tarantino of New York was registered at the Hotel Presidente. At Boris's suggestion, I had vacated the Villa Igeia in favor of the Hotel Politeama, but I also maintained a room at the Presidente to support my cover legend. Once my bona fides had been established with DiMaggio, he agreed to introduce me to Badalamenti.

The meeting took place in a coffee bar in the town of Cinisi, several miles outside of Palermo. DiMaggio escorted me inside and led me to a back room where Badalamenti was seated at a table. I didn't see anyone else around. A chair was waiting for me. I sat down. DiMaggio brought me a cup of espresso and then departed. It was so dark inside, I couldn't even make out Badalamenti's face.

"You are from America?" he asked rhetorically.

"Yes," I affirmed.

"What do you need?"

"I'm looking for some *farina*," I told him in Sicilian. *Farina* was the word the Mafia used for heroin. "Just a small sample. I'm looking for a good laboratory. I have access to large amounts of morphine base from the Far East."

Of course, the story was meant to open negotiations that would lead back to one of his labs. By approaching him in this way, I hoped to establish a relationship that was somewhat more sophisticated than a mere seller-buyer transaction. If he bit, I might be looked on as an equal.

"Where are you staying?" the mafioso asked.

"The Hotel Presidente," I replied.

Abruptly ending the conversation, he said, "Somebody will get in touch with you."

Nobody ever did.

He had made me. He knew I was an agent. Perhaps not during our meeting, but certainly after his people had checked out my story. This wasn't an Old Country rube. Badalamenti was every bit as sophisticated as his American counterparts—perhaps more so.

Boris was pissed when he found out I had met with Badalamenti. He was angry that I hadn't informed him prior to the approach. I explained that security for my operation necessitated the secrecy. Gentleman that he was, he forgave me.

A few days later, Boris confirmed that my cover had been compromised.

"Everyone on the streets is talking about the big U.S. agent in Palermo," he explained.

I asked him how it happened, but I never received an intelligent answer. I naturally concluded that the leak must have come from one of Boris's people in the INP. I trusted Boris and people like D'Antone and Vasquez who were in his inner circle, but beyond that, anything was possible. It was also possible that the leak could have come from someone at the U.S. Consulate or at my hotel, but Boris's reticence strongly suggested that the information had originated within the ranks of the INP.

We initiated a wire on Badalamenti, one of fifty-nine telephonic intercepts that would be activated in Sicily during my time there. In addition, six intercepts would go up in France to support the joint DEA-INP operation in Palermo.

Conceding the blown cover, I abandoned it. I gave up the room at the Presidente and adopted a more open approach focused on cultivating other informants. I wanted to insert an undercover asset into Badalamenti's organization, a Greek ship captain who had been previously recruited by Special Agent James Porten. The captain had established bona fides with several traffickers as a Mediterranean transporter of morphine base and other illegal commodities, and he had developed contacts with Greek nationals who were working with Badalamenti's people.

In the course of a previous INP investigation supervised by Boris, the activities of Turkish chemist Ismet Kostu had been monitored. Kostu was well known to the DEA and other Mediterraean law enforcement agencies as a specialist in the heroin-manufacturing process. When he checked into a hotel in Palermo, Boris picked up his trail. By interrogating Kostu's cab driver, Boris was able to track some of the chemist's movements on Sicily. Boris determined that Kostu, accompanied by some Greeks, had arrived in Sicily in possession of six kilograms of pure heroin. He had been summoned by Badalamenti after his own chemists had botched one of their first attempts at heroin production. Under Kostu's supervision, the lab tried unsuccessfully to salvage the previous deficient quantity. Finally, Kostu just mixed the six kilos of good heroin with six kilos of the tainted dope. Boris's investigation of the Kostu episode had been instrumental in confirming DEA and INP suspicions that the Sicilian Mafia was expanding its involvement in the heroin business by setting up its own processing laboratories, previously the all but exclusive province of Marseille-based Corsicans and Frenchmen.

I directed the new investigation with Boris's full support and cooperation. Our ship captain now approached the Badalamenti group through the very same Greek nationals who had accompanied Kostu. He had heard that Gaetano Scavone was expecting a shipment of two hundred kilograms of morphine base. Scavone was in business with Rosalino Savoca and his uncle Giuseppe Savoca, highly placed mafiosi involved with Badalamenti's heroin-manufacturing enterprise. Through the captain and his contacts, we tried to buy the finished heroin yield that would derive from the two hundred kilos of base. However, that approach had to be abandoned when Savoca's representatives repeatedly claimed that shortages of morphine base had dried up their heroin supply.

The intelligence was relayed to Rome and from there to DEA headquarters in Washington. Headquarters then came up with a different angle. I was to approach Boris with the notion of selling morphine base—which supposedly was in short supply—to Savoca's people. Instead of buying the finished product, we would sell the raw material in a reverse undercover operation. Then, through an intense surveillance effort, we would attempt to follow the morphine base back to the clandestine laboratory.

Boris's answer was a flat, unequivocal *no*.

"What you are suggesting is illegal in Italy," he argued.

"Not too long ago, undercover work by DEA agents on Italian soil was also considered illegal," I pointed out.

Under the so-called *agent provocateur* laws that were prevalent in countries governed under the old Napoleonic Codes, undercover agents and their activities were severely restricted. By 1978, some of that had changed, but there were still many limitations on what could be done on an undercover basis. Search warrants and wiretaps were done routinely, oftentimes with paperwork executed after the fact, but selling morphine base to a drug trafficker was still considered taboo.

"It's the same as secretly putting a bag of heroin into a man's pocket and then arresting him," Boris went on.

"I agree," I said reluctantly, conceding to the subtleties of the Italian judicial system.

"Besides," he added, "that's just not done here. We have an unwritten code. We have to abide by it, just as the Mafia has to abide by it. If we don't, they're going to shoot me down in the street like a dog."

I wired the Rome office, indicating our objections to the new plan. The Rome office wired back, summoning Boris and me to Rome on the following day for a meeting with Mike Antonelli and officials from DAD. There we were told that judicial exception had been granted for the reverse undercover op. Like it or not, we had official permission to go ahead. They gave me four kilograms of morphine base from a seizure in Paris.

Boris was worried—and with good reason. There were the rules of justice and the courts, and there were the rules of the streets.

Omertà.

Vendetta.

And the smoky gray code of honor that defined how far cops and criminals could go.

Now the rule book was being thrown away. The gloves were off. Anything could happen.

Porten and one of our informants met with Scavone and Giacomo Pirrone and gave them the morphine base. Surveillance officers tailed the suspects as they took an overnight ferry to Naples.

The INP had deployed more than fifty officers to the detail. Undercover officers were positioned in Palermo, in Naples, and on the ferry. The Italians weren't big on electronics; they favored "eyeball" surveillance, even though the opposition often employed countersurveillance personnel. The Italian authorities frequently put their people in cabs as drivers and passengers. They utilized female surveillance officers far more than we did at the time. Often male and female undercover officers would station themselves on a park bench, embracing like lovers.

The suspects drove all around Naples before returning to the ferry for the return trip to Palermo. A fresh INP undercover team accompanied them. Back in Palermo, they gave the morphine base back to Porten without explanation. Evidently, they had made the surveillance before the first ferry ever docked in Naples. We hadn't traced the morphine base back to the lab, but we were able to assemble prosecutorial evidence against sixteen suspects.

The ferry episode was not the first time that the mainland port city of Naples had figured into our investigation. Shortly after the phone taps on the Badalamenti group had been installed, we started to trace a number of calls to and from a known member of the Neapolitan Camorra, the Neapolitan equivalent of the Mafia. Other calls were traced to a coffee shop on the Via Santa Lucia that was a favorite hangout for the Camorristi, perhaps even serving as their base of operations. Our informant arranged a meeting with one of the Sicilian traffickers that was to take place at the coffee shop.

I went into Naples a few days early to check things out. I wanted to see the layout of the coffee shop so I could better plan the surveillance. Venturing into the coffee shop, I wandered over to the counter and ordered a cup of coffee.

No problem.

The counterman poured the strong, dark brew and set the cup down in front of me. I paid him.

No problem.

I looked for the sugar jar. Not finding one, I asked the counterman for some sugar and a spoon.

Big problem!

In the older parts of Naples, where there are still traces of influence left from Spanish rule of centuries past, coffee is brewed *with the sugar already in it.* I could have just as easily jumped on the counter and yelled, "I'm an outsider! I don't belong here!"

The patrons of the coffee shop needed no such overt display. My faux pas had been duly noted. One of them, a tough-looking punk with a shaved head who was built like a fire hydrant, marched up to the counter and pressed in beside me, as close as he could get without actually touching me. This guy must have been a wrestler or a weight lifter. Solid, squat, all muscle—he took root at the counter and gave me the once-over.

My thoughts quickly gravitated to the Colt Commander .38 Super that was in my leather shoulder bag. *Was there a round in the chamber or not? Was the safety on? Was there even time to get the automatic out of the bag?*

I turned and looked out the plate glass window. On the street outside the shop, glaring at me, was a well-dressed man and six young punks in their twenties—no doubt, the local Camorra enforcement unit.

I figured I was done for. On my tombstone they'd write, *Killed in the Quest for Sugar.*

I inhaled the damn coffee and bolted out of the place. The hydrant followed. I headed for the bay, about one hundred yards away. The hydrant was gaining on me. I cut a quick left into a courtyard and hugged the wall. Seconds later, the hydrant turned the corner. I hit him with the hardest right I ever threw, catching him on his left ear and temple. He went down, and I lit out down the Via Partenope. The other six hoods continued to follow me. After I had decked their buddy, I'm sure they were eager to get a piece of me. I made sure I kept to busy streets, where there were lots of people milling around. Perhaps curious to see where I was staying, they stuck with me a while, before finally dropping off.

Never—before or since—have I feared for my life like I did that evening in Naples. I don't think the Camorristi made me as a narcotics agent or even as anyone connected in one way or another to their activities. They had reacted simply because I was an outsider. It was strictly a turf thing.

Almost anticlimactic was the actual meeting between our informant and the traffickers. The INP in Naples arranged an ingenious surveillance utilizing cabs and motorcycles, but still the Camorristi made them. Those guys on the Via Santa Lucia knew everything that belonged there. Every face. Every vehicle. Again, I couldn't help but be impressed with the intelligence and cunning of the Old World mobsters.

Although the Camorristi had detected the surveillance team, they didn't seem to suspect our informant. He was later able to continue his penetration and succeeded in orchestrating the precedent-setting deal that had so frightened Boris.

One of the other informants I developed was Calabrese like myself. I would sometimes meet him at the Greek ruins at Segesta about twenty-five miles from Palermo. High up on a windswept hill that discouraged tourists, the old temple and theater provided a secure, isolated vantage point from which I could see for miles in all directions, making it easy to determine if either of us had been followed.

Another meeting spot, chosen for similar reasons, was in the little town of San Fratello, nestled in the shadow of Mount Etna high in the Apennines. I started out for one meeting in shirtsleeves. As I drove up the long, winding mountain road, the skies darkened and it began to drizzle. As I climbed further up the mountain, the rain turned to flurries, then to heavy snow. I couldn't believe it. I was in the middle of the Mediterranean, damn near in the tropics, and I was plowing through a blizzard. Before I knew it, my car was stuck in two feet of snow. Luckily for me, the heater was working, because it was at least an hour before a tow truck pulled me out. The informant never did make it.

My Calabrese informant wasn't very successful in his efforts to penetrate the group of heroin traffickers, but in the course of his undercover work, he did meet an individual who offered to sell him a priceless stolen work of art. *Adorazione dei Pastori coi Santi Francesco e Lorenzo* (The Adoration of the Shepherds with Saints Francis and Lorenzo) by Caravaggio had been stolen nine years previously from the Oratory of St. Lorenzo in Palermo. The painting was offered at 100 million lire (about $115,000 U.S. at the time) to my informant. When I told Boris about the offer, he was very excited at the opportunity to recover one of Sicily's most-treasured historical artworks. Unfortunately, subsequent attempts to cut one of Boris's undercover agents into the deal never clicked, and the painting continued as an art world MIA.

Prior to and during the time I was in Sicily, agents from the DEA and the FBI in the United States were making great progress on a significant money-laundering investigation. The principal in the case was Salvatore Sollena, who also happened to be an Operation Caesar target because of his heroin-trafficking involvement with the Badalamenti group. Over time, we were able to dovetail the Sollena investigation into Boris's probe of the Di Cristina murder. The paper trail seemed to lead over the same ground. The same banks and the same names kept popping up in both investigations.

Things were starting to come together. By April of 1979, Boris and I starting thinking in terms of a large conspiracy prosecution. We envisioned it in three separate phases, each phase to be kicked off with a roundup of several defendants. Given our limited resources, in order to maximize our search, seizure, and interrogation effectiveness, the enforcement actions would be staggered a few days apart from each other.

The first phase was targeted on the Savoca group. We had identified sixteen mafiosi whom we could tie into the reverse undercover op involving the morphine base. Justice Domenico Signorino issued the arrest warrants.

A few days later, Justice Luigi Croce was scheduled to issue eleven warrants. These were to target Sollena's people and the operation that laundered narcotics money flowing between the United States and Sicily.

Shortly after that, Justice Francesco Scorzari would issue ninety-seven warrants related to the Di Cristina murder investigation and money laundering within Italy.

At 3:00 A.M. on May 5, 1978, we started making the first arrests. The Mafia was caught completely off guard. By midmorning, half of the Phase One defendants were already in custody, and enforcement teams were zeroing in on those still at large. I was with Boris in his office, when at about 9:00 A.M., he was called away. He returned in no more than five or ten minutes. Ashen-faced, he asked me to accompany him into the hall. He had something private to discuss with me.

"At times like this," he stated grimly, "we start getting phone calls. We've received some threats against me and against you. From now on, don't go anywhere without calling me first. Don't leave your hotel. Don't go to meet friends. I want to know where you are at all times."

About noon, I returned to my hotel. Having been up since about 2:30 A.M., I wanted to shower and freshen up. Three hours later, I was ready once again to venture out. I called Boris as he had instructed.

"Don't go anywhere for at least a half-hour," he said.

I waited as he had asked. When I did walk down to the lobby, I was instantly aware of a radical change in the hotel staff's attitude. Previously, they had been helpful and friendly; now they looked at me with dread and resentment. Outside I found three unmarked INP cars waiting for me, each manned by two officers. I got into my Fiat 132. The INP teams followed me everywhere I went.

Over the next couple of days, I limited my movements basically to the hotel and INP headquarters. At all times, the INP bodyguards were nearby. On May 8, Boris told me that I had to change hotels.

"More phone calls," was his terse explanation.

Boris didn't even want me to go back to the Hotel Politeama. He made arrangements to have my things picked up and brought to the fortress-like Villa Igeia. It occurred to me that in returning to my original Sicilian accommodations, I was, in effect, advancing to the rear. At Boris's urging, I spent the next few days holed up like a prisoner behind the Villa's massive stone walls.

On Friday night, Boris met me at my hotel. Over dinner, he told me that I had to leave Sicily the next morning. He sketched out a precise route that I was to follow. I was to depart at precisely 5:00 A.M.

The following morning I did exactly as Boris had instructed. The streets were empty. They had been blocked off by the INP. I drove along the prescribed route, every couple of blocks passing an INP patrol car. The officers waved as I passed. Once I made it to the *autostrada*, a helicopter tagged along overhead. More police units were stationed at strategic intervals. At Termine Imerese, about ninety miles from the ferryboat docks at Messina, the helicopter circled, buzzed me, and flew off. I took the ferry to the mainland and proceeded on to Rome. Boris had even arranged for INP escorts on this part of the journey.

Alone in the Fiat, I could feel only a deep sense of sadness. I realized that Boris's precautions had probably saved my life, but still I regretted leaving Palermo. The hasty departure had separated me abruptly from one of the best friends I had ever known. And it had interrupted the work we had done together—before we had been really able to see the fruits of our labors.

I told myself that our work in Sicily was not over.

26

CALLS IN THE
NIGHT

I cooled my heels in Rome for a few weeks. Only once did I risk
returning to Sicily. I was in and out of Palermo the same day. A
security detail picked me up as soon as I hit the island. I met with
Boris at police central and with the judges at the Tribunale (courthouse).

In late May 1979, I returned to the States. I was assigned to the
Special Action Office for Southwest Asian Heroin (SAO/SWA), an
operational unit that had been established with White House funding. Our targets were any and all groups dealing in heroin that originated in Southwest Asia. In addition to Turkey, which was on the
decline as a provider of morphine base, we targeted heroin-related
activities in Pakistan, Afghanistan, Iran, Iraq, and India. Eventually,
the target country list was expanded to include Greece, Syria, Turkey, Bulgaria, and Yugoslavia. Since a healthy portion of the Southwest Asian morphine base was going to Sicily for processing, the

assignment to SAO/SWA was a natural extension of the work I had done in Palermo. By the time the unit was disbanded in 1981 because of lack of funding, I was the SAO/SWA acting director.

During my tenure with the Special Action Office, I ran a couple of task forces to Italy and Greece, essentially interdiction efforts that enjoyed limited success. The cooperation of the international community, in general, and the Italians, in particular, was noteworthy.

Once, during the Iranian hostage crisis, while in Trieste, I was awakened by the Italian customs authorities at about 4:00 A.M. They had detained four Iranians at a checkpoint along the Yugoslav border and felt I might be interested in witnessing their inspection procedures.

The Italian customs facilities were impressive. They had three large garages where vehicles could be lifted on hoists for detailed inspections. If necessary, they had the equipment to dismantle and reassemble an entire vehicle. Their inspections were carried out in view of the arriving travelers. By contrast, inspections on the Yugoslav side of the border were limited to poking long-handled mirrors under vehicles.

The Italian officials had located a trap between the backseat and the trunk of the Iranians' vehicle. Only trace amounts of heroin had been found, but it was enough to warrant an arrest. Clearly, there was evidence that the vehicle had been used for drug smuggling. There was also a large quantity of propaganda handouts found in the vehicle. The Iranians were between the ages of thirty-two and forty-five, yet they were all students at the University of Padua. All in all, they fit the classic terrorist profile.

The customs people strip-searched the Iranians, three guys and a female. It was the middle of winter, and there was no heat in the garage. The Iranians were allowed to freeze their asses a good long while before their clothes were returned to them. The Italians asked if I wanted private interrogation privileges. I told them that I was obliged to refuse. The customs authorities decided it would be easier all around to just deny entry visas, rather than to make arrests.

The Iranians were sent back across the border. The Yugoslavs, not to be outdone and feeling embarrassed that their own inspection had proved deficient, performed another strip-search of the Iranians. Then they contacted border stations in Greece and Turkey, arranging for similar receptions at every checkpoint.

When I first returned from Italy, I had many phone conversations with Boris. He kept me up-to-date on the progress of Operation Caesar, and I helped as best I could with information and advice. The danger of Mafia reprisals had not diminished. I could usually detect the concern in his voice. He explained that the second and third phases of the roundup had been delayed for political reasons and because of the need for still more investigative work. He was quite excited about the Di Cristina phase and about the discovery of $500,000 in an unclaimed suitcase at Punta Raisi Airport that he had been able to trace back to Salvatore Sollena.

Early in July 1979, Boris called me. He sounded extremely worried, even more so than he had on previous calls. On July 9, he had met with Milan lawyer Giorgio Ambrosoli after a court proceeding in Rome where Ambrosoli had caucused with Italian and American prosecutors regarding the ongoing Mafia cases. Two days later, Ambrosoli was executed in full view of his wife as he entered his apartment. Ambrosoli, several years previous, had been appointed by the Treasury Ministry and the Bank of Italy as liquidator for Banca Privata Italiana, one of five banks that Michele Sindona controlled through his holding company, Fasco, A.G. During their last conversation, Boris and he had discussed the Di Cristina investigation, especially how it related to Sindona and the P2.

Realizing the mounting danger of the situation and Boris's concern, I tried to cheer him up. Half-joking, I told Boris that if things got any worse in Sicily, he and his family would always be welcome at my house. We went on to discuss plans for his son, Alessandro, to visit me and attend a local Jesuit school.

On the morning of July 21, 1979—ten days after Ambrosoli had been assassinated—Vice Questore Giorgio Boris Giuliano was shot dead in a Palermo coffee bar.

As was his custom, Boris had gone to the Cafe Lux for a cappuccino and a *cornetto* (horn-shaped pastry). On this particular morning he arrived about twenty minutes earlier than usual. His bodyguard, who daily met him there, hadn't arrived yet. After Boris paid the cashier, a punk ran up and pumped seven shots from a 7.65mm automatic into him. It was a professional hit. The first bullet went to Boris's right shoulder, incapacitating his arm so that he couldn't draw his own gun. The last shot went to his head to finish him.

After the murder, it was learned that Boris had received a phone call shortly before 8:00 A.M., after which he immediately left the house for the Cafe Lux. It was a peculiar change of routine, for Boris was fastidious in his punctuality, neither being late nor early. You could set your watch by him. Yet, on the last morning of his life, he arrived at the coffee bar twenty minutes before his bodyguard was due and during a period when he had more reason than ever to exercise caution. The circumstantial evidence suggests strongly that someone close and trusted set Boris up in classic Mafia style. I believe that someone he knew called him and changed the plans. Someone Boris trusted, perhaps a fellow police officer or another prosecutor, sent him to his death.

I received the news in the middle of the night. The phone rang at about 3:00 A.M. At first I thought it was another of the strange calls I had been receiving. For several weeks, I had been getting calls at all hours from someone who would hang up just as soon as he confirmed that he was speaking to Tom Tripodi. At first I thought nothing of the calls, but ever since Boris had told me about the Ambrosoli hit, I started to be more concerned. This time it was Mike Antonelli calling from Rome with the shattering news about Boris.

My friend was dead.

The Mafia had cut down one of the most dedicated and fearless law enforcement professionals it has ever been my privilege to know.

I had taken the call in my family room, standing in front of the sliding glass patio doors. As soon as I hung up the receiver, I realized what a great target I was presenting to any would-be assassins outside. Quickly, I moved away from the glass and pulled the drapes shut. If someone was out there, I wasn't about to make it easy for him. From that night on, whenever I was in a vulnerable situation—walking to my car in a dark parking lot, venturing alone down a deserted street—I always had a gun in my hand.

I was overcome with alternating waves of sorrow and anger. My grief for my friend mixed with the rage I felt for his murderers. I made reservations to go to Palermo. I would attend the funeral, and then I would work with the INP to find his killer.

Over the next several hours, I received calls from headquarters, from the U.S. State Department, and from Italian police officials. Antonelli had already told me to be on the alert, that Boris's murder was quite likely related to Operation Caesar, that I might be "on the list." Now I was told flat out not to go back to Italy. The Italian authorities had specifically informed headquarters that if I did return to Italy, under no circumstances would I be allowed to travel to Palermo. They didn't want a bloodbath on their hands.

What they wanted and what they got were two different things. In September of 1979, world-famous Mafia-busting Judge Cesare Terranova came out of retirement to direct the investigation of Boris's murder and other related matters. On his first day back in public life, after reviewing the case files, Terranova was assassinated as he sat in his car mired in a traffic jam. Almost four years later his replacement, Rocco Chinnici, was killed by a car bomb.

The Mafia murdered the owner of a restaurant where Boris, his wife, and I frequently ate dinner. At the INP's request, the owner, a wonderful old man who had become a good friend, had allowed undercover detective Vasquez to work in the restaurant as a waiter.

In January 1980, Piersante Mattarrella, the president of the Region of Sicily, was killed. He had strongly supported Operation Caesar and the appointment of Terranova.

The following May, the Mafia eliminated Capt. Emanuele Basile of the Carabinieri. He had headed the Carabinieri's involvement in Operation Caesar. In June of 1983, his replacement, Capt. Mario D'Aleo, also was assassinated. Senior Judge Gaetano Costa of Palermo was murdered on August 6, 1980.

The killings eventually provoked the central Italian government in Rome to take a stronger stand regarding the Mafia in Sicily. They gave Carlo Alberto Dalla Chiesa, general of the Carabinieri, expanded enforcement powers, including the ability to suspend constitutional rights in certain circumstances. Soon after beginning a crackdown in Palermo, Dalla Chiesa was murdered on September 3, 1982.

Shortly after the murder of Judge Costa, I happened to be eating lunch with his replacement, Giovanni Falcone; Gianni De Gennaro; and a senior DEA official at Tre Moschettieri in Rome.

Jokingly I said to Falcone, "You're next."

He shook his head. "No," he disagreed. "They have to get you first because you started this whole thing."

"Why Tripodi?" the senior DEA man asked, evidently feeling left out. "He's going back to Washington where he'll be safe. What about me? I'm here in Rome."

"Why should they kill you?" Falcone asked. "You never hurt anyone."

Falcone went on to become one of Italy's most successful Mafia-busters. On May 23, 1992, Falcone, his wife Francesca, and three others were killed by a bomb that was remotely detonated under a section of a Palermo highway. Italian officials estimated that over a ton of high explosives were used in the ambush that destroyed Falcone's armored-plated car and blew apart six other vehicles. In July 1992, the Mafia killed Falcone's possible successor, Judge Paolo Borsellino, and his five police bodyguards. The bomb destroyed a neighborhood in Palermo and injured many innocent people.

Had Boris and the others lived, they would have taken great pride in the ultimate results of what we had started in Operation Caesar. Our ground-breaking work set in motion a series of joint operations with Italy that eventually led to the arrests of more than one thousand mafiosi. The vast majority of the defendants were convicted and incarcerated. One case in Sicily had more than three hundred defendants. A case in Naples saw four hundred suspects indicted. The joint operations also shut down nine heroin laboratories in Italy and France. More than one thousand kilograms of heroin were seized.

Beyond some coordinating efforts, I had limited involvement with the investigations that followed Operation Caesar. Tremendous work was done by law enforcement officers—with major participation by the DEA and the FBI—in the United States, in Italy, and in France. Without in any way detracting from their considerable achievements, I think it's still fair to say that the way was paved for them with the blood and the determination of brave men like Boris Giuliano. Operation Caesar had started the ball rolling.

During the period I was in Sicily, there were absolutely no seizures at JFK International Airport of heroin that had originated in Palermo. Prior to July of 1978, the DEA had been making seizures on almost a monthly basis. From then until August of 1979, the DEA did not seize even one gram. I don't for a minute think that the lull in shipments was due solely to my presence in Palermo, but I do believe without a doubt that the supply stoppage was related to the overall efforts of all those involved with Operation Caesar.

Shortly after Boris's murder, I received another anonymous phone call. This time, the caller had a bit more to say: "Get your affairs in order. Your time has come."

Not too long after that, DEA agent—and former CIA agent—Lou Conein informed me that Washington restaurateur Antonio Tripoli wanted to get in touch with me. Conein was a regular at Antonio's restaurant.

Antonio was a friend. We had known each other for some time. Antonio spent six months of the year running his restaurant and the other six months back in his hometown of Messina in Sicily. When in Sicily, he spent much of his time—according to his wife—with his *amici* in Palermo.

"There's a reporter in town from New York who wants to see you," Antonio explained. "I thought I could make the arrangements."

It sounded fishy.

"Have him contact the DEA's PR people for clearance," I responded. "I can't talk to a reporter unless I get their okay."

Antonio was a bit flustered. He tried a different approach. "I need to talk to you, myself, on a very important matter. Can you meet me at the restaurant later tonight?"

Curious, I agreed.

I contacted my old and trusted friend Abe Azzam, who was now director of SAO/SWA. He agreed to accompany me to the restaurant.

The building that housed Antonio's restaurant was scheduled to undergo demolition. That evening, when we arrived there, we found the restaurant closed to the public. Furniture was stacked up, ready for removal. Not all the lights had been turned on. There was nobody around except for Antonio standing behind the bar, fidgeting and looking very nervous. Azzam gravitated to a spot that provided a reasonable vantage point. He had an Uzi ready under his raincoat. I had my Colt .38 Super in my left hand inside my coat pocket.

If ever there was a setup, I figured this was it.

I opened the conversation with the usual cordialities, asking about his family, his health, and so on.

"I just got back from Palermo," Antonio stammered. "I saw many of your . . . friends . . . over there."

"What friends?" I asked.

"If I was you," Antonio continued, "I would never return to Sicily."

"Did someone tell you to tell me that?" I inquired.

"If I was you, I would never return to Sicily," he repeated, his tone as solemn as an undertaker's.

"Why?"

"If I was you, I would never return to Sicily!"

To each and every one of my questions, I received the same broken-record reply.

Somebody in Palermo had really put a scare into Antonio. Evidently, our friendship was known to my enemies in Sicily. The Mafia used Antonio to deliver a message: they had put a contract out on me.

I have no way to know for sure, but my feeling is that the contract does not extend beyond the shores of Sicily. I've been to Italy several times since Antonio delivered the Mafia's message, but I have not ventured back to Sicily.

Not yet.

27

THE P2

There were three theories prevalent regarding Boris's assassination. The first and most obvious was that he had been killed because he had been the most visible Italian authority associated with Operation Caesar. The second possibility related to the reverse undercover operation Boris had been so reluctant to implement. The final theory—and perhaps the most intriguing—centers on Boris's probe into the P2.

The biggest insights into the P2 during the last fifteen years probably trace back in one way or another to Mafia banker Michele Sindona. As it turned out, many of the joint investigations that followed Operation Caesar demonstrated links to Sindona's operations and to the P2.

Michele Sindona was born in 1920 near Messina in Sicily. He managed to dodge Mussolini's draft and was able to earn a law degree from the University of Messina. After the arrival of the Allies, he went into the black-market produce business, shipping his goods from the port of Palermo to other Sicilian towns and villages, an enterprise that could not exist without the blessing of the Mafia. None other than Italian-American mobster Vito Genovese, the infamous fugitive from U.S. justice and a former Gestapo informant, was his benefactor. After the war, Sindona moved to Milan where he set up a lucrative law practice. When clients couldn't pay him for his services, he allowed them to sign over shares of stock in companies they owned. He amassed a fortune and, in 1960, bought the Banca Privata Italiana. Almost immediately, the Vatican started funneling huge deposits to Sindona's bank. Eventually, Sindona was appointed as a financial adviser to the Vatican. With help from the P2, Sindona's financial juggernaut continued. His holding company, Fasco, A.G., acquired interests in five banks and 125 companies spread out over eleven countries. In North America his holdings included the Montreal Stock Exchange Building, Paramount Studios, and the Watergate Hotel complex. Sindona used his international network of financial institutions and companies to launder Mafia narcotics money. He became the primary go-between for the Mafia and the P2.

Following the collapse of the Sindona-controlled Franklin National Bank, the twelfth largest bank in the United States, Sindona was arrested and indicted on ninety-nine counts of fraud, perjury, and misappropriation of bank funds. He was allowed to post bail, and he was released from jail. On August 2, 1979—less than two weeks after Boris's murder—Sindona disappeared from New York. Within days of his disappearance, the media began receiving ransom demands in the amount of $36 million from persons unknown who claimed to have kidnapped the banker.

In reality, no kidnapping had ever occurred. Sindona, disguised with a wig, mustache, and beard, and carrying a phony passport in the name of Joseph Bonamico, had fled the United States. He flew from JFK Airport in New York to Vienna and then on to Athens. In Greece he boarded a ferry headed across the Strait of Otranto to Brindisi, on the Adriatic coast of Italy. From there he traveled by automobile and ferry to Palermo, where he was the houseguest of brothers Rosario and Vincenzo Spatola, both Operation Caesar targets.

The kidnapping ruse continued, although no one in law enforcement believed it for a second. In a modern variation of the old Italian shell game, P2 figure Licio Gelli arranged to have Roberto Calvi, another P2 member, pay the enormous ransom to the "kidnappers." In June of 1982, Calvi, who by then had been implicated in P2-related money laundering and banking scandals, was found hanging from the Blackfriars Bridge in London. In Mafia terms, he had been *suicidato*—"suicided."

While Sindona was in Palermo, New York mafioso "Big John" Gambino flew to Palermo with his physician, Dr. Joseph Miceli Crimi, a reputed member of the P2. To lend credence to the kidnapping fiction, Crimi shot the banker in the leg with a .22 pistol, being careful to direct the bullet in such a way as to render the wound superficial yet authentic looking.

A Gambino lieutenant then drove Sindona to Vienna. Sindona flew to Frankfurt, then back to JFK. Again, the banker employed a disguise and a phony passport. In New York, a girlfriend of Gambino picked up Sindona at the airport and dropped him off at Central Park, where he was found "wandering around in a dazed condition." He told the New York police that he had been shot while escaping from his kidnappers. He had the bullet wound to prove it.

On March 27, 1980, Sindona was convicted in New York of charges stemming from the Franklin National Bank swindle. On June 13, he was sentenced to twenty-five years in prison.

In the meanwhile, the INP was intensifying its investigation of the Spatolas, as well as Gambino and Crimi. When the INP interrogated Crimi in March of 1981 about a mysterious six hundred–mile trip he had taken to the northern Italian town of Arezzo while Sindona had been in Sicily, he told his questioners that the journey had been prompted by a toothache. He claimed he had traveled six hundred miles to see his dentist. The story was about as believable as Sindona's kidnapping yarn. Under further questioning, Crimi broke down and copped to having visited P2 big shot Gelli in Arezzo on a mission for Sindona.

A couple of days later, the INP raided Gelli's home in Arezzo and his office in nearby Castiglion Fibocchi. They found boxes full of classified government documents as well as damaging bank and financial records, many of them relating to Sindona's failed empire. Most importantly, they discovered a master list of the secret P2 lodges throughout Italy and a roster of the members' names. For the first time, authorities had uncovered solid evidence of the extent of the P2's reach into the Italian government, military, intelligence community, law enforcement establishment, and even the Vatican.

The Gelli seizures propelled the INP investigations, providing links to many of the Mafia targets we had identified in Operation Caesar. As the investigation progressed, the picture of Sindona's involvement in Mafia money laundering clarified. It also became clear that Sindona's banking network had processed several arms deals and other commercial activities for P2 members. By the end of 1981, the Italian authorities had even tied Sindona to the murder of Ambrosoli, the Milan lawyer whose death had preceded Boris's by less than two weeks.

Both Ambrosoli and Boris had been involved in P2 probes. They had met and discussed their investigations just shortly before both of them were assassinated. With Sindona now implicated in Ambrosoli's death, it became easier to entertain the P2 connection as a viable explanation for Boris's murder.

Although Sindona was behind bars in the United States, the Italian courts indicted him for Ambrosoli's murder. Later, in January 1982, he was also indicted, along with more than eighty others—including Big John Gambino, the Spatola brothers, and several members of the Inzerillo family—on charges of conspiracy in a $600 million heroin-trafficking operation. The Inzerillos were also former targets of Operation Caesar, as well as being defendants in some stateside narcotics cases.

Within a month of the indictment, Pietro Inzerillo was found in New Jersey in the trunk of a car belonging to his cousin, Erasmo Gambino. A five-dollar bill was found in his mouth. Two singles were discovered in his crotch. Shortly after the body was found, the FBI sponsored a big meeting in New York to discuss the killing and its possible relationship to the various investigations that were in progress. Various theories were expounded by the "organized crime experts" in attendance, none of whom had the firsthand experience with the Mafia that I could claim. Virtually all of their "expert" theories linked Inzerillo's killing to money laundering or drugs. Finally they got around to asking for my opinion.

"I don't think it had anything to do with dope or with money laundering," I said. "The killer left signs that are recognizable only to other Mafia members. He's letting them know who he is and why he killed this man. This hit was personal. There was money in Inzerillo's mouth and in his crotch. That tells me he was screwing somebody's wife or girlfriend or mother or daughter or sister or somebody. And he was talking about it."

The United States and Italy had recently concluded a new extradition treaty that allowed for the exchange of prisoners for investigative purposes. The treaty had been designed for the express purpose of enabling Sindona's return to Italy, where he was tried and convicted. On March 22, 1986, he died in an Italian jail cell after drinking coffee that had been laced with cyanide.

One more mafioso had been "suicided."

28

THE BONO CASE

After the Special Action Office disbanded, I worked at DEA head-quarters in Washington coordinating investigations in the United States and Italy. I also acted as liaison to the FBI on cases of mutual interest. Occasionally I'd receive a request to assist on an undercover operation.

During May 1982, our office in Brussels developed an investigation on a southern European diplomat. Through an informant, the Brussels office learned that the diplomat was free-lancing on the side for a South American cocaine-producing country. The diplomat had asked the in-formant to find him a customer who could purchase large amounts of cocaine on a continuous basis. Furthermore, the diplomat indicated that the cocaine cost him nothing, but with the proceeds from the sale, he was to purchase five surplus fighter jets from the Belgian govern-ment. Once more, I was faced with a situation where drug trafficking had been incorporated into a covert intelligence operation.

I was elected to play the customer. A DEA undercover pilot leased a Lear jet and flew it down to Miami to pick up the diplomat. I flew in another small jet to a landing strip at a fancy resort near White Sulphur Springs, West Virginia. The diplomat's plane arrived a few minutes after mine. He exited and walked over to my jet, duly impressed by the surroundings and the elite travel arrangements that had been made on his behalf. In a suitcase, I had a million dollars—for flash. I also had a Smith and Wesson 9mm submachine gun stashed close by—just in case.

I popped open the suitcase and showed him the cash. He went bug-eyed at the sight of all that money. He was absolutely certain that I was the big-time cocaine buyer he needed. We quickly cut a deal. Then, he flew back to Miami in the same Lear that had brought him down. Other agents picked up the investigation in Florida.

My DEA undercover pilot had to get my plane back to New York. He dropped me off at Baltimore-Washington International on his way home. It was raining, and no one from the DEA was there to pick me up. I wrapped the Smith and Wesson in a plastic garbage bag, the only camouflage I could find on the jet. With the suitcase full of cash in one hand and the bagged submachine gun in the other, I headed out across the rain-soaked tarmac toward the terminal building.

It was the era of hijackings and terrorist bombings. Police and security guards were everywhere. More than a few eyeballed me as I wandered around nervously, waiting for someone from the DEA to show. To the cops, I must have looked like a character straight off the streets of Beirut. When it became clear that nobody had been detailed to pick me up, I made a few angry phone calls and arranged transportation. Had the police actually stopped me, I'm sure I could have talked my way through the situation, but I was in no mood for polite explanations and the inevitable long wait as the local authorities verified my story. I turned in the money the next day, and others continued on this case.

On another occasion, William Nelson, a DEA supervisor in Baltimore, asked me to accompany an informant to Miami, where we would negotiate a cocaine buy. As it turned out, the informant and I looked remarkably alike. We could have passed easily for brothers. We flew down together in a Cessna 721. In Miami, the informant cut me into the trafficker, a Colombian national. He stated his prices: $4,000 per kilo if delivered in Colombia, $10,000 per kilo if delivered in Panama, and $18,000 if delivered in Miami. The tiered pricing structure relevant to point of delivery was more or less typical. The farther the dope was transported, the higher the risk. The higher the risk, the higher the price. I settled on delivery in Panama. In the follow-up investigation, we seized three hundred kilograms of cocaine and arrested more than a dozen traffickers.

Nelson also requested my help on another undercover case. I was to be the Italian heavy from New York. *What else was new?* I played the uncle of Leonard Athis, the undercover agent who had made contact with a group of Colombian cocaine traffickers. Athis was attempting to set up a major buy from the suspects who had been dealing in the Baltimore area. To impress the Colombians and show them that I was behind "my nephew," I arrived at Baltimore Harbor aboard a luxurious yacht we had previously confiscated in a seizure. We royally entertained the Colombians on the yacht, then took them to an Italian restaurant in Baltimore's Little Italy section for continued wining and dining. We cut the deal. Subsequently, when the suspects delivered the cocaine, agents seized a significant amount and busted several traffickers.

We had surreptitiously videotaped the meeting on the yacht. I understand that the tape has been shown to Organized Crime and Undercover Operations classes at the DEA and FBI training academies. Following its presentation to one DEA class, the instructor told the trainees, "You are liable to see Tripodi pop up in any office around the world. If he does, you don't speak to him first. If he wants to talk to you, he'll start the conversation."

In May 1982, I was assigned to assist the Venezuelan intelligence services on an investigation they were running. All I knew was that, in the course of an internal security investigation, the Venezuelans had determined that their subjects were in telephonic contact with people in the United States and Italy. Thinking at first that the contacts related to undercover intelligence activities, the Venezuelans alerted the CIA. The agency begged off and referred them to the DEA country attaché in Venezuela, John O'Connor.

The information was sketchy. As I began the long flight from Miami to South America, following a previous long flight from Washington, I reflected on the situation. Specifically, I wondered if I was being set up. Given my unsettled situation with regard to the charge against me, I had to be especially careful to avoid even the slightest appearance of wrongdoing. Whenever I was given such scant information prior to an assignment, I had to consider the possibility that I could be compromised—intentionally or not—in an undercover encounter with another agent. If another agent's account of an undercover encounter was different from my own, I could once again be put in the position of defending myself.

I managed to get myself upgraded to first class and settled in for the long trip. I was looking forward to a peaceful, comfortable ride. Since my school days, I had always sought out quiet, relaxing places when I had serious brain work to do. The sparsely peopled first-class cabin seemed like an ideal spot for a long, undistracted assessment of the Venezuelan situation.

The flight attendant, pretty though she was, had a different idea. She pestered me incessantly. *Did I want a pillow? Did I want a drink? Did I want a blanket?*

After about six such interruptions, I snapped, *"No, thank you!"* My words were polite. The tone of my voice was not.

She got the message. Not skipping a beat, she asked, "Would you like some blood plasma? Maybe some counseling or medication?"

I had it coming, I guess. She was just doing her job, after all. We had a good laugh, and she left me alone for the rest of the trip.

Able to concentrate on my assignment, I recalled that as long ago as 1961 I had been aware of a connection between Caracas and Sicilian heroin trafficking. While working the Settimo Accardi fugitive case—the investigation that took me to Toronto in the undercover guise as a mob hit man—we had discovered that much of the money Accardi had sent to his family had been routed through banks in Caracas. It was apparent even then that the Sicilians must have had people in Caracas helping them launder money.

John O'Connor met me at the airport in Caracas. The following day, we met with a Venezuelan intelligence officer at a coffee shop a few miles away from the American embassy. From there we went to an upscale apartment building that housed their covert site. In one of the apartments, tables had been set up for dozens of cassette recorders that were being used to copy and filter original tapes of telephonic intercepts. The walls were lined with shelves holding the cassettes themselves, all of them catalogued and indexed as to subject, date, time, officers assigned, and so forth. In a side room were several additional tapes that the Venezuelans needed my help with. Apparently many of the recorded conversations were in Sicilian dialects that the Venezuelans could not translate.

I listened to a few of the tapes and recognized dialects indigenous to Palermo, Catania, and Agrigento. Others I couldn't identify. From what little I could understand, it was clear to me that the conversations dealt with cocaine and heroin trafficking.

In one conversation, a suspect in Venezuela said he was shipping "fish" to Sicily. Each "fish" weighed one kilogram. There were twenty "fish" to a box and fifty boxes overall. Undoubtedly, "fish" was the code word for cocaine. The shipment being discussed involved one thousand kilograms.

On another tape, a caller from Italy mentioned that he had just returned from a real estate hunt "up north." He had found a quiet spot with no neighbors close by. There was a dock that projected at least twenty meters into the sea. In the house they could "wash things and take baths." I understood this conversation to mean that a lab site for processing heroin had been located; the pier was to facilitate the off-loading of morphine base and the shipment of finished heroin.

The tapes were of very poor quality, making the process of translation from the obscure Sicilian dialects that much more difficult. Because of security factors, the Venezuelans had used remote transmitters on the phone lines, rather than tapping in and running a land line back to a listening post. Their receiving equipment was in mobile vans. What they gained in security, they lost in quality. The conversations were basically being relayed by mini-radio transmitters, with all the attendant problems of interference and reception deficiencies.

I remained in Caracas for a couple of weeks, transcribing as many of the tapes as I could, but the quality problems—and my lack of familiarity with some of the more remote dialects—worked against making any significant progress. Returning to Washington, I contracted out for retired Agent Anthony Mangiaracina to tackle the transcriptions. I also worked with our technical people to have the audio quality of the tapes enhanced as much as possible. Some of the tapes I retained myself for after-hours and weekend "homework." A steady stream of new tapes came in weekly from Caracas.

The case that I had worried about soon began to look like one of the potentially biggest cases I had ever worked—an irony I had begun to realize even when first confronted with the tapes in Venezuela. Massive quantities of cocaine were going to Italy. Huge amounts of heroin were coming into Venezuela. The cocaine was priced in Italy at about $100,000 per kilo, around ten times its value in Caracas. Conversely, heroin was going into Venezuela at about $200,000 per kilo, better than twice its value in Italy. Each side was getting what it needed and didn't have. Unfortunately, the system of codes and other security measures employed by the traffickers was extremely sophisticated, preventing us from ever ascertaining the exact place and time of a shipment sufficiently in advance for us to effect a seizure. It appeared that our best shot was to pursue a conspiracy investigation.

I directed the ensuing multinational investigation. Eventually it spread through Caracas, Maracaibo, Honduras, Costa Rica, Miami, New York, Palermo, Agrigento, Naples, Rome, Milan, Nice, Paris, Vienna, Brussels, Frankfurt, Canada, Belize, and Brazil. The central figure of the case, which now bore his name, was mafioso Giuseppe Bono of Palermo.

Bono had interested us for years. A rising star in the Sicilian Mafia, he had been sent early in his career to Milan to oversee its interests in the banking center of Italy. Later, he came to New York, evidently to cement relationships with the New World factions, who, over the years, had separated themselves from the traditional Sicilian Mafia. With the establishment of heroin laboratories in Sicily, there was a need to organize North American distribution capabilities. With the French traffickers on the wane, the Sicilian sphere of influence was growing, a development that appealed to mafiosi both in New York and Palermo. The Sicilians wanted to restore order in the ranks of their American brethren, as well as reassert through diplomatic means the supremacy of the traditional strongholds in Sicily and in Italy. Bono was the guy chosen to pull everything together. In effect, he acted as Palermo's ambassador to the Italian crime groups in New York.

While in America, Bono married an Italian-American girl. The wedding was elaborate. Anyone who was anyone in Italian organized crime was invited. The FBI arranged to have covert photographs taken of the guests, but then had trouble making identifications. They asked for help from the DEA. We went to the actual wedding photographer whom Bono had hired and borrowed his negatives along with the matching captions that identified the pictured guests. Sometime after the wedding, Bono returned to Italy, where he continued to rise as a Mafia power.

The primary focus of the Bono case in Venezuela was the powerful Cuntrera crime family headed by Pasquale Cuntrera and his brother Gaspare. In addition to other nefarious activities, the Cuntreras controlled an international network of commercial and banking entities that were involved in laundering drug proceeds. We also went after the Giovanni Caruana family. The Cuntreras and the Caruanas had a long history of associations with the Montreal and Toronto Mafia organizations.

In New York, the investigation centered on a number of reputed mafiosi including Salvatore and Francesco Catalano, Giuseppe Ganci, and Filippo Casamento, all of whom, except for Salvatore Catalano, would be also indicted in the more publicized Pizza Connection case.

The father-and-son team of Antonio and Angelo Mongiovi had our attention in Miami. The cover for their drug operation was a network of international companies transporting lumber and other legitimate materials.

In Brazil, there was former Operation Caesar top-target, Gaetano Badalamenti, and Tommaso Buscetta, who would later testify as the government's star witness against several mafiosi in the Pizza Connection case. Both Badalamenti and Buscetta were then fugitives from Italian justice.

In Italy, besides going after Bono, we also developed evidence against several other powerful mafiosi—among them, Alfredo Bono; Gerlando Alberti; four members of the Salamone family; Nunzio and Salvatore Barbarossa; Giuseppe and Giovanni Liguori; Pasquale and Lorenzo Nuovaletta; Nunzio Guido; and Michele and Salvatore Zaza. As in Operation Caesar, there was significant evidence of cooperation between the Sicilian Mafia and the Neapolitan Camorra.

In situations such as the Bono case, where large numbers of suspects are implicated in several different countries, I've always felt that it was best to pursue prosecution in the country (or countries) that offered the best enforcement yield. There was no room for nationalism. As far as I was concerned, it didn't matter to me if the case went to court in New York or Caracas or anywhere else just as long as we got the results we were looking for. The country that offered the best prosecutorial chances for the Bono case was clearly Italy. It was there that we had the best evidence, and it was there that we had the strongest anti-Mafia laws to work with.

However, there was a hitch. The Venezuelans had from the very start prohibited us from sharing any of the tapes or intelligence that had originated in their country. They feared that doing so would compromise the larger—in their minds—internal security investigation they were working. All attempts to get them to reconsider ran into a stone wall.

During the Bono investigation I made several trips to Italy to meet with those who were leading the Italian effort against the Mafia—Gianni De Gennaro, Giovanni Falcone, Tonino De Luca, Enzo Portaccio, Bruno Contrada, and others. Individually and in groups, they also visited me in Washington. We discussed the cases we were working on and shared intelligence. However, due to the restrictions, I couldn't pursue any of the leads that had originated in Venezuela. In the normal course of the discussions, however, I noted that the Italians mentioned several of the same people that were popping up on the Venezuelan intercepts. It soon became apparent that the Italians, independent of anything the Venezuelans were doing, had tapped into many of the same phone calls. Law enforcement officers in two different hemispheres, unbeknownst to each other, had been eavesdropping on the very same conversations.

Now that the Italians had surfaced the information, I was free to pursue my leads with them. They cooperated enthusiastically. In February 1983, 160 suspects were charged with violation of the Italian anti-Mafia codes and with conspiracy to traffic in narcotics.

The following month, I traveled to Brazil to pursue more leads. The attaché at Brasília asked if I was free to interrogate a Sicilian who had been arrested for trafficking in cocaine. The next morning we set out from São Paulo in a VW Beetle for the prison at Baoru near the Bolivian border. It was a grueling eight-hour ride. The facility itself was one of several Brazilian "mini-prisons"—small, walled facilities that house perhaps fifty inmates and an appropriate number of guards and administrative personnel.

We arrived toward evening. Baoru was dry, dusty, and hot. Guards patrolled in khaki uniforms and knee boots, revolvers strapped to their hips. I didn't get the impression that rehabilitation was high on their list of priorities.

There was no interrogation room on the premises. The guards ushered us into the clinic. Then they brought in the prisoner. The poor bastard was shackled hand and foot. Seven guards hovered over him. The room we were in had no door to close, and several other prisoners milled about just outside the passageway.

Yeah, this guy was going to be real talkative.

Just as I figured, the prisoner gave me nothing. There was no way he was going to give the slightest impression to fellow prisoners that he was cooperating with us. Seeing the jam that the guy was in, I can't say that I really tried very hard. After a while, I dismissed him.

As he was being led from the room, he whispered in Italian to me, "All the big ones are in São Paulo."

He was right—as I was soon to learn.

29

THE PIZZA CONNECTION

The "big ones" referred to by the prisoner in Baoru were none other than top Operation Caesar target Gaetano Badalamenti and notorious Mafia outcast Tommaso Buscetta. Before authorities could track him down in São Paolo, Badalamenti fled to Spain, where he was ultimately apprehended. Buscetta's travel options, however, were more limited. He was on the run from U.S. and Italian law enforcement authorities—and he was hiding from the Mafia.

For reasons that never became perfectly clear, after decades of Mafia involvement, Buscetta had suffered a falling out with the leadership in Palermo. When Buscetta fled for his life to South America, the Mafia decided to inflict its most severe form of punishment. The mob killed every male member of his family it could find. In September of 1982, it murdered his two sons, Antonio and Benedetto. The following December saw the assassinations of three of his nephews, his son-in-law, and his brother. The Buscetta family name was being wiped out while the real target of their wrath was left alive, helpless to do anything about it.

In 1983, close friend Gianni De Gennaro, the top anti-Mafia official in the INP, and members of his staff conducted inquiries in Brazil regarding a fugitive hunt for mafiosi Antonio Bardellino and Raffaele Scarnatto, both of whom had been charged in the Bono case. In response to an INP request, the Brazilian police put together a catalogue of mug shots of several Italian mafiosi, including Tommaso Buscetta as well as the two fugitives in question. The Brazilians showed the pictures around in areas thought to be frequented by the Italians. When they came to an apartment building that was owned by Bardellino's wife, the manager failed to recognize Bardellino or Scarnatto, but he was sure he had seen Tommaso Buscetta. The lead was pursued, and on October 22, 1983, Buscetta was captured in São Paulo.

Immediately, there began a three-way tug of war over who would get Buscetta first. The Italians had wanted him for a long time on a number of serious charges. The U.S. attorney for the Eastern District of New York (in Brooklyn) wanted to try Buscetta for importing a large amount of heroin back in 1973. The U.S. attorney for the Southern District of New York (in Manhattan) needed Buscetta's testimony on a case that was becoming a media favorite.

The Pizza Connection case marked the entry of the FBI into the war on drugs. As such, it received heavy media attention, perhaps more than it deserved relative to other ongoing and previous cases. Even its name had a PR razzle-dazzle that was more sizzle than steak. Some of the defendants happened to own pizza parlors. Hence, the *Pizza Connection*. If they had owned service stations, I guess it would have been called the *Gasoline Connection*. Interestingly enough, there was little if any connection between the pizza shops and the criminal activities of the defendants. But relevance wasn't as important as image. The *Pizza Connection* evoked memories of the *French Connection*, which everyone knew was a big case because Hollywood had made a film about it. And it was catchy—not unlike *La Cosa Nostra*, that other addition to the criminal lexicon given to the world two decades earlier by the FBI.

Basically, the Pizza Connection case saw the prosecution of several New York Mafia notables on charges primarily related to trafficking of Sicilian heroin. The investigation could trace its roots all the way back to 1971 when the BNDD provided intelligence to the Customs Service alerting it to a large shipment of inbound heroin secreted in an automobile. The resulting seizure netted about eighty kilograms. The mule that accompanied the car, Francesco Rappa, flipped and assisted in a "controlled delivery." The ensuing investigation revealed Gaetano Badalamenti as the probable source of supply in Palermo. It also turned up a long list of Italians in the United States who were involved with either pizzerias or restaurant supply firms that dealt with pizzerias. The list of pizza business owners included, among others, Operation Caesar target Salvatore Sollena, his brother Matteo, and Filippo Casamento.

Operation Caesar had already targeted Badalamenti and the Sollenas. When Boris Giuliano seized the suitcase containing $500,000 at Punta Raisi Airport in June of 1979, the cash traced back to Salvatore Sollena's pizza shop in the States. That same year, Mafia big shot Carmine Galente was gunned down in New York. The FBI investigation that followed the gangland murder led back to the same group of pizza shop owners. Numerous phone taps were established.

Among the thousands of calls monitored by the FBI were ones between Giuseppe Ganci and Benedetto Zito. Ganci was a subject of the FBI investigation into Galente's murder, as well as being a defendant in the Bono case. Zito was a known drug trafficker operating in the Philadelphia area. During some of the conversations, Zito arranged for a heroin delivery for his customer, Steve Hopson. Unknown to both Zito and Ganci was that Hopson was an undercover agent for the DEA.

After several unsuccessful attempts, Hopson finally succeeded in buying a kilogram of heroin from Zito. Soon thereafter, Hopson's DEA investigation was integrated with the FBI's. The FBI recorded several calls that Ganci made to others concerning the Hopson buy. The heroin DEA Special Agent Hopson purchased from Zito wound up being the only substantive evidence presented in the Pizza Connection trial. It sat on a table in full view of the jury throughout the long trial.

When the Southern District's prosecutors heard of Buscetta's apprehension in São Paulo, they realized that if Buscetta could be convinced to cooperate, he would represent the biggest Mafia defection ever. Buscetta was a powerful figure whose reach had been international in scope. He was known in New York, in Canada, in South

America, and, of course, in Italy. His knowledge of the international Mafia was thought to be extensive, ranging from the streets of New York to the banking centers in Milan. His PR value was enormous. He would be showcased at important trials such as the Pizza Connection case. Although Buscetta was not thought to have had direct involvement in the specific criminal actions under indictment in the Pizza Connection, his presence in court would lend great weight to the prosecution's case. He would be, in effect, *the* top-ranking mafioso to have ever testified on behalf of the U.S. government. He was seen as the ultimate expert witness, one who could provide the court with an unprecedented inside view of the Mafia and its drug operations.

But there were the Italians to deal with—not to mention the Eastern District prosecutors, who were anxious to press forward with their case against Buscetta. The Italians clearly had the strongest case against Buscetta, but the United States had more clout with the Brazilians, who were in a position to play both sides against the middle. Offers came from all quarters, and the Brazilians acted as brokers. No matter what happened, they were going to win a concession from one of the interested parties.

Buscetta knew that he faced certain conviction in Italy and that imprisonment there was tantamount to a death sentence. There was no jail cell within Italy that was safe from the reach of the Mafia. Sooner or later, it would find him and kill him. Being in prison would only make the assassin's job that much easier. Buscetta had plenty of motivation for wanting to come to America. He certainly knew about the Federal Witness Protection Program, and it must have looked pretty good compared with the alternative. In the program, he could have his wife and surviving children with him. He would enjoy a modicum of freedom. Most importantly, he would be alive. But he couldn't just snap his fingers and transport himself into the security blanket the Americans could offer. First of all, they hadn't offered it. Not yet. And even if they had, the Italians wanted to try him in his homeland.

The deal-makers went to work. It was decided that the Italian case took precedence over the old 1973 New York case. U.S. extradition requests were dropped. In reciprocation, the Italians dropped their extradition request for Gaetano Badalamenti, who was sitting in a Spanish jail waiting anxiously to see if he would be sent to Italy or to the United States, where he faced charges stemming from the Pizza case. Buscetta was extradited to Italy. American prosecutors felt that after spending a few nervous months in Italian jails, Buscetta would be even more receptive to the idea of cooperating with them. The Eastern District agreed to plea bargain on the old 1973 charges as well as some others, contingent on Buscetta's cooperation with the government. Under the same treaty that had allowed P2-Mafia go-between Michele Sindona to be sent to Italy, Buscetta would be sent to America.

On July 21, 1984, Buscetta was flown to Italy, where he was housed in the maximum-security wing of the Rebibbia Prison in Rome. Immediately, Mafia-fighter Giovanni Falcone began a vigorous interrogation process. Shortly thereafter, the Italian authorities extended interrogation privileges to U.S. enforcement personnel.

On September 16, I met with the group of assistant U.S. attorneys and agents who were assigned to the case. From JFK we flew together to Rome, our party taking up most of the upper section of a 747. In the plane was Eastern District Assistant U.S. Attorney Charles Rose; DEA Agent Tony Petrucci; FBI Special Agents Carmine Russo and Charles Rooney; and Southern District Assistant U.S. Attorney Richard Martin, who would prosecute the Pizza Connection case along with Louis Freeh and Robert Bucknam.

In Rome it was decided that only two of us would be allowed to meet with Buscetta. Charles Rose and I were selected. Falcone and De Gennaro introduced us to the prisoner.

"I already know of you," Buscetta told me.

"How's that?" I asked.

"I know of your presence in Palermo," he explained. "I understand that you were very close with Boris Giuliano. You respect his memory."

"Highly," I affirmed.

"I don't share your respect," he said.

"Why not?"

"His reputation in Palermo is not so good."

I pressed for clarification, but he refused to elaborate on the insinuation.

"Who killed him?" I asked. "I'm interested in knowing who actually did it, who ordered it, and how it was set up."

"I don't know," he answered.

After a few go-arounds on that issue, his eyes drifted away from mine for the first time during the interview. He knew the answers. And he knew that I suspected he was lying. When we left Buscetta later that afternoon, De Gennaro said one word to me as we walked from the interrogation room: "Patience."

The following day was taken up with discussions of the legalities relating to his coming to America. I saw no reason to participate. With Russo and Tommy Angioletti—a DEA agent who had previously worked in Italy with me on task force assignments—I drove to Naples. There we searched out and found one of Angioletti's old informants. Upon questioning, the informant further confirmed conclusions we had drawn from the Bono investigation. A few months later, Angioletti's informant was gunned down in Naples.

Shortly before Christmas in 1984, Buscetta was flown to New York in a U.S. Air Force C130-B military transport. Security arrangements were elaborate, but word leaked out anyway. A swarm of reporters and TV crews descended on La Guardia Airport where the plane was expected. To evade the press, the jumbo transport was diverted to a nearby military field. Buscetta and his family transferred into a smaller DEA plane that could more easily complete the journey unnoticed to La Guardia's marine terminal.

Buscetta was remanded into the control of the DEA, but the FBI, the IRS, the Customs Service, and various U.S. attorney offices had almost unlimited access to him. In early 1985 I was assigned to participate in Buscetta's debriefing. I had also been selected to testify during the Pizza Connection case as an expert witness. Basically, I was to help prepare him for his testimony, and he would do the same for me.

Buscetta was housed at a covert site in an upper-class neighborhood about sixty miles from New York City. Authorized visitors had to go to a remote section of Newark International Airport, where they were met by a DEA pilot, usually John Falanga. The pilot flew the visitors in a small plane to a dirt airstrip. DEA Agent Tony Petrucci picked them up in a van and drove them to the site. The visitors sat in the back of the van, which was partitioned off from the driver's section. All the side and rear windows were blacked out.

At the site, Petrucci and Agent Mario Sessa pretty much ran the show. Their operation was efficient and secure. Buscetta was made to be as comfortable and relaxed as possible. He was provided with a private bedroom and bathroom and given access to exercise equipment. Arrangements were made to allow occasional visits from his wife and remaining children.

Until spring of 1986 I continued with Buscetta's debriefings. Eventually, I was allowed to bypass many of the security precautions and drive directly to the site. When I retired from the DEA in August 1985, I was retained by the U.S. Department of Justice to continue my work as an expert witness on a consultant basis.

Buscetta claimed no more than an eighth-grade education, yet his command of language and manners were impeccable. This struck me as curious, and I often asked him about it. He was flattered, but he never offered any explanation. I concluded that his work for the Mafia must have brought him into contact with upper-crust types—perhaps bankers and the business elite. I surmised that he had picked up his refinements from hobnobbing with his "betters."

He also proved reticent to talk about his falling-out with the Sicilian Mafia. He claimed that the reprisals against his family had been solely because of his reluctance to join forces with Badalamenti in a feud against the Corleonesi faction of the Mafia. I never bought it. I thought it highly unlikely that one mob chieftain would order the virtual eradication of another's male family members simply over a refusal to participate in a gang war. I felt that Buscetta's transgression must have involved some grievous betrayal, something he was perhaps ashamed to talk about.

Neither did he offer any further elaboration regarding his comments about Boris. There had been rumors circulating for years about the suitcase belonging to Salvatore Sollena that Boris had confiscated. The speculation was that the suitcase had actually contained $1 million, not just the $500,000 that had been turned in. No one had ever been able to lend any credence to the street gossip, but I suppose that some may have concluded that Boris or his people had diverted $500,000. Maybe that's what Buscetta believed. It's not what I believe.

Buscetta often referred to himself as *"un uomo di onore"*—a man of honor. On several occasions I asked him how he had achieved such status. His explanations always focused on his organizational and political acumen. However, his description of how others had earned the appellation always involved the commission of murder. Likewise, in my previous experience, my understanding of becoming a "made man" in the Mafia had always entailed killing someone. Buscetta was suspected of several murders, including the killings of five Carabinieri officers, but even after repeated questioning, he never admitted that he had ever killed anybody. I suppose that, having lost so much, Buscetta just could not humble himself any further.

Where Buscetta helped me the most was in interpreting Mafia telephonic intercepts. Superficially, most of the conversations seemed to be about mundane, everyday affairs. But masked beneath the pleasant chatter was the communication of drug dealings. The details were there for someone who understood the code. Buscetta knew the lingo, and he was quite helpful. He also assisted with myriad background details. Although my work in Palermo on Operation Caesar qualified me as an expert witness, Buscetta's information did much to fill in the blanks of my understanding of the complexities of the various criminal organizations and enterprises.

In the spring of 1986, passage of the Gramm-Rudman bill forced cancellation of most federal consultant contracts. My contract was one of those that fell to the cost-cutting ax. The information I had prepared was incorporated into the testimony of DEA Agent Frank Tarallo, an experienced veteran and professional whose knowledge of the Mafia was comparable, if not superior, to my own.

Buscetta's actual trial testimony was anticlimactic. Several of those who had been instrumental in bringing him to the United States actually felt let down. As expected, he offered no direct testimony. He did provide much in the way of solid background information. He told the jury how things worked, how deals were cut. He defined the nature of various organizations. In effect, he drew the template into which the defendants neatly fit. His testimony was authoritative and believable. All of the defendants who survived the trial were convicted.

During the trial, defendant Giuseppe Ganci died of a heart attack. Defendant Gaetano Mazzara was tortured and murdered. Defendant Pietro Alfano was shot several times; he survived, paralyzed from the waist down.

As of this writing, Buscetta continues to live safely within the Federal Witness Protection Program under the protection of the U.S. Marshal's Service. He still ranks as the leading international mafioso to have ever cooperated with the U.S. government. So far, he has succeeded in evading the assassin's bullet.

Occasionally I hear from him. He's not happy with his treatment, and he has complained that the DEA reneged on some of the money promised to him. I looked into his claims.

The DEA contends that it has provided Buscetta more than he bargained for, even having secured employment for his wife.

Unhappy though he is, I think Buscetta prefers his present circumstances to life—or death—in an Italian prison cell.

30

A PROMISE TO KEEP

Una mentàlita.

Of all the definitions of the Mafia I've heard throughout my life, of all the explanations for its continued existence, of all the analyses I've listened to or endeavored to offer, perhaps those few words shed more light than any others. Boris Giuliano was the first, in my experience, to coin that phrase as an attempt to explain, at least in part, the phenomenon that is the Mafia: *a state of mind.*

To embrace the criminal lifestyle of the mafioso requires, first and above all else, a state of mind. On the part of the individual, there must initially be the inclination to pledge one's self to the Mafia's value system, which is, itself, a shared state of mind enforced by ethnic kinship. The Mafia initiate must be predisposed toward a perspective that supersedes legalities, family, taboos, and traditional morality. The Mafia—and the other, less-heralded Italian secret criminal organizations such as the Neapolitan Camorra and Calabrian 'Ndrangheta—create themselves according to the evolving design of a shared mind-set. In such a way does the Mafia perpetuate itself and evolve.

It should be obvious that the vast majority of Italians and Italian-Americans have no relationship with the Mafia. Put in the simplest of terms, they don't share the state of mind. They just don't have what the Mafia would consider to be "the right stuff." Yet, unfortunately, sometimes an entire nationality is painted with the same broad and damning brush.

I hope that in the pages of this book, much of which has dealt with Italian criminal organizations, I have made it clear that there are many Italians—in America and in Italy—risking their lives every day in an attempt to eradicate the Mafia. Italian and Italian-American law enforcement officers have been unsurpassed in their efforts against their own nationality. I myself have jailed more Italians and Italian-Americans than any other ethnic or racial group.

The growth of the Mafia has been directly proportional to the opportunities afforded it. The period following World War I saw the decline of the Mafia in Italy as Mussolini rose to power. The repressive measures of his Fascist regime left little operating room for the Mafia. In contrast, the same period in America offered fertile ground for immigrant mafiosi. Prohibition made the public willing accomplices. The police, the political system, and the courts were all corruptible. And there was the emergence of the lawyering class, a development that allowed the American Mafia to institutionalize itself and incorporate itself into the fabric of "legitimate" American life. For a fee, the New World mafiosi found that their new accomplices, the attorneys, could often achieve more with their briefcases than could be achieved with a gun.

By the end of World War II, the American Mafia, strengthened by its post-Prohibition rackets in gambling, prostitution, and the black market, ruled the criminal world. In Italy, where the Mafia had been devastated by the war, the underworld received a needed shot in the arm from the American government; the political interest of stopping the spread of communism was exploited by the Mafia, and it rebuilt its base of power.

Both the American and Italian Mafias entered the drug trade. Both found it rewarding—and dangerous. As the American Mafia drifts away from drugs—leaving it to other factions that are organized along ethnic or racial lines—the Italian Mafia struggles to rebuild its position in the traffic after being weakened in recent years by the ongoing law enforcement efforts that began with Operation Caesar.

As powerful as the international Mafia is, as integrated into legal enterprise as it has become, it is still not nearly as organized or as big as it has been portrayed. There is no single man sitting in Palermo wearing a black fedora and pulling strings that trigger an assassination on the south side of Chicago. Any such description of centralized Mafia power is a myth. Crime is organized, but not that organized. If it were anywhere near as large and controlled as some would have us believe, how do we explain the continued infighting, the hits, the power struggles, the defections?

Always counterbalancing the organizational goals of the Mafia is the overwhelming allure of free enterprise. Like other businessmen, mafiosi are out to enlarge their own piece of the pie. Unlike most other businessmen, they're willing to break the law to get what they want. But essentially, they are driven by the same forces that drive legitimate commerce—namely, greed. Factions and individuals continually try to better their lot at the expense of others. Homogeneous, far-reaching, centralized organizations tend to stifle grass-roots self-betterment. A huge, centralized Mafia would be no different. Mafiosi share a state of mind and little else.

That is not to say that real organized crime does not exist in America. It does. Beside it, the Mafia shrinks in significance. The crimes of the Milkens and the Boeskys, the S&L bandits, and the defense industry thieves are to the Mafia what the Brinks robbery is to a convenience-store heist. These are the world-class players in the game of organized crime. Instead of hit men they employ politicians, lobbyists, and lawyers. Lots of lawyers.

For the most part, these white-collar criminals have had opportunities not available to their counterparts in the Mafia—upbringing, heritage, education, connections. It would seem logical to say that they must have known better, that crime was not the only avenue open to them. It would follow that punishment for such transgressors would be the stiffest allowable under the law. After all, they have no socioeconomic excuses to fall back on, no prejudice to blame, no lack of alternative opportunity to bewail. Yet when caught, these archcriminals, whose crimes ultimately victimize millions, are given the lightest sentences in the most benign institutions—that is, when they don't just skip away with suspended sentences. Many leave their minimum-security jails in the best physical condition they have ever known, having utilized fitness equipment provided at taxpayer expense. Others write memoirs, which New York publishers line up to purchase for outrageous advances.

Today, federal agents have to adapt to a world where foreign intelligence operations routinely involve drug trafficking, where the ever-volatile mix of drug money and armaments is the engine of finance and politics, where the refinement of money laundering on an international scale increasingly spreads through world commerce, where concepts of "legitimacy" erode as white-collar executives dabble in crime and hoodlums buy their way into legal businesses.

Yet the emphasis, unfortunately, will remain on law enforcement via headlines. Multitarget raids and occasional big seizures will continue to be made. These media events should be accepted for what they really are—unwitting indications of how immense the drug problem actually is. Whatever tonnage of contraband is seized and displayed for the television cameras, it is but a tiny percentage of the total traffic. It's the tip of the iceberg. The bigger the tip, the bigger the iceberg.

It doesn't have to be that way. The drug problem can be licked. Since the Civil War, we have fought our wars on foreign soil, yet we persist in fighting the war on drugs in the streets of Harlem and in the barrios of East L.A. There's no reason to allow the battle to be brought to our doorstep. We can interdict drugs before they ever cross our borders. We have the technology, and we have the manpower. All we lack is the will.

With the dissolution of the USSR and the virtual worldwide collapse of communism, our military suddenly finds itself all dressed up with nowhere to go. Why can't we mobilize it to defend us against the drug traffickers who attack our youth, our economy, our national productivity?

We have satellites in orbit that can detect an enemy aircraft on the ground as soon as a pilot turns on the engine. Why can't we target them on the clandestine airstrips of South and Central America?

We have weapon systems that can carry ordnance over incredible distances and deliver them through apertures as tiny as a smokestack. Why can't we fire them at the drug runners' planes and boats or at least force them to areas where they can be searched and arrested?

The war on drugs should be fought in our territorial waters and in the airspace adjacent to our borders. Those who worry that a program of interdiction by the military portends troops on boulevards and tanks in town squares have already surrendered to the idea that the drug war is a war that we must fight on Main Street. We're already losing the war on Main Street. It's time to attack the enemy's supply line. We have the capability. We can win.

But it's extremely doubtful that interdiction will ever get a real chance. The lawyers will scream about constitutionality. Of course, their real concern will be their own livelihoods, for there is a formidable army of attorneys whose jobs depend on the ever-growing bureaucratization of crime-fighting.

In the not-too-distant past, it was commonplace not to involve prosecutors in a criminal investigation until such time as an arrest or a seizure had been made. A year or more of street work might have occurred without any involvement of the legal profession. Law enforcement officers did their jobs, then turned the cases over to prosecutors, who did theirs.

Today, an agent is obligated to advise a prosecutor at the time of case initiation. From that moment forward, the prosecutor must be copied on all memorandums and reports stemming from the investigation. The agent must confer with the prosecutor, keeping him abreast of all developments and heeding his advice with regard to legalities and rights. The briefings pose obvious security and efficiency problems. The "lawyering" tends to restrict investigative creativity. The emphasis has shifted to "prosecutability," as opposed to law enforcement.

The increased involvement of attorneys in law enforcement is supposedly meant to raise productivity by ensuring that more investigations result in successful prosecutions. Yet, even though investigations are now tempered by concerns for constitutional rights, there are more acquittals today than ever before. Investigations take longer and require more manpower, yet the results are worse than in the days when less time was spent worrying about such things as illegal wiretaps and insufficient probable cause. While not suggesting that we embrace a law enforcement process that ignores individual rights, I do maintain that the current approach is an abysmal failure—except, of course, if you happen to be a lawyer whose livelihood depends on it.

In the current system, where attorneys are allowed to oversee and supervise law enforcement, the fox caught in the chicken coop never goes to trial unless there is a witness to the "poultricide." Dead chickens are everywhere and feathers cling to his blood-stained muzzle—it doesn't matter. The case just isn't prosecutable. The fox walks. Sooner or later he finds another chicken coop.

There is something intellectually dishonest about a system that ignores truth. But as I said early on, truth is not the province of the lawyering class. Theirs is the realm of procedure. Of course, procedure begets bureaucracy, which always prioritizes to maintain the status quo. It would be interesting to give the lawyers badges and guns and turn them loose on the streets. Would they do as they preach? Or would we soon find them tossing junkies on fishing expeditions for information?

These were the thoughts that ran through my mind at a recent DEA agent graduation ceremony. I had been honored with a request to present credentials to Jeanette Ferro on the occasion of her appointment as a special agent. I had worked with her father, Joseph, years ago in New York.

I thought, too, of DEA intelligence analyst Mona Ewell, who had assisted me with research and analysis during task force assignments in Italy, a time when females were not nearly as accepted in U.S. law enforcement circles as they are today. Jeanette never knew Mona, but Mona, through her dedication and professionalism, had helped pave the way for her. Cancer took Mona in 1989.

I wondered if Jeanette would be forced to work with fewer cards than I had been dealt. I suspected as much. I knew she wouldn't be given the same latitude I was afforded when I first hit New York in 1960. It was going to be harder for her. She was not going to be allowed to develop and maintain the kind of street presence I had. She wouldn't be permitted to work informants like I did, to gather the intelligence directly from the people involved in the traffic, to force them to cooperate.

One card that hopefully will never cross her hand is the card of corruption. I have full confidence in Jeanette's character and believe that she will resist the temptations that have so bloodied the history of narcotics law enforcement. But what if she's asked, as I was, to conduct anticorruption investigations within the DEA? Some day, will she find herself working for the very same people she investigated? Will she fall prey to the same inequities that blunted my career? I sincerely hope not.

Jeanette enters a DEA that continues to evolve. As Attorney General Ramsey Clark had warned in 1968, the DEA was eventually subordinated under the FBI. Today, the agency is in the process of separating itself from the FBI. Once more it will have the opportunity to work as an independent entity.

I never wanted to be a *crusader*, yet—like it or not—my work became a *crusade*. I found myself pitted against corruption, against my country's enemies both at home and abroad, against the nameless, faceless, gutless wimps who hide in the bureaucracy of government and divert our mission for their own self-interest. I could not have survived without constantly invoking those principles I accepted as a child growing up in Cliffside Park and swore to uphold when I first became a federal agent in 1960. A crusade does not permit doubts, equivocation, or compromise. This was the road I took. I suffered for it, but I prevailed.

Since retirement, I have lived in a rural community not too far from Camp David. I coach high school football and track, and occasionally I work as a consultant for the DEA or the FBI. I fish and hunt whenever I can. During the warm months I enjoy raising tomatoes, peppers, and basil in my garden—at least to the extent that the Japanese beetles will permit.

Recently, a former colleague brought to my attention an article that had run in the *Giornale di Sicilia* in January 1992, eleven years after Boris's assassination. It was an interview of Maria Leotta, the widow of Boris Giuliano. She expressed her dissatisfaction with the lack of justice in the investigation and prosecution relative to her husband's assassination. She mentioned that shortly before his death, Boris had interrogated Badalamenti and met with Ambrosoli, whom she referred to as the liquidator of Sindona's banks. She went on to say that these encounters had occurred without the presence of other law enforcement personnel. She then pointed out that Boris often met with someone else without involving his co-workers, "an Italo-American, a certain Tripodi," whom she identified as a U.S. agent. She recounted a conversation we had after Boris's death:

He said to me, "Madam, I owe my life to Boris. We worked together, and shortly before his death we understood the danger we were in and he—against my wishes—made me leave Palermo." I asked him for more details, and Tripodi assured me he knew little else and then he said to me, "Please do not ask me to die in Italy as it is not my homeland."

There is much that I left unfinished when I retired in 1985. Such is the nature of intelligence and law enforcement work. Whether via compartmentalization or reassignment, one is often forced to leave a case prior to its completion. Sooner or later, you learn to live with the situation, to accept that you can do only so much, that when you're pulled from a case, it's over for you.

There is one piece of unfinished business, however, that even retirement cannot prevent me from completing—a solemn promise that I must fulfill: Mafia contract or not, I must return to Sicily and lay flowers on the grave of Giorgio Boris Giuliano.

INDEX